How Music
and Mathematics Relate

David Kung, Ph.D.

THE
GREAT
COURSES

PUBLISHED BY:

THE GREAT COURSES
Corporate Headquarters
4840 Westfields Boulevard, Suite 500
Chantilly, Virginia 20151-2299
Phone: 1-800-832-2412
Fax: 703-378-3819
www.thegreatcourses.com

David Kung, Ph.D.
Professor of Mathematics
St. Mary's College of Maryland

Professor David Kung is Professor of Mathematics at St. Mary's College of Maryland, the state's public honors college, where he has taught since 2000. He received his B.A. in Mathematics and Physics and his M.A. and Ph.D. in Mathematics from the University of Wisconsin–Madison. Professor Kung's academic work concentrates on topics in mathematics education, particularly the knowledge of student thinking needed to teach college-level mathematics well and the ways in which instructors can gain and use that knowledge.

Professor Kung began violin lessons at age four. In middle school, he quickly progressed through the violin repertoire under the tutelage of Dr. Margery Aber, one of the first violin teachers to bring the Suzuki method to the United States. He attended the prestigious Interlochen music camp and, while completing his undergraduate and graduate degrees in mathematics, performed with the Madison Symphony Orchestra.

Deeply concerned with providing equal opportunities for all math students, Professor Kung has led efforts to establish Emerging Scholars Programs at institutions across the country, including St. Mary's. He organizes a federally funded summer program that targets underrepresented students and first-generation college students early in their careers and aims to increase the chances that these students will go on to complete mathematics majors and graduate degrees.

Professor Kung has received numerous teaching awards. As a graduate student at the University of Wisconsin, he won the math department's Sustained Excellence in Teaching and Service Award and the university-wide Graduate School Excellence in Teaching Award. As a professor, he received the Homer L. Dodge Award for Excellence in Teaching by Junior

Faculty, given by St. Mary's, and the John M. Smith Teaching Award, given by the Maryland-District of Columbia-Virginia Section of the Mathematical Association of America. His innovative classes, including Mathematics for Social Justice and Math, Music, and the Mind, have helped establish St. Mary's as one of the preeminent liberal arts programs in mathematics.

In addition to his academic pursuits, Professor Kung continues to be an active musician, playing chamber music with students and serving as the concertmaster of his community orchestra. ∎

Table of Contents

Table of Contents

How Music and Mathematics Relate

Scope:

Great minds have long sought to explain the relationship between mathematics and music. This course will take you inside a fascinating subject filled with beautiful symmetries and simple mathematical explanations of musical sounds you hear every day. Exploring the connections between math and music, while assuming little background in either subject, will help you understand the seemingly simple sound of a vibrating string, the full sound of a symphony orchestra, an intricate Bach canon, how music is recorded, and even the voice of a loved one on the other end of the phone. Throughout the course, the central goal will be to reveal how mathematics helps us understand the musical experience.

Structured around the experience of listening to music, the course will start where all music starts: with vibrating objects. Whether a metal string, a tube of air, or a circular membrane, every instrument vibrates in particular ways, producing not only the frequency we notice most clearly but also a set of predictable overtones. The structure of these overtones, analyzed with mathematics appropriately called "harmonic analysis," leads to myriad fascinating topics: why different cultures choose particular musical scales, how to tune such scales, why some intervals sound more dissonant than others, how to fool the mind with auditory illusions, and why Western scales (and pianos) are always out of tune.

In addition to scales and intervals, rhythm forms a fundamental component of all music. The mathematics of rhythm is sometimes obvious, as in the time signature that closely resembles a fraction, but it sometimes hides itself well, as when a composer implicitly uses number theory to create a sense of instability in the music.

Self-reference sometimes plays a role in composition, as famously noted by Douglas Hofstadter in his classic book *Gödel, Escher, Bach*. We explore both mathematical and musical examples of self-reference, showcasing their sometimes mind-bending weirdness.

Having seen how mathematics helps explain the choice of notes and their lengths, we will turn to the ways composers use mathematics in writing compositions. Although modern composers, notably the 12-tone composers of the early 20th century and later avant-garde composers, explicitly used mathematical ideas from probability and other fields, musicians back to the Baroque period employed mathematical principles when manipulating melodies and harmonies. Understanding the probability and group theory behind their methods—many details of which were not written down by mathematicians until long after they were used in music—will help us understand the mathematical structures hidden in the music we hear every day.

After a composer completes a piece and an ensemble performs it, the final product is most often delivered to our ears digitally, via an MP3 file or a CD. In either case, mathematics plays a crucial role behind the scenes to make the listening experience an enjoyable one. In the case of MP3 (and similar technologies), the harmonic analysis of overtones helps in the compression of files that would otherwise require more lengthy downloads or larger drives. In the case of CDs and DVDs, error-correcting codes and other mathematical techniques are used not only to detect the errors that are unavoidable in the disc-writing process but actually to correct those errors! Incredibly, these mathematical algorithms ensure that the more than 50,000 errors that occur on a typical audio CD will be corrected before sound comes out of your stereo system! In fact, the digitization of music (and musical scores) allows us to accomplish tasks hardly imaginable a generation ago, including fixing out-of-tune notes on the fly and finding a composition knowing only a short melody.

In the final stop on our tour of the musical experience, we will delve into the available evidence for how the brain processes both mathematics and music. By examining similarities between the two subjects on many different levels, from infant development, to how the brain works with patterns, to the level of abstraction, to creativity and beauty, we will arrive at the ultimate connection between the subjects: that similar patterns of thought underlie both mathematics and music.

Throughout our journey, from the origins of single notes to the mental processing of music, the mathematical concepts that help explain musical phenomena will be illustrated with examples, primarily on the violin. Not only is the violin one of the most popular instruments in the orchestra, but it provides a way to visualize much of the mathematics in this course. The shifting in each lecture between interesting mathematics and engaging musical examples enables each subject to illuminate the other, helping us gain a better understanding of, and appreciation for, both mathematics and music. ■

Overtones—Symphony in a Single Note
Lecture 1

T his course is structured around a single central question: How can mathematics help us understand the musical experience? Mathematics and music might seem to be separate topics, but our philosophy in this course is to show the connections between these two beautiful subjects. When we see mathematics, we will illustrate the math with musical examples. When we hear music, we will explain the underlying mathematics to help us understand the music better.

Frequency and Wavelength

- Instruments look different, but they all have something in common. When an instrument plays, something is vibrating, which causes a wave of pressure changes that travels through the air and reaches your ear. Mathematicians have studied vibrating objects extensively, and their work helps us understand the sounds produced by instruments.

- When we play a note, such as an A on a violin (440 A), what frequencies are produced? In this case, the answer is 440 hertz (Hz). The higher the frequency, the more times the waves are vibrating per second. For 440 Hz, the waves are vibrating 440 times per second.

- When we look at the spectrum for this note, we see that the peaks have different heights. The spectrum shows us that the string vibrates at many different frequencies, all at the same time. If we play a note at 100 Hz, we see frequencies of 100, 200, 300, and so on—the higher the frequency, the higher the pitch. The lowest frequency produced is called the "fundamental."

- In addition to frequency, we can also look at wavelength. Here, we're measuring from the peak of one trough to the peak of another.

o   Sounds are actually pressure waves. Parts of the air are compacted, and parts of the air are rarefied. A 100-Hz note has a wavelength of about 3.4 meters.

o   If we measure the wavelength of the overtones instead of the frequency, we get, in this example, 3.4 meters for the fundamental, 1.7 meters, 1.13 meters, and 85 centimeters. If we take that largest one, 3.4, as our measuring stick, we see that those are in a ratio of 1, 1/2, 1/3, 1/4, 1/5, 1/6, and so on.

•   The frequencies and wavelengths satisfy a key equation: The frequency multiplied by the wavelength is a constant, the speed of sound.

•   If we play a 440 A, what frequencies are produced? We can see the answer in the spectrum: 440 Hz, 880 Hz, 1320 Hz. These are all multiples of 440. The fundamental frequency is 440, and then we just add that repeatedly. Mathematically, we talk about this as an arithmetic sequence. The important thing for us is that it's additive. To get from one to the next, we simply add the fundamental frequency each time.

•   A string vibrates at many different frequencies. Listening to a single string vibrating is like sitting in front of an orchestra of the jump ropes we've used here for illustration, each one vibrating in a particular mode.

•   Note that there's a difference between pitch and frequency. Pitch is the perceived highness or lowness of a note, whereas frequency is this physical vibrating.

•   The mathematical term "harmonic sequence" comes from the harmonics you can play on a string. The relative frequency of each overtone is in a ratio of 1:2, 1:3, 1:4, 1:5, and so on.

•   Recall that the key equation here was that the frequency multiplied by the wavelength gives the speed of sound: $f\lambda = v$. If we look at the relative wavelengths versus the relative frequencies, we can see this equation working. If we multiply the frequency by 3, we have to divide the wavelength by 3 in order for them to multiply and get the same velocity, the speed of sound.

Differential Equations

- We need calculus (the study of change) in order to understand this, but we also need differential equations, which use calculus to predict the future. In particular, we need partial differential equations, which have more than one variable.

- There are three steps to understanding and using any mathematical model to predict the future.
  o The first step is to create a model: to use variables, talk about assumptions, and mathematize the situation.

  o The second step is to connect the variables, for which we use equations.

  o Finally, we have to solve the system. We have to use the equations to predict what will happen in the future, to get a function that represents what will happen for all time.

- If we do this well, then the result the model predicts closely follows what we see in reality. If we don't do it well, then the prediction doesn't closely match reality. We have to go back to step 1, change the variables, change the assumptions, tweak the model, and go through the whole process again.

- To construct a mathematical model for a vibrating string, we let x represent the distance along the string at the bridge (assume $L = 1$ unit), t represents time, T represents the tension on the string, and ρ stands for the mass per unit length (weight). The height of the string at position x and time t is $u(x,t)$.

- The next step is to connect the variables using equations. In this case, we will use Newton's equation $F = ma$. When we translate that to this particular situation, we get that the tension (T) multiplied by the second partial of u with respect to x is equal to the weight (ρ) multiplied by the second partial with respect to t. In mathematics, this is called a "wave equation."

- Taking into account boundary conditions and initial conditions, the next step is to solve the partial differential equation, and when we do so, we predict the future. In this case, given any initial condition F that we deform the string into, the mathematics will tell us what's going to happen for $t > 0$ for all time in the future.

- The power of differential equations is this: If you can model the forces that act on a system, the mathematics predicts what will happen in the future.

- The mathematics is telling us that the string is vibrating in a series of modes. Mathematically, we're getting a sum of sine waves; musically, we're getting a series of overtones.

The Universality of Mathematics

- The beauty of mathematics is that it's universal. Once we have a model for a situation in one field, it can be used in many different fields. In our area of interest, wind and brass instruments involve vibrating air columns, but the mathematics of the situation is almost identical to that for vibrating strings.

- Like a string, a tube of air resonates in particular modes, and what we hear is a combination of those modes—literally, a sum of those modes. If we swing a simple plastic tube, we hear a particular sequence of vibrating modes, perhaps 400 Hz, 600 Hz, 800 Hz, and so on. It's another arithmetic series.

- As we listen to an A played on a series of instruments, the spectrum shows us that we hear a sequence of different frequencies: the overtones.

o   Notice that each of these instruments produces more than one frequency. There is a fundamental, and then there are many other peaks in the spectrum.

o   Each instrument has essentially the same patterns of frequencies, which again, are additive. They are just multiples of the fundamental. The ratios are 1:2, 1:3, 1:4—the natural numbers.

o   If we're looking at wavelengths, we get the reciprocals of those: 1, 1/2, 1/3, 1/4, and so on. The mathematics we use—differential equations—correctly predicts that we will get those particular sequences of numbers.

Visualizing Modes
- To get a different set of overtones, we have to move from one-dimensional objects—strings, vibrating columns of air—to something that's two-dimensional. We are essentially moving from the strings, brass, and winds in an orchestra to the percussion.

- When we play a drum head, we get different vibrating modes, just as we do on a string. But when we look at the spectrum of a timpani, we can see that it doesn't have the same structure as that of the other instruments. There isn't one fundamental with overtones above it. The peaks in the spectrum of the timpani aren't nearly as clear.

- We can use a frequency generator to see the different modes in which the timpani can vibrate.
    o   Notice that when we change the frequency, we're not changing the amplitude, although the volume seems to change dramatically. That's not because the drum is vibrating in greater and greater amounts. Instead, it's simply because this particular drum has particular resonances.

    o   Note, too, that when you hit a drum head, you don't hit the center (the nodal line), because the drum head doesn't move there. Instead, you hit near the side, away from the nodal lines.

- Once we understand the overtone sequence of an instrument, we can then start playing the instrument. We can vary the frequency of the fundamental. If we couldn't do that, music would be very uninteresting; it would have only a single note.

The Frequency of the Fundamental

- How does the frequency of the fundamental depend on such things as, in the case of a violin, the weight of the string, the tension, and the length?

- Qualitatively, we can say that if the weight of the string increases, the vibrations will slow down. We also know that if the tension increases, the speed of the vibrations will increase. And if the length increases, the vibrations will slow down.

- Differential equations give us a more quantitative answer. The formula here is: $f = \dfrac{1}{2L}\sqrt{\dfrac{T}{\rho}}$.

- In this formula, L is the length of the string, T is the tension, and ρ is the weight. We can see this formula at work. If we increase the tension on the string, the pitch goes up. That's because the tension, T, is in the numerator of that fraction. When T increases, the square root also increases, and the frequency goes up. We can also see the formula at work with the weight and length.

- How does the fundamental frequency depend on T, ρ, and L? To answer that, we do exactly what we did before: go through the three steps to make a mathematical model and then solve it. Once we've solved the equation, we can create melodies in predictable ways.

- As you listen to "Twinkle, Twinkle, Little Star," think about how each note is made of many different frequencies—the overtones—and how we're creating a melody by changing the frequency of the fundamental. The way to do that on a violin is by changing the length and the weight of the strings.

Changing Pitches

- To change the pitch on a vibrating column of air, we change the length of the column. We see this in a demonstration with the "Wonder Pipe 4000," an instrument consisting of a PVC pipe and a bucket of water. As we move the pipe lower into the water, the column of air that is vibrating gets shorter. If we raise the pipe almost out of the water, we get a much higher frequency.

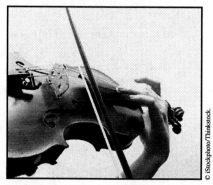

The vibrato motion on a violin slightly changes the length of the string and lends a wavering sound to the pitch.

© iStockphoto/Thinkstock.

- Mathematics predicts this difference between a pipe in water and a pipe out of water.
  - o The mathematics of a vibrating column of air, for instance, a flute, is similar to the mathematics of a vibrating string. When we looked at a string, $u(x,t)$ represented the height of the string at position x and time t. When we look at a column of air, $u(x,t)$ represents the difference in atmospheric pressure in this particular tube at position x and time t.

  - o When we put this into equations, what we get is another version of the wave equation: c^2 (c = speed of sound) multiplied by the second partial of u with respect to x is equal to the second partial of u with respect to t. This comes from fluid dynamics.

- For a flute, the column of air is open at both ends; this fact tells us that the boundary conditions are 0 at both ends.
  - o The key difference between a violin and a flute is that when a violin vibrates, there's a sort of middleman in the process. The string vibrates, and that vibrates the air.

- o In contrast, when a flute is vibrating, there is no middleman. The air within the instrument is vibrating. The length of the instrument determines the wavelength of the sound.

- o We can predict what the wavelength of sound will be from a flute exactly as we did for a violin.

- The lowest note on a clarinet is something around 160 Hz. That's much lower than the 240 Hz on a flute. To understand why clarinets play so much lower, the key is to understand the boundary conditions.
  - o A flute, remember, is open to the air at both ends. There is atmospheric pressure at the end and at the mouthpiece.

  - o In contrast, a clarinet is open at the bottom, but it's closed at the top. The clarinet player puts the reed entirely in his or her mouth. Pressure can build up against the reed, and that changes the mathematics of the situation.

  - o Rather than having boundary conditions of 0 at both ends, we have 0 at the bell end—there is no pressure change—but at the closed end, there is maximum pressure change. There's nowhere for the air to go. It can't vibrate because it comes up against the edge of the reed.

  - o The mathematics tells us that one end of the clarinet is like one end of the jump rope: It's held fixed. The other end of the clarinet has a place where the jump rope has to be flat. The mouthpiece, in other words, is located in the middle of the loop of rope when we think about this jump rope. We can use that to figure out the lowest wavelength that a clarinet can produce.

  - o A clarinet is about 0.6 meters long. The lowest frequency produced by the clarinet should be, according to this mathematical model, the velocity, 340 meters per second, divided by 4 times the length. That gives us 2.4 meters. When we do the calculation, we get that the lowest frequency a clarinet should be able to produce is about 140 Hz, which is not far off.

- This same mathematics also explains the Wonder Pipe 4000. We realize that a flute cannot play very low because it's an open tube at both ends. A clarinet can play lower because it's closed on one end. When we put the Wonder Pipe down in the water, we're representing the closed mouthpiece, and we get a lower pitch. When it's out of the water, it acts like a flute and has a higher pitch.

- As we've seen in this lecture, a note played on almost any instrument includes many different pitches, different frequencies, called overtones or harmonics. For most instruments, those overtones are related to a harmonic series. In terms of wavelengths, that's 1, 1/2, 1/3, 1/4. In terms of frequencies, those are 1, 2, 3, 4, 5, and 6. We make different pitches by changing the vibrations in mathematically predictable ways.

Suggested Reading

Benson, *Music: A Mathematical Offering*, chapters 1, 3 (for the mathematically advanced).

Fletcher and Rossing, *The Physics of Musical Instruments* (for those with a significant physics background).

Harkleroad, *The Math behind the Music*, chapter 2.

Loy, *Musimathics*, vol. 1, chapters 1–2, 4–5, 7–8; vol. 2, chapter 7.

University of New South Wales, http://www.phys.unsw.edu.au/music/.

Wright, *Mathematics and Music*.

Questions to Consider

1. What is the overtone series of a vibrating object?

2. How is mathematics used to predict the overtone series for a vibrating object?

Overtones—Symphony in a Single Note
Lecture 1—Transcript

Welcome to a class about two subjects very close to my heart, and I hope to yours: Mathematics and music. I'm a professor of mathematics at the St. Mary's College of Maryland. That's Maryland's public honors college. I've been there for more than a decade, but I've been playing violin for three decades in orchestras, quartets, and various groups.

Now, the opening music that I was playing was Bach's Prelude from Partita Number Three. We're going to have music throughout this course illustrating mathematics, but first I want to tell you a little bit about how mathematics and music are connected for me. When I interviewed for the position at St. Mary's College, Richard Stark interviewed me. He's a short, Austrian gentleman. The first thing he said to me, he said, "I see you play the violin." He's very proud of his accent. Playing the violin is at the end of my résumé with all the extra things.

The next question he asked was, "Can you play the Bach Chaconne?" If you don't know about the Bach Chaconne, Bach wrote Six Partitas and Sonatas for solo violin with nobody else on stage. The Chaconne is sort of seen as the pinnacle of all of this. It's 15 minutes of incredibly challenging music. It was actually once described by Brahms in the following way, "On one staff for a small instrument, the man writes a whole world of the deepest thoughts and most powerful feelings."

That was the piece that Richard was referring to when he asked me about the Bach Chaconne. Now, this was an interview, and I didn't want to admit that I couldn't play it. I said I could play other unaccompanied Bach. Then I did admit that I could not play the Chaconne, to which Richard responded, "Well, you cannot have the job." Apparently, nobody with a PhD in mathematics that year could play the Chaconne, and they gave me the job at St. Mary's College. The point here is that math and music are intimately connected for me. I hope by the end of this course they will be for you, too, no matter if you're coming more from the math side or from the music side. Or like myself, from both.

Every course of mine at St. Mary's is structured around a single central question. This course is no different. The central question for us is the following: How can mathematics help us understand the musical experience? When I say musical experience, I mean the entire musical experience from the single vibrating string or a vibrating tube of air like a violin or a flute. Putting those notes together to get a scale or a chord and putting multiple instruments together to get some complex Bach piece—a sonata, a partita— to finally how music is delivered to us digitally in this day and age, on a CD or downloaded as an MP3.

Now, the philosophy of this course is maybe a little different from the math you had in school. In school, mathematics and other topics tend to be taught in isolation. Mathematics and music might seem to be very separate, and they certainly were in school for me. Our philosophy is different. It is to show the connections between these two beautiful subjects. When we see mathematics, we're going to illustrate the math with musical examples played on my violin or with other recordings. When we hear music, we're going to explain the underlying mathematics to help you understand the music better.

Throughout this, we're going to draw on many different connections from different disciplines. We're going to talk about different areas of mathematics. We're going to talk a lot today about physics. We're going to talk about music history, history in general. We'll talk a little bit about music theory, and we'll, in fact, talk a little bit about art. If some of these are unfamiliar, that's okay. The key here is the connections among these things.

Where should we start? Let's start where we usually start, with an A. Here is an A on a violin. That's called a 440 A, and we're going to talk about what that means in a bit. Now, instruments look different, but they all have something in common. When an instrument plays, something is vibrating causing a wave of pressure changes that travel through the air and finally get to your ear. The mathematicians have studied vibrating objects extensively, and their work helps us understand the sounds produced by all of the instruments in the orchestra. Eventually that will help us understand music.

When we hear something vibrating, what are we actually hearing? When we play a 440 A—and here it is again—we might ask what frequencies are produced. Well, we call it 440 hertz (Hz) , and that's after the 19th-century German physicist, Heinrich Hertz. The higher the frequency, the more times the waves are vibrating per second. In particular, for 440 Hz, the waves are coming 440 times per second. You might think that what's happening is the string is just sort of going up and down 440 times per second. Surprisingly, it's a much more complicated motion than that, and there are a lot of implications to that. With help from Gordy in the audio booth, I'm going to play an A, and we're going to see the spectrum; we're going to talk a little bit more about the spectrum later.

Now, what you're going to see is that we have peaks, and the peaks come at different frequencies, and they have different heights. Here again is an A. What the spectrum is showing you is that the string vibrates at many different frequencies all at the same time. Let's look at the frequencies that are produced when you hear a particular note. Let's do a quick example of this. If we were to play a note at 100 Hz, so something vibrating back and forth 100 times per second, the frequencies, when we looked at the spectrum, would be at the following numbers: They would be at 100, 200, 300, 400, 500, 600, on and on up. The higher the frequency, the higher the pitch.

Now, pitch is what musicians talk about to talk about the lowness or highness of a note. And these higher frequencies are higher in pitch. They're more in the soprano range and less down in the bass range. The lowest frequency produced, in the case of this example, the 100 Hz, that's typically called the fundamental. When we say a 440 A, 440 Hz is the lowest frequency produced.

If instead of looking at frequency, we wanted to look at wavelength, we could do that as well. When we talk about wavelength, you should think actually of ocean waves. When we talk about wavelength, we're measuring from the peak of one through the trough to the peak of another; a full cycle of that. You could also measure from the trough back to another trough or from some midpoint back to the midpoint. You have to take a full cycle into consideration when you talk about the wavelength.

Now, sounds are actually pressure waves. Nothing is going up and down. It's the pressure that's coming. Parts of the air are compacted, and parts of the air are rarified. A 100-Hz note has a wavelength of about 3.4 meters. If we measure the wavelength of the overtones instead of the frequency, we see that those are things like 3.4 meters for the fundamental, and then 1.7 meters, and then 1.13 meters, and 85 centimeters. If we take that largest one, 3.4, as our measuring stick, we see those are in a ratio of 1, 1/2, 1/3, 1/4, 1/5, 1/6, on and on and on.

The frequencies and wavelengths satisfy a key equation that the frequency times the wavelength is going to be constant. In fact, the constant is equal the speed of sound. Now of course, the speed of sound isn't exactly constant. It changes depending on the pressure. For instance, if you go up to altitude, the speed of sound will be slightly different. In any one place, the speed of sound is roughly constant.

If we play a 440 A, what frequencies are produced? Well, we now know that, and we can see that in the spectrum, it's 440 Hz, and then 880 Hz, 1320. These are all the multiples of 440. The fundamental frequency is 440, and then we just add that again and again. Mathematically, we talk about this as an arithmetic sequence. The important thing for us is that it's additive. To get from one to the next, we're just adding the fundamental frequency each time.

How is it that a string vibrates in so many ways at the same time? Well, we actually have a demonstration to show you that. It requires a jump rope. We're going to take this jump rope. This jump rope is going to—we're going to act like this jump rope is my vibrating string. Imagine this vibrating string blown up to the size of this jump rope. When we vibrate the string, the mathematics is telling us that it vibrates at many different frequencies. We can see that on the string. The fundamental way the string vibrates is like this. It's the way we think of a jump rope.

Now, musically this is called the fundamental. What you want to notice is that there's a flat place in the middle. There's a place where the string is exactly horizontal. We can actually get the string to vibrate in a different mode, and that looks like this. Mathematically we are talking about the second harmonic. Musically we are talking about the first overtone. They are always off by one when you describe that, and you'll notice that is has one note in the middle. There's a place where the string isn't moving at all. It also has two flat places. These are places where the string is exactly horizontal. We can get a third mode vibrating here. Here's the third mode. Now, there are two places where the string isn't moving. Those are the two nodes, and there are three places where the string is horizontal. This is called the third harmonic, or it's called the second overtone if you're talking to musicians.

I think it's quite surprising that our violin string is doing all of these simultaneously. Listening to a single string vibrating is like sitting in front of an orchestra of jump ropes. Each one is vibrating in one of these particular modes. That's why we talk about it as a symphony in a single note. A single vibrating string is actually many, many different frequencies. Let's actually hear what these sound like. Remember this is what the mathematics is telling us, is we're getting different frequencies all vibrating at the same time. Those are giving us different pitches, how high and low these different overtones are.

Now, you have to be careful when you talk about pitch and frequency. Pitch is actually the perceived highness or lowness of the note, whereas frequency is the physical thing. We'll see in lecture three when we talk about auditory illusions that pitch and frequency are actually different. In this case, the overtones vibrate at different frequencies. We hear a single pitch, and the spectrum shows us all of their different frequencies that are vibrating.

I want to play for you all of the frequencies that you're hearing, or at least the first eight or nine. Here is the fundamental. Here is the first overtone, also called the second harmonic. Here is the next one; after that. I want you to note that all of those notes are on the notes that you can find on a piano, except the seventh harmonic. That's an interesting fact that we're going to come back to a little bit later.

We can look at the frequencies and the wavelengths of these. If you look at the wavelengths, what you see is exactly what we saw on the jump rope. We see that the fundamental has a wavelength of the full string. In fact, it's double that, but we're going to talk about sort of one loop of that. One loop of that is the full string. Then the next mode, the next harmonic, vibrates so that the loop is just half the string. The next one is just a third of the string, and then a fourth of the string, a fifth, a sixth.

Mathematicians have a name for this. If you've had calculus, you would have heard this. It's called the harmonic sequence. It's sort of ironic. Mathematicians teach this all the time, and many times without noticing that that's where the name comes from. It comes from the harmonics that you can play on a string. The relative frequency of each overtone is now in a ratio of the following: It's in a ratio of one, to two, to three, to four, to five.

If you remember back, the key equation here was that the frequency times the wavelength gives you the speed of sound. Mathematicians write this $F \times \lambda$, the Greek letter lambda, is equal to v. V stays constant in any one place. If you look at the relative wavelengths versus the relative frequencies, you can see this equation working. If you multiply the frequency by three, you have to divide the wavelength by three in order for them to multiply and get the same velocity, the same constant, the speed of sound.

What mathematics do we need in order to understand this? Well, first we need calculus. Calculus is the study of change, but we also need something called differential equations, which uses calculus actually to predict the future. That's sort of the point of differential equations: To be able to predict what's going to happen in the future. We need a subfield of differential equations called partial differential equations. Partial differential equations are when you have more than one variable going on. Now, we're not going to go in depth with this mathematics. I just want to give you an idea of what's going on when we look at this mathematics and what the results of this mathematics tell us.

There are three steps to understanding and using any mathematical model in order to predict the future, to sort of numerically and with functions, understand a situation. The first step is always to create a model, to use variables, to talk about your assumptions, to figure out what's going on, and to mathematize the situation. The second step then is to connect the variables. We have to figure out how these variables are related. We use equations, and sometimes we'll use physics and things like that in order to connect the variables. Finally, the third thing that we have to do is, we have to solve the system. We have to use these equations to predict what's going to happen in the future; to get a function which represents what will happen for all time after that.

Now, if we do this well, then the result predicts it actually closely models what happens when we see it in reality. If we don't do it well, then our prediction doesn't closely match reality. Then we have to go back. We have to go back to step one, change our variables, change our assumptions, tweak the model a little bit, and go through the whole process again.

What does this look like for a vibrating string if we do this process of mathematical modeling? In our case, x is going to represent the distance along the string where $x = 0$ right here at the bridge, and $x = $ —well, we'll just call it l here at what's called the nut of the violin. Let's just assume that's one for now to make our calculations easier. Now, we're also going to have other variables in here: t we're going to use for time, and T we're going to use for the tension on the string, because these pegs are holding this string in with a particular tension. We also have to talk about the weight of the string, and we usually use ρ for that, another Greek letter. That stands for the mass per unit length. We're going to just call it weight.

Now, if we want to talk about this moving, we need to give that a variable. We talk about $u(x, t)$ being the height of the string at position x and time t. $u(x)$ would be some number that tells us how high the string is. One of the assumptions that we make is that we're going to at least initially assume that our string just vibrates up and down. That's of course not what it really does. It sort of moves in a circle like this, but that'll actually be close enough for our purposes.

The next step is to connect the variables. If we want to connect the variables, we need some equations to do that. In this case, we're going to use Newton's Laws. One of Newton's Laws is that force equals mass times acceleration. When we translate that into this particular situation, we get that the tension times the second partial of u with respect to x is equal to the weight times the second partial with respect to t. Mathematicians give this equation a name it comes up so frequently. We call this a wave equation.

We actually need a little bit more information. We need boundary conditions. The boundary conditions for this particular problem are fairly simple. We know that the string is never going to move here. This is the position x: $u(0, t) = u(1, t) = 0$ for all time, t. We also need another thing called initial conditions, and that's the following: If we were to deform this string into some shape, some function f and then let go, we could use this model to predict what's going to happen. Again, the initial conditions are to deform the string and then to just let go.

The next step in our process is to solve the partial differential equation. Now, we're not going to go into the details of solving a partial differential equation. If you're interested, the reading list suggests several readings that would do exactly that. A partial differential equations course in an undergraduate mathematics program would do this as well. The point here is that when we solve these partial differential equations, we predict the future. Given any initial condition f that I deform my string into, the mathematics tells us what's going to happen for $t > 0$ for all time in the future. The power of differential equations is exactly this: If you can model the forces that act on a system, the mathematics predict what will happen in the future. That's an amazing thing that mathematics does.

Let's look at the solution that we get when we solve this particular PDE. We get $u(x, t)$ is equal to the sum, the capital letter Σ stands for sum. What we get is that it is a sum of sines and cosines. One of the assumptions we've made before we solved this is that the tension, the length, and the weight are equal to one for now. We'll come back later and revisit this model in the case that they're not one. This mathematics is telling us that the string is vibrating in a series of modes. Mathematically what we're getting is the sum of sine waves. Musically what we're getting is a series of overtones.

Now, these numbers a_k that you see out in front of these. Mathematically, these are the Fourier series coefficients. These are just numbers. Each a_k is a single number. Musically that's telling us how much of each overtone is produced. When I take my violin and I pluck a single string, just like this, this mathematics is telling us we already saw in the spectrum: that we hear a symphony of different frequencies when I just pluck this single string.

What about other instruments? The beauty of mathematics, one of the wonderful things about mathematics is that it's universal. You know, once we've developed addition so that we can add two apples to three apples and get five apples, we can do that same addition with bananas or any other fruit. Once we have algebra that models a biological situation, that same algebra can be used in economics. It can be used in lots of different fields. It models the same thing. The algebra stays the same. Interestingly, wind and brass instruments involve vibrating air columns, but the mathematics of the situation is almost identical. Like a string, a tube of air resonates in particular ways, modes, much like the jump rope that we had up here earlier. What you hear is a combination of those modes, literally a sum of all those different modes.

We can hear this in an interesting example of just a single swinging tube. I want you to think about this swinging tube as modeling a wind or a brass instrument. Here's my tube. I actually bought it at the local pool store. It's just a plastic corrugated tube. It has these bumps in it. When we swing it at different speeds, we find the resonant frequencies and you can hear it. First, I'll play a few of these notes. Again, you get a particular sequence of vibrating modes just like we heard on the violin. Again, they're additive. What we're hearing are maybe 400 Hz, 600 Hz, 800 Hz, 1000 Hz. What we see is that they're additive. They're differing by the same amount every time. It's another arithmetic sequence.

Now, it turns out that we're missing the 200 Hz, and that has to do with technical physics reasons with corrugated tubes. But like strings, brass instruments and wind instruments produce a symphony of different sounds in a single note; a symphony of different frequencies. Those are the vibrational modes. Now, one of the things that you can do on a corrugated tube like this is you can play simple songs. In fact, you can play taps. It's actually not surprising that you can play a song like "Taps".

You see, "Taps" is traditionally played not on a trumpet, but on a bugle. A bugle has no valves. You can't change the length of pipe that's in a bugle. It's just a single vibrating tube, and the mathematics of that is very similar. You get exactly these overtones. Those are exactly the things you can play on a bugle, and those are exactly the notes that we can get on this particular vibrating tube.

Let's look at the spectrum of other instruments. We're going to listen to a couple of different instruments and see them played. Each instrument is going to play an A, and the spectrum is going to show us that we hear a sequence of different frequencies: the overtones.

I want you to notice a couple of things about this. All of these produce more than just one frequency. There's a fundamental, and then there are many other peaks in the spectrum. Each instrument has essentially the same patterns of frequencies. Again, it's additive. It's just multiples of the fundamental. How much of each overtone? That we're going to talk about in lecture two.

Let's listen to a couple of As from different instruments. Here's an A on a clarinet. Here's an A on a flute. Here's another. Here's a bass guitar. Here's an A on a trumpet. Here's an A on a piano. I hope what you saw in those is that any instrument is going to produce a sequence of overtones, and there's a pattern to those frequencies. For most instruments, that's called the harmonic sequence. When we're looking at frequencies, those are just multiples of the fundamental. The ratios are one to two, to three, to four, to five, to six, to seven; just the natural numbers. If we're looking at wavelengths, we get the reciprocals of those. Fractions flipped over. We get ratios of 1, 1/2, 1/3, 1/4, 1/5, 1/6. The mathematics that we use, differential equations, correctly predicts what's going to happen; correctly predicts that we get these particular sequences of numbers.

Now, I want to show you an instrument with a different set of overtones, and we have one here. This is a timpani. We have to move to get a set of different overtones. We have to move from one-dimensional objects—strings, vibrating columns of air; these are all one dimensional—to something that's two-dimensional. We are essentially moving from the strings, brass, and winds in an orchestra over to the percussion. This drum head here is two-dimensional. It's flat.

When you play the drum head, you get different vibrating modes just like we do on a string. Now, I can play this here, and I'll play it for you here. We can look at the spectrum and see exactly what it looks like. When you look at the spectrum of a timpani—when you look at that spectrum, you see that it doesn't have the same structure of the other instruments we've had.

There isn't one nice peak, nice fundamental, and then overtones above that. It still has some structure, but the peaks are not nearly as clear. They're much more chaotic. You simply don't have this nice one-two-three-four-five-six pattern. The timpani still has different modes that it can vibrate in, and we can actually use this setup to see them.

Now, one of the things I want you to note, and we're going to explain this in a minute, is that when you play a timpani, you hit it out here somewhat close to the rim. You don't put it in the center, and you can actually hear the difference. Here is when you play out here. If I were to hit the timpani in the center, it sounds much more dead. You don't get that nice reverberation.

Let's look at what the modes on a timpani look like. What I have set up here is I have the timpani. Then it's connected to this vibration mechanism, which vibrates this piston up and down; up and down in a particular way. What this is connected to is it's connected to a frequency generator. When I turn this on, this frequency generator is going to vibrate this at exactly particular frequencies. I'm allowed to change the frequencies on this setup. I can change the frequencies. One of the things that's interesting about this is, I'm not changing the amplitude at all. When we turn this on, you're going to hear that the volume you hear changes dramatically. That's not because this is vibrating at greater and greater amounts. Instead, that's simply because this particular drum has particular resonances. That's the setup we have going here.

Let me turn it on for you. Now, this drum head already has a line drawn on it on the top. To allow us to see these modes, I'm going to sprinkle poppy seeds on the top. What's going to happen is, when the drum head vibrates in a particular mode—say if the drum head is vibrating like this, then each half of it is going to go up and down. There's going to be a line in the middle where the drum head isn't moving at all, and we can actually see that because these poppy seeds will accumulate in the places where the drum head isn't moving. Let's see if we can see that.

Now, one of the things you'll notice about this is that most of these patterns actually go through the center. What that's telling you is that the center of this drum contains most of the nodal lines. Now, when you hit a timpani—

when you play it, you play away from that point. You see, if you play at a nodal line, that's where the drum head is not going to move at all. What you want to do is you actually want to hit in a place where the drum head is moving a lot. You don't hit at the center where all the nodal lines are. You hit here near the side where it's in the middle of these modes, and that causes the drum to vibrate in exactly those modes.

Once we understand the overtone sequence of an instrument, we can then start playing an instrument. We can vary the frequency of the fundamental. If we couldn't do that, music would be very uninteresting. We would have only a single note. That's not very interesting music. How do we change the pitch of a single note? That question it turns out is highly mathematical. How does the frequency of the fundamental depend on things like, in the case of a violin, the weight of the string, the tension, and the length?

Let's look at some qualitative answers first. If the weight of the string increases, the vibrations are going to slow down. That makes sense. If you make some heavier, it goes slower. You can also see that my G string here is a much thicker string than my E string over here. The G string is a much lower note. Here is the G, and here is the E. We also know that if the tension increases, the speed of the vibrations has to speed up. We can do that. We can tune something. Here's my D string. If I tune it up—if I increase the tension, you hear the frequency going up. We also know that if the length increases, the vibrations are going to slow down. The frequency will go down. Think about cellos and basses. Those have long strings. Those produce low frequencies.

Differential equations give us a more quantitative answer. The question, again, is how does the frequency of the fundamental depend on the string weight, the tension, and the length? Here we actually have a formula. The mathematics gives us this formula. The frequency is equal to 1 over $2L$ times the square root of T over ρ. Again, L is the length of the string, T is the tension, and ρ is the weight. We can see this formula at work. Again, if I increase the tension, the pitch goes up. That's because the tension, the T here, is in the numerator of that fraction. When T rises, the square root also rises, and so the frequency goes up.

If we increase the weight, the pitch goes down. We can see that going from my E string here, which is the lightest string, to my G string, the heaviest one. When we increase the weight, the weight ρ appears in the denominator. When the denominator gets bigger, that fraction gets smaller, and the frequency is going to go down.

Now, you might ask about the tension. We actually have roughly the same tension on my G string and my E string. If we didn't have the same tension, then over time my violin would be pulled to one side or the other. We know that instruments, especially Italian instruments, have lasted hundreds of years. That tells us that the tension has to be about the same. If you do the math, it turns out that the G string is about 10 times the weight of the E string.

We can also look at length. When you increase the length, L is going up, and L is in the denominator. That tells us that the frequency goes down. The pitch is going down. You can think about that in terms of larger instruments: Violas, cellos, or basses. You can also look at the strings of a harp. If you look carefully at the strings of the harp, the lower ones are long. Up higher, the higher ones are much shorter. You can see this inside of a piano as well.

Where does this formula come from? It comes from differential equations. Remember, before we assumed the tension, the ρ, and the length were all equal to one. When we looked at that equation, and we took k equals to 1, we got the fundamental. The fundamental frequency, how does that depend on T, ρ, and L? Well, we could go back and run these calculations again and do exactly what we did before; the three steps going through and making a mathematical model and then solving then. If we do that, here is the more complicated equation we get that involves now T, ρ, and L.

What does this equation mean? Well, this equation is saying that, again, it vibrates in many different modes. That's the summation. We have different overtones. k equals 1 is going to give our fundamental. When we look just at the k equals 1 part, we get the sine of πx over L times the cosine of this complicated expression. You can see that complicated expression looks a little bit familiar. That complicated expression is exactly giving us the fundamental frequency of our vibration. It's giving us that the frequency is equal to 1 over $2L$ times the square root of T over ρ. That's coming from the cosine term. If you're wondering about the 2 and the π that aren't there, that has to do with the fact that the natural frequency, I'm sorry, the natural wavelength, of a cosine is 2π.

Now that we've solved this, mathematically we can create melodies in predictable ways. I wanted to show you how we do that on a violin with a piece, the first piece I ever learned. I was four when I started playing the violin, and the first piece I ever learned was "Twinkle Twinkle Little Star." I want you to think about how each note is made of many different frequencies, the overtones, and how we're creating a melody by changing the frequency of the fundamental. The way we're doing that on a violin is by changing the length. I'm going to put my fingers on the string. That effectively shortens the string and makes a shorter string vibrate. We're also changing the weight. I'm doing that by switching from my E string to my A string to heavier strings. Here's "Twinkle Twinkle Little Star."

Now, that was very simple. Let's think about a more complicated piece. Let's go back to the Bach Prelude that we opened this talk with. Think about how quickly I'm changing the length and the weight of the strings that are vibrating. I'm creating music. I want you to know that if we had a professional violinist here, they would be even more accurate in changing the length. They would be even more accurate, within fractions of a millimeter, as to where they're putting their fingers on the string. Now, I haven't played for professionally for as long as a professional violinist would have, so I'm going to be a little bit less accurate. I also want you to notice that I'm using what's called vibrato. When my finger does one of these, motions like this, mathematically what's going on is that we're slightly changing the length of the string. What that's doing is giving us this sort of wavering sound to the pitch. That vibrato sort of takes the edge off of a note, and it gives a sort of a slightly sweeter sound to it. Here again is the Bach Prelude.

Now I want to move from changing pitches on the string to changing pitches on a vibrating column of air. Before we dig into the mathematics of a vibrating column of air, I actually want to demonstrate one of the instruments that some of my students made. They had a name for this instrument. They actually called it the Wonder Pipe 4000, but it's a fairly simple instrument. It just involves a PVC pipe and a bucket of water. Now, on a violin, we were changing the length of the string. That was changing the pitch. On the Wonder Pipe, what we're going to do is, we're going to change the length of the column of air that's vibrating, and that's going to change the pitch.

What happens is, as we move this pipe lower and lower, the water level stays at the surface of the water. The column of air that's vibrating is short and shorter. They've put lines on here to indicate where you should play a scale. Now an interesting thing happens with the Wonder Pipe 4000. When you take it out of the water, here it is with just barely the end in the water. If I lift it out of the water, you get a much higher frequency. Let's go back and forth. Here it is in the water and out of the water. This difference actually explains a key difference between flutes and clarinets, and we're going to talk about that in a minute.

Mathematics predicts this strangeness, this difference between a pipe in water and a pipe out of water. Now, what I said before is true. The mathematics of a vibrating column of air, for instance a flute, is very similar to the mathematics of a vibrating string. When we were looking at a string, u (x, t) represented the height of the string at position x and time t. When we're looking at a column of air, u (x, t) is now going to represent the pressure, the difference from atmospheric pressure that's in this particular tube at position x and time t. When you put this into equations, what you get is another version of the wave equation. You get that c^2 times the second partial of u with respect to x is equal to the second partial of u with respect to t. Here c is the speed of sound. We're getting that from fluid dynamics.

For a flute, which is open to the air at both ends, one end that's obvious. At the other end, you'll notice that a flutist is not covering the mouthpiece entirely. The mouthpiece is open to the air, and they're blowing across that. For a flute, the column of air is open at both ends. That tells us that the boundary conditions are zero at both ends. u $(0, t)$ is equal to u (l, t) is equal to 0 for all time t. Now, there is a key difference between a violin and a flute. That difference is that when a violin vibrates, there's the sort of middleman in this process. The string vibrates, and then that vibrates the air. In contrast, when you have a flute that's vibrating, there's no middleman. It's the air within the instrument, within the flute, that's doing the vibrating. The length of the instrument actually determines the wavelength of the sound.

Let's look and predict what the wavelength of sound is going to be from a flute. The wavelength of sound here, if we have a flute which has length *l*, then we think about setting up a wave within that. We're going to set up exactly what we had with the jump rope. We're going get something which is zero on both ends. Those were the boundary conditions. Then if we want to know the wavelength, we actually have to extend that. That's just half of that. That's going up, and now we have to go back down to get an entire wavelength.

If we have a length of tube here, think about a flute. We know that the lowest possible frequency, the lowest note that we're going to have, is going to have wavelength which is about double the length of the flute. We can check this. The lowest note possible on a flute—a flute is about 0.7 meters long. We know that the frequency times the wavelength is going to give us the speed of sound. Well, the speed of sound is roughly 340 meters per second, and so we can solve for the frequency. The frequency should be the velocity divided by the wavelength. We should get 340 meters per second divided by 2 times the length, which is 1.4 meters. When we do that, we see that the lowest frequency a flute should produce is about 240 Hz. If we check and try to play a note on a flute, the lowest note on a flute is a B below middle C. That's what musicians call it. It's about 247 Hz. We're incredibly close.

Now, what about clarinets? Clarinets play much lower. You might remember from hearing an orchestra that a clarinet has a much lower range than a flute. If you think of the quintessential clarinet solo, it might be the opening of Gershwin's "Rhapsody in Blue" where the clarinet goes. It's this beautiful glissando. Now, that might be a little bit weird because a clarinet and a flute are about the same size. Why is it that a clarinet can produce sounds so much lower than a flute? The lowest note on a clarinet is something around 160 Hz. That's much lower than the 240 Hz that we had for a flute. To understand this difference, we have to understand the boundary conditions. That's the key.

A flute, remember, was open to the air at both ends. We got atmospheric pressure at the end and at the mouthpiece. In contrast, a clarinet is open at the bottom, the bell end of the clarinet, but it's completely closed at the top end. The clarinet player puts their reed entirely in his or her mouth. Pressure can build up against the reed, and that changes the mathematics of the situation. Before the boundary conditions with it, you had zero at both ends. Now when we take into account the fact that it's closed at one end, we get that it's zero at the bell end. There is no pressure change at the bell end, but at the closed end, we get that there's actually maximum pressure change. We get that u_x, the derivative and x, $(x, 0)$ is always equal to 0. That's telling us that we have no displacement. There's nowhere for the air to go. It can't vibrate anywhere because it's coming up against the edge of the reed.

We can actually see this if we think back to the jump rope. The mathematics is telling us that one end of the clarinet is like one end of the jump rope. It's held fixed. The other end of the clarinet is different. The other end of the clarinet has a place where the jump rope has to be flat. It has to be horizontal. The mouthpiece, in other words, it's located in the middle of the loop of rope when we think about this jump rope. We can use that to figure out the lowest wavelength that a clarinet can produce.

What is that wavelength? We can think about a clarinet here. Here this end will be the mouthpiece, and this end will be the bell. You can follow the rope. The rope has to be not moving here, but it has to have maximum motion here. It has to have a flat point here. If we wanted to look at the wavelength, here is the length of the instrument. We would have to go up and back down here, and that's only half the wavelength. The wavelength has to go up, and then down, and then finally get to the end. It has to do a full cycle. The length of the clarinet was only 1/4 of that length. That tells us that λ, the wavelength for a clarinet, has to be four times the length of the clarinet.

We can check this. A clarinet is about 0.6 meters long. The frequency produced, the lowest frequency produced by the clarinet should be, according to this mathematical model, the velocity, 340 meters per second, divided by 4 times the length. The length was 0.6 meters, and that gives us 2.4 meters. When we do the calculation, we get that the lowest frequency a clarinet should be able to produce is about 140 Hz, and that's really not far off. Let's compare a clarinet and a flute for a second.

A flute and a clarinet, again, are about the same length, but a flute can produce only notes as low as 240 Hz or so. A clarinet can go much lower, 140 Hz. They're about the same size, but a clarinet plays much lower. If you want to think about how much lower, we're going to have to study things like intervals. We can study those mathematically, and we're going to do those in later lectures.

The scientists at the University of New South Wales have done some very cool work related to acoustics and vibrating tubes of air. You can see what they've done on YouTube if you search for a flute–clarinet hybrid. What they've done is, they've taken a clarinet mouthpiece and mounted it on a flute. If you take a clarinet mouthpiece and put it on a flute, you now have what looks mostly like a flute, except that it's now closed on one end because it's a clarinet mouthpiece. It turns out that can play much lower notes. They've also taken a flute mouthpiece and put that on a clarinet. What you get then is an instrument which looks mostly like a clarinet, except now it's open on both ends and it no longer plays low.

Let's go back to our Wonder Pipe 4000 now that we understand the mathematics. That explains why we can do this. Now when you see a flute play, you should realize that it's an open tube at both ends. It cannot play very low. When you hear a clarinet play, you know that it's closed on one end. This end down here would represent the mouthpiece where it's closed, and we get a much lower sound. Out of the water, higher pitch it's a flute. In the water, lower pitch it's a clarinet.

I want to talk about one of the assignments I give to students, which is to use mathematics to build instruments. They build really interesting instruments. One is the Wonder Pipe 4000 that they had here. Some of them will build things like flutes. One student, Ben Love, built something much more complicated out of PVC pipe. I think this is just a rubber glove that he found in the kitchen. All of their instruments have to use mathematics to produce sound at different frequencies.

Let's see what we've figured out today. What we've figured out today is a note played on almost any instrument includes many different pitches, different frequencies called overtones or harmonics. For most instruments, those overtones are related to a harmonic sequence. In terms of wavelengths, that's 1, 1/2, 1/3, 1/4. In terms of frequencies, those are 1, 2, 3, 4, 5, and

6. We make different pitches by changing the vibrations in mathematically predictable ways.

Now, I want to leave you with an interesting question to ponder, and that's exactly this. The mathematics of differential equations explains some of the differences between these instruments. Among other things, a clarinet and an oboe, the mathematics is not the same because they're both closed on one end. But the hole inside of an oboe is actually a cone. It's not a cylinder. Inside of a clarinet it's a cylinder, so you get different mathematics. Now, what we said today is that flutes and violins have the same exact mathematics. Why don't flutes and violins sound exactly the same? The answer has to do with resonance and timber. That's the color of the sound, and that's the subject of lecture two.

We're going to finish this lecture the way we'll finish many of the lectures, with a sort of coda. That's the end part of a musical piece. We're going to end here with a piece by Vittorio Monti. It's a piece called Csárdás. It was inspired by the Gypsies of Eastern Europe. I want you to think about how I'm changing the attributes of a vibrating string to produce different pitches, and we're using that to produce music. Here's Csárdás.

Timbre—Why Each Instrument Sounds Different
Lecture 2

In the first lecture, we learned that a note played on any instrument includes many different frequencies, called overtones or harmonics. For many instruments, these overtones are related to the harmonic sequence. In wavelengths, that's 1, 1/2, 1/3, 1/4, 1/5, 1/6; in frequencies, those are the ratios 1:2, 1:3, 1:4, and so on. We make different pitches on different instruments by changing the vibrations in mathematically predictable ways, whether it's shortening the string on a violin or putting holes in a flute to shorten the length of a vibrating tube of air. We know that if we play the same note on a flute and a violin at the same loudness, we would still know the difference between the two instruments. The reason we do is the subject of this lecture: timbre.

Defining Timbre

- According to the *Grove Dictionary of Music*, timbre is: "A term describing the tonal quality of a sound. A clarinet and an oboe sounding the same note at the same loudness are said to produce different timbres. Timbre is a more complex attribute than pitch or loudness, which can each be represented by a one-dimensional scale (high-low for pitch, or loud-soft for loudness). ... Timbre is defined as the frequency spectrum of a sound."

- A negative definition of timbre comes from the American National Standards Institute: "everything that is not loudness, pitch, or spatial perception." Spatial perception means that you can tell where a sound is coming from. If you hear a sound on your left side, how do you know it's on your left side? Your brain does an amazing calculation to give you this information.

- The mathematics we'll look at in this lecture is the Fourier transform, which breaks a complicated wave into simpler sine and cosine waves. The human ear does this sort of complicated mathematics in differentiating a flute from a violin.

Using Mathematics to Understand Timbre

- To begin, let's look at the sine wave (pressure variations) at 440 Hz.
  - The horizontal axis is time; the scale from one peak to the next is 1/440 seconds. The vertical axis is pressure. The 0 in the middle is atmospheric or ambient pressure.

  - Where we have a peak, that's where we have higher pressure, where the air molecules are compressed. Where we have a trough, that's below ambient pressure; the air molecules are more spread apart, and that's called "rarefaction."

- The *Grove* definition of timbre was the "frequency spectrum of a sound." What is the spectrum? It's the answer to the following question: How would you make this wave by adding up pure sine waves of different frequencies? In other words, the spectrum tells you what the "recipe" is to cook up a particular sound—a particular wave—using sine waves as the ingredients.

- What does it mean to add up sine waves? It turns out that sound waves add just like functions. To add a 440-Hz sine wave and a 500-Hz sine wave, at every point in time, we add the pressure values from the two waves. If they're both high, then when we add them, we get something even bigger. If one isn't a peak and one isn't a valley, then they cancel each other out, and we get something near 0.

- We can also do this process in reverse. What sine waves do we add to get a 440-Hz sawtooth wave?
  - Given the fact that it's a 400-Hz sawtooth wave, we know we need to add up sines that have the same period. In other words, we need sine functions that repeat every 1/400 seconds. That gives us some idea of which sine waves we should take. In fact, if f is the frequency, then the period is $1/f$, and we should take $\sin(2k\pi/ft)$ for $k = 1, 2, 3$, and so on. All of those have the correct period.

○ We might try to add up and get a sawtooth wave $s(x)$ by taking $\sin(2\pi/ft) + \sin(4\pi/ft) + \sin(6\pi/ft)$. We might think about taking different amounts of each, and those amounts are a_1, a_2, a_3, and so on. Now, we've reduced the problem to a different question: How much of each ingredient should we take? What should a_k be for $k = 1, 2, 3\ldots$?

○ Solving for the amount of each ingredient is a mathematical trick called "orthogonality." It turns out that if we take the $\sin 2j\pi t$ $\sin 2k\pi t$ and integrate (that is, sum all the ingredients) from 0 to 1, we always get 0 unless j and k are the same number. Mathematicians say that those two functions, the $\sin(j\pi t)$ and $\sin(k\pi t)$, are orthogonal, which is a version of perpendicular.

○ We can actually think of those functions as being vectors in some abstract function space, and those particular vectors are perpendicular. On the other hand, if $j = k$, then those two vectors are parallel.

The Fourier Series
• This is all the work of Joseph Fourier, a mathematician born in 1768. He was studying various problems when he came up with these Fourier series. He was looking for a recipe to write any periodic function as the sum of sines and cosines. Fourier did this work in the context of studying heat flow and metal plates.

• His work is used to solve a wide variety of problems in differential equations, anything from signal processing to quantum mechanics. Most

The mathematics of the Fourier transform is key to virtually all signal analysis, including AM-FM transmission.

problems involving periodic functions use Fourier series or Fourier transforms.

- Let's return to the sawtooth wave problem. We figured out that the ingredients for the sawtooth wave were probably certain sine functions. Interestingly, unlike regular recipes in the kitchen, this recipe looks like it goes on forever. It's an infinite series. Now we're trying to answer the question: How much of each one of the ingredients should we take?

- That's where we turned to the orthogonality trick, and the answer we got from that is that we should take the first sine wave with amount 1, the next one with amount 1/2, the next one with amount 1/3, and so on. We've seen that before. That's actually a copy of the harmonic series!

- We can check this answer both graphically and with sound. As we add more terms (more ingredients in the correct proportions), the function looks and sounds more like the sawtooth wave.

- So far, we've talked about Fourier sine series, for which there are two important generalizations.
  - o The first is that we could use sines and cosines but stay with even multiples of π for our frequencies: π, 2π, 3π. If we use sines and cosines with those as the argument, those are called Fourier series in general.

  - o The second generalization we could make is to allow any frequency, not just integer multiples of π. If we do that, we get the mathematics called the Fourier transform. In all of these cases, the point is to break down a complicated periodic function into simple sine waves that we understand much better.

The Fourier Transform
- The mathematics of the Fourier transform is incredibly advanced. But for this lecture, what we need to know is that the Fourier

transform takes a complicated wave and breaks it down into component sine waves of different frequencies. We call that the spectrum.

- It's also important to know that this is reversible. We can go from the wave form to the spectrum and back. Mathematicians call that going from the function side to the Fourier transform side and doing the inverse Fourier transform to get back. That's what our ears do: a Fourier transform.

Understanding Instrument Sounds

- Let's return to the simple sine wave A at 440 Hz. Again, peak to peak, we see a gap of 1/440 seconds. The spectrum of this, if we take the Fourier transform, shows a single peak at 440 Hz. In theory, it's a single infinitely tall point. It's a delta function. In practice, the computational issues smooth this out, so you see a peak sort of smoothing out to the sides.

- Does this sort of pure sine wave ever occur? Does anything vibrate in just a sine wave?
  - It turns out that some bird calls, such as that of a black-capped chickadee, are very close. Its wave form looks remarkably like a simple sine wave. Its spectrum is nearly a single peak at 3850 Hz. All of the other overtones are much smaller.

  - It's important to note that the vertical scale of the spectrum is logarithmic. Each line is 10 decibels, and the scale is multiplicative. When something is three lines below (30 decibels below), that's actually $10 \times 10 \times 10$ less. It's 1/1000 as powerful. The chickadee is singing almost a pure sine wave. All the other frequencies are much softer.

- Let's return to the spectrum of the sawtooth wave. We already figured out the recipe for this wave. When we look at its spectrum, it shows us visually the recipe we use to get it; we take each of the frequencies in smaller and smaller proportions. That's the harmonic series that we saw in our recipe: 1, 1/2, 1/3, 1/4, and so on. This confirms our idea of the correct recipe for the sawtooth wave.

- When we look at the wave form for an A on the violin, we see that it repeats, and the gaps are, again, 1/440 seconds. Its spectrum has peaks at multiples of 440. Here, we're concentrating on the heights of those peaks: How much of each harmonic are we hearing? The second harmonic, the one that's at 880 Hz, is actually 20 decibels below the fundamental. That means it's 100 times lower. On the other hand, the fifth harmonic is almost as loud as the fundamental.

- The spectrum of an A on a trumpet also shows peaks at multiples of 440, but the heights of those peaks form a different pattern from the spectrum of a violin. The clarinet spectrum shows that all the odd overtones of the clarinet A are much louder than the even ones. This relates to the fact that one end of the tube is closed in a clarinet.

- Why should we care about the spectrum or the Fourier transform? It's how we distinguish different instruments and different voices from different timbres. It has to do with the heights of the various spectrum peaks. How our ears do this has a fascinating mathematical component to it.

Resonant Frequency
- Deep inside the ear, on the other side of the ear drum, is an organ called the cochlea. It's conical-shaped—different sizes at different places. That means that different places resonate at different frequencies.

- If a particular sound comes in—if a particular sine wave comes in—there is some place in the cochlea where that resonates very loudly. The basilar membrane is inside the cochlea, and it picks up those vibrations and sends that message to your brain. In this way, your ear is figuring out a recipe for that sound.

- When an A is played on a violin, the sound wave hits your ear. Each overtone on the spectrum—each ingredient in our recipe—

resonates the cochlea in a different place and with a different amplitude, producing a different force on the basilar membrane. The ear then does exactly what the Fourier transform does. It separates a complicated wave into simple sine functions and sends those to your brain.

- Your brain has stored-up patterns of spectra from various instruments. Your brain knows that a spectrum of a particular pattern is a violin or a clarinet. The brain then does pattern matching.

- The caveat to all this is that the spectrum changes over time. The spectrum of the very beginning of the note (the "attack") is crucial. If we remove the attack electronically, it becomes difficult to distinguish the instrument. The timbre of the attack is particularly important.

- We hear four different ways of playing A 440 Hz on a violin: pizzicato, open A, A played on the G string, and ponticello. Looking at the spectra of these four sounds after the attack reveals differences. For example, the pizzicato is all about the lowest overtones. The attack would have higher overtones, but they die out fairly quickly. The open A has a rich set of overtones in most ranges.

Harmonics
- String harmonics are different from the harmonics that describe the modes of vibrations, the overtones. The idea here is that we lightly stop the string from vibrating at a particular point. If we do this in the fundamental mode, where the whole string is vibrating, the string will be completely disrupted.

- If we stop the string in the middle of the second harmonic, the first overtone, there's no disruption. The string can continue to vibrate on each side (each loop) even if the string is lightly stopped in the middle. Notice that all the even modes have nodes in the middle, which would mean no disruption. All of the odd nodes would be disrupted because they are moving in the middle.

- The spectrum of an A that is lightly stopped in the middle acts exactly like the mathematical description. The harmonic gives us only the even overtones; all of the odd ones are damped out. Notice, too, that this changes the fundamental. The lowest frequency is no longer 440 Hz; it's now 880 Hz, double the fundamental frequency of the original.

- If we stop the string two-thirds of the way up, we would hear only the modes where there's a node at that place. The fundamental doesn't have a node there, nor does the next mode. In fact, only the multiples of 3 will have nodes at two-thirds. We should hear only every third overtone.
  - When we do this, the timbre and the fundamental change. The timbre changes because we eliminate some of the overtones. The fundamental changes because the lowest frequency we hear is three times the original fundamental's frequency.

  - Stopping the string one-third of the way up sounds almost exactly the same as stopping it two-thirds of the way, again, because we're looking at only the multiples of 3 in the original overtone series of the A.

Pianos and the Seventh Harmonic
- If you're designing a piano, you have a choice about where on the string the hammer should hit. Different choices will give you different timbres.

- Remember that when we were looking at the overtones, we looked at the seventh of those. The seventh harmonic was not a note that was on our 12-tone scale. When we're making a piano, we can choose to put the hammer in a place so that the seventh overtone is less audible.

- Using partial differential equations, we can actually predict how much of each overtone we will hear for a given hammer position. To avoid the seventh harmonic, we position the hammer exactly one-seventh of the way up the string.

- To understand this, think back to the jump rope. The seventh harmonic has seven loops and will have a node one-seventh of the way up the string. If we hit it there, we will disrupt that mode, so we won't hear any of the seventh harmonic. This is actually the way that pianos are made.

How Composers Use Timbres

- The primary way that composers use timbre is by choosing different instruments for different parts. Think about the piece *Peter and the Wolf* by Prokofiev. The bassoon represents the grandfather, the oboe represents the duck, and so on. These are different timbres for different instruments because of the storyline.

- A more subtle way of doing this is not by having different instruments play different things because of the difference in timbre, but by having a single instrument play in different ways—plucking, bowing, or playing harmonics.

- This takes us back to the opening music for this lecture, Bach's "Air on the G String" from his Orchestra Suite No. 3 in D Major. A German violinist, August Wilhelm, adapted this piece just for violin and piano. He changed the key to C, brought it down an octave, and had the violinists play entirely on the G string, which gives the music a darker quality. We perceive the lower, darker overtones via a Fourier transform.

Suggested Reading

Benson, *Music: A Mathematical Offering*, chapter 2 (for the mathematically advanced).

Fletcher and Rossing, *The Physics of Musical Instruments*.

Harkleroad, *The Math behind the Music*.

Loy, *Musimathics*, vol. 1, chapters 2, 6, 8; vol. 2, chapters 3, 6.

University of New South Wales, http://www.phys.unsw.edu.au/music/.

Wright, *Mathematics and Music*, chapter 10 (an excellent, less mathematically technical discussion).

1. How is the timbre of a note related to the spectrum, overtone series, and Fourier transform?

2. In what sense does the ear perform a Fourier transform before sending information about a note on to the brain?

Timbre—Why Each Instrument Sounds Different
Lecture 2—Transcript

Welcome back. That was Bach's Air on the G String. We're going to talk about that again at the end of the lecture, and I hope that this lecture helps you understand it a little bit better.

In the first lecture, we played a note on any instrument. We played many of them, and we found that a note on any instrument includes many different frequencies. As we learned, those are frequencies and not pitches. Pitch is the musical term for how or low a note is. These are called overtones or harmonics. For many instruments, these overtones are related to the harmonic sequence. In wavelengths, that's 1, 1/2, 1/3, 1/4, 1/5, 1/6. If we look at frequencies instead, those are the ratios 1 to 2, to 3, to 4, to 5, to 6, on and on and on.

Now, we make different pitches on different instruments by changing the vibrations in mathematically predictable ways, whether it's shortening the string on a violin or putting holes in a flute to shorten the length of a vibrating tube of air. On the Bach Air that we opened with, all of those notes are on the G string. That's what it means, Bach on the—the Air on the G String. It's all on my lowest string right here. We're shortening the G string to get different notes.

Why did they decide to put it on the G string? That's today's topic, and that's timbre. I want to start by giving an informal definition of timbre. Timbre is the quality of sound that allows one to distinguish between two notes of the same pitch on the same loudness. If you play a flute and a violin, they could play the same note and the same loudness, but you would still know the difference between a flute and a violin. Why do you know that difference? Timbre.

Here's a more formal definition. If you want to know a formal definition for any musical term, you turn to the *Grove Dictionary of Music*. If you look up in the *Grove Dictionary*, it says this. Timbre is, and I quote, "A term describing the tonal quality of a sound. A clarinet and an oboe sounding the same note at the same loudness are said to produce different timbres. Timbre is a more complex attribute than pitch or loudness, which can each be represented by a one-dimensional scale (high-low for pitch, or loud-soft for loudness);...."

I have to interrupt at this point to say we are actually going to find out that the high-low for pitch isn't as easy as it might sound, and we're going to hear that in lecture 3 in auditory illusions. The end of the *Grove Dictionary of Music* definition includes the following line: "Timbre is defined as the frequency spectrum of a sound." Spectrum, that's where the math comes in. That's what we saw last time. We saw graphs showing how much of each vibration you heard, how much of each overtone. That's the mathematical connection to timbre.

I also want to give you what's a negative definition of timbre. It comes from the American National Standards Institute, ANSI. They define timbre as, "everything that is *not* loudness, pitch, or spatial perception." That's a different one; spatial perception. Neither of the other definitions mentioned that. Spatial perception is that you can tell where a sound is coming from. If I hear a sound on my left side, how do I know it's on my left side? Interestingly, your brain does this amazing calculation. That sound reaches my left ear first; it comes over and reaches my right ear a little bit later.

The reason I know that it's not two sounds is that my brain decides that's not two different sounds, one before the other. Instead, my brain realizes that it's one sound. Because it hit my left ear first, it must be coming from the left. Now, today's topic, timbre, interestingly also has—there's a brain aspect to this. There's a combination of brain and your ear that combine to tell a flute from a violin. The surprise here is that your ear and not your brain does the complicated math.

The mathematics we're going to talk about today, and the mathematics we need to understand to get through the mathematics of timbre, is the Fourier Transform. What the Fourier Transform does is it breaks a complicated wave into simpler sine and cosine waves. Amazingly and somewhat unexpectedly, the reason we care about this is that the human ear does a Fourier Transform. It does that sort of complicated mathematics. You hear the difference between a violin and a flute because your ear is doing this complicated math and sending the results of that complicated math to your brain. Once we understand timbre and how to change it on a violin, then we can actually use at the very end, I'll show you how violinists use fractions in order to show off.

Let's listen to some examples. The definition suggests that we can distinguish among different instruments playing at the same pitch and the same loudness. Let's try. Here are four As in a row. Ask yourself, what instrument is each one of those? Here is the first, here is the second, here is the third, and here is the fourth. In order, those were a trumpet, a violin, a clarinet, and a pure sine wave. That last one wasn't actually an instrument at all.

Let's use mathematics to help us understand timbre. We can look at the waveform. Let's look at the sine wave first. The sine wave is the pressure variations. The horizontal axis here is time. The scale here is that from one peak to the next is 1/440 seconds. This is a sine wave, which was at 440 Hz. The sine wave was going back and forth 440 times per second. One complete cycle of that takes 1/440 seconds. Now, the vertical axis here is pressure. The zero in the middle is atmospheric or ambient pressure. When you have a peak, that's where you have higher pressure, where the air molecules have compressed, and it's higher pressure. Where you have a trough that's below ambient pressure, that's where the air molecules are more spread apart. That's called rarefaction.

If we look at a violin waveform, we can hear this on an A. We can hear it on the A of a violin. Here is an A on a violin. Here is the waveform that goes with it. You can see, it's much more complicated than just a sine wave, but it is also periodic. How frequently does it repeat? Well, if you look from one peak to the next, it's exactly 1/440 seconds. That's because this A was a 440-Hz A.

How do we look at the spectrum? Remember, the *Grove* definition was the "frequency spectrum of a sound." What is the spectrum? The spectrum is the answer to the following question: How would you make this wave by adding up pure sine waves of different frequencies? In other words, the spectrum sort of tells you what the recipe is to cook up a particular sound, a particular wave, using sine waves as the ingredient.

Now, you remember—sine waves you probably remember from a high-school trigonometry course. These are the simple building blocks of trigonometry. If you had a right triangle, it would be the length of the opposite side over the hypotenuse. If you were working on the unit circle, you'd be looking at the y coordinate on the unit circle. When we graph a sine wave, it looks like this. It's sort of simple, regular, going back and forth. Now, we can stretch and squeeze a sine wave. We could instead of just taking sine of x, we could take A sin(Bx), or even A sin(Bx)+C. Those are all variations of a sine wave. The A increases the amplitude, the B squishes and shrinks it this way, and the C shifts it over left and right.

What does it mean to add up these waves? We said we're looking at the recipe, how to sort of cook up a sound. To do that, we combine these ingredients with addition mathematically. It turns out that sound waves add just like functions. Let's hear a 440 A, again a sine wave. Here's a 500-Hz sine wave. Now, we're going to add them together. Here, let's listen to it first. Here's a 440-Hz sine wave plus a 500-Hz sine wave. Mathematically, we're simply adding those together. At every point in time, we're going to take the pressure value we get from the 440 Hz and the pressure value from the 500 Hz. We're going to add those together. If they're both high, if they're both in their peak portion, then we're going to add and get something even bigger. If one isn't a peak and one isn't a valley, then they're going to cancel each other out and get something near zero.

That's an example of taking two ingredients, the 440-Hz A and the 500-Hz A and putting them together to get a particular dish, the sum. Let's see if we can go in reverse. Take the dish, and then figure out what is the recipe that gave us that? Here is a particularly interesting dish. This is a sawtooth wave. Let's hear the sawtooth wave. Notice that the timbre is very different from the other As you heard. It sort of has an edge to it. The question we're asking is which sine waves would you add up to get that.

Now, we have some clues here. We played a 440-Hz sawtooth wave. That means we would need to add up sines that have the same period; that fit nicely within the same period that the sawtooth wave is vibrating. In other words, we need sine functions that repeat every 1/440 seconds. That gives us some idea of which sine waves we should take. In fact if F is the frequency, we should take $\sin(2k\pi/f\,t)$ for k=1, 2, 3, on and on up. All of those have the correct period. We have an idea what the ingredients should be. We might try to add up and get a sawtooth wave $s(x)$ by taking $\sin(2\pi/f\,t) + \sin(4\pi/f\,t) + \sin(6\pi/f\,t)$. We might think about taking different amounts of those, and those are the a_ks. Now we've reduced it to a different question. How much of each one those ingredients should we take? What should the a_ks be?

Now, this is a quick math aside for those of you who know calc. because the way you figure out the a_ks is this really wonderful mathematical trick called orthogonality. It turns out that if you take the $\sin 2j\pi t$ $\sin 2k\pi t$ and integrate from zero to one, you usually get zero. In fact, you always get zero unless j and k are the same number. Mathematicians say that those two functions, the $\sin(j\pi t)$ and $\sin(k\pi t)$, are orthogonal. It's a version of perpendicular. We can actually think of those functions as being vectors in some abstract function space, and those particular vectors are perpendicular. On the other hand, if j is equal to k, then those two vectors are perfectly parallel. They're the same vector. That allows us to do some interesting mathematics. If you're interested in this, look up orthogonality and Fourier Series online. There's wonderful work on that.

This is all the work of Joseph Fourier. Who was he? It turns out that he was a mathematician born in 1768. He was one of at least 19 kids. We're not exactly sure how many kids there were. He was orphaned at age 8. He was very active in the French Revolution. He was not only an expert in mathematics, he was also an expert in Egyptology. Interestingly, it was Fourier who first discovered the greenhouse effect, this effect of gases on the earth's atmosphere keeping heat in. He didn't, of course, know about climate change at that point. Now, the word is—the story is that in 1830, he actually died in the somewhat ironic way sort of like the greenhouse effect. He would wrap himself in blankets instead of turning on the heat, and he quite possibly fell down the stairs when he tripped on one of the blankets and died in 1830.

Fourier was studying various problems when he came up with these Fourier series. The idea is that given any periodic function, he was looking for a recipe to write it as the sum of sines and cosines. That was what he was doing. He was doing this in the context of studying things like heat flow and metal plates. His work, Fourier Series and later Fourier Transforms, is used to solve a wide variety of problems in differential equations. Anything from signal processing uses Fourier Series and Fourier Transforms. Mathematically, we call things the Heat Equation or the Wave Equation because they model heat transfer or wave equations when they model what happens to waves as they move. Quantum mechanics uses Fourier Series and Fourier Transforms to study the topics that they're looking at. Most problems involving periodic functions use Fourier Series or Fourier Transforms in order to figure them out.

Let's go back to the problem we were working on. We we're looking at a sawtooth wave. Here, let's listen to it again. We had figured out that the ingredients for the sawtooth wave were probably these sine functions. Interestingly, unlike regular recipes in the kitchen, this recipe looks like it goes on forever. It's an infinite series. Now we're trying to answer the question: How much of each one of the ingredients should we take?

That's where we turn to this orthogonality trick. The answer we get from this orthogonality trick is that we should take them in the following amounts. The first sine wave we should take with amount 1, and the next one 1/2, and the next one 1/3, 1/4. We've seen that before. That's actually a copy of the harmonic series. Isn't that amazing? Mathematics is like that. The same things come up again and again and again. Now that we have an answer, let's be good math students and check to see if that works. Interestingly, we can check both graphically and with sound. As we add more terms, as we add more of these ingredients at the correct proportions, does the function look more like the sawtooth wave and does it sound more like the sawtooth wave?

The key idea here is approximation. We're going to approximate the sawtooth wave by taking more and more terms in the series, by taking more and more ingredients in our recipe. Let's look at this. Here's just the first sine wave. When we add another term, we get something that looks closer. When we add another term, we're getting even closer. Every time we add another piece of our recipe, we're getting closer and closer to our sawtooth wave. By the time we added a lot of them, we're actually getting very close to the sawtooth wave. That looks good. Graphically, it looks like we're getting closer to the sawtooth function as we add more and more ingredients in our recipe.

Let's ask the related question, does the same thing happen with sound? If we add up more and more ingredients—if we put more ingredients in the pot, does it sound more and more like the sawtooth wave? Well, let's listen. When we put the first ingredient in, that's just a sine wave. Let's listen to that. When we put the second ingredient in, we're only taking half of that— half of $\sin(4\pi/f\ t)$. Now when we add those together, here's what we get. With three ingredients, we get this, and four ingredients, five ingredients. We'll cut. Here's the first 10 ingredients all added together. Just to compare, that's sounding more and more like the sawtooth wave. Here's the sawtooth wave that we're aiming for.

Now, let's look at related mathematical questions. You can already see that this is working. This recipe is giving us the function, but mathematicians asked a lot of different questions about this once they figured this out. Mathematicians since Fourier have answered many of these questions about approximations. Let's look at a function g and think of it as writing it as the sum of different sine waves. When we add up the sine waves, do we always get g? Do we get g everywhere? You'll notice in that sawtooth wave there was this jump when we got from the top of the sawtooth wave to the bottom. If you look closely, the approximations actually overshoot that jump a little bit.

What's going on with that particular point? How quickly will our recipe converge to the dish we're looking for? How quickly will the sum converge? Can you estimate the error if you take only n terms, maybe a hundred terms? How far off are you going to be from the eventual function that you're trying to approximate. If two functions have the same Fourier expansion, are they necessarily the same? Interestingly, this is what Georg Cantor was working on when he came up with his theories about different sizes of infinity. It was actually Fourier's Series that he was working on.

Let's look at a couple of important generalizations of Fourier's Series and how we use them to understand musical sounds. So far we've talked about what are called Fourier Sine Series. We're only using sines. Now, there are two important generalizations to this. The first is that we could use sines and cosines, but stay with these even multiples of π for our frequencies: π, 2π, 3π. If we use sines and cosines with those as the argument, those are called

Fourier Series in general. The second generalization we could make is to allow any frequency, not just integer multiples of π. If we do that, we get the mathematics called the Fourier Transform. In all of these cases, the point is to breakdown a complicated periodic function into simple sine waves that we understand much better.

Now, I don't want to get into the details of this, but I do want to tell you a little bit about the tools that you would need to understand in order to get into this mathematics. It's beyond the scope of our course here. The mathematics is incredibly advanced. It would take semesters to cover, but you need things like complex numbers. You need exponentials. You actually need something, a generalization of functions called generalized functions, the most famous of which is the delta function. You may have heard about that if you've taken a physics class. The idea, again, is that you have your waveform on the time side, the pressure wave in terms of music, and you also have the spectrum, the frequency side. It's this wave side versus the frequency side that becomes really important.

The spectrum shows us what frequencies of sines and cosines make up the waveform. This mathematics is key to virtually all signal analysis, including AM-FM transmission. AM is on the wave side, and FM is on the Fourier Transform side, and sound compression, which we'll talk about in lecture 11. The key mathematics in quantum mechanics is actually exactly this. It's Fourier Transforms. You may have heard of the uncertainty principle, the key behind the uncertainty principle is a particular Fourier Transform. That's a lot of complicated mathematics.

What do you need in order to follow this particular lecture? Well, you need to know that the Fourier Transform takes a complicated wave and breaks it down into component sine waves of different frequencies. We call that the spectrum. It's important to know also that this is reversible. You can go from the waveform to the spectrum and back. You're going from the waveform, the function, to the frequency, and back. Mathematicians call that going from the function side to the Fourier Transform side, and the doing the inverse Fourier Transform to get back. You also need to know that that's what our ears do. Our ears are doing a Fourier Transform.

The rest of this lecture is going to be using these tools to understand instrument sounds starting with an A. Let's return to this simple sine wave A at 440 Hz. Here it is visually. That's a sine wave. Again, peak to peak we're looking at a gap of 1/440 seconds. The spectrum of this, if we take the Fourier Transform, is showing a single peak right at 440 Hz. Now in theory, it's a single infinitely tall point. It's a delta function. In practice, the computational issues smooth this out, so you see sort of a peak sort of smoothing out to the sides.

Does this sort of pure sine wave ever occur? Does anything vibrate in just a sine wave? It turns out that some bird calls are very close. Here's the call of a black-capped chickadee. If we look at its waveform, that looks remarkably like just a simple sine wave. It didn't have the complications that a violin or a trumpet had. Its spectrum is nearly a single peak right at 3850 Hz. All of the other overtones are much, much smaller. Now, it's important to note that the vertical scale here is logarithmic. Each one of these lines is 10 decibels. Ten decibels doesn't mean you subtract 10 from something. It's multiplicative. When something is three lines below, 30 decibels below, that's actually 10 × 10 × 10 less. It's 1/1000 as powerful. This chickadee is singing almost a pure sine wave. All of the other frequencies are very much softer.

Let's go back to the sawtooth wave and look at its spectrum. The sawtooth wave looks like this, and we already figured out the recipe for this sawtooth wave. When we look at its spectrum, it shows us visually the recipe we use to get it. It shows that each one of these frequencies we take in a smaller and smaller proportion. That's the harmonic series that we saw in our recipe: 1, 1/2, 1/3, 1/4, on and on. This is confirming our idea of the correct recipe for the sawtooth wave being exactly what we figured it out to be.

Let's look at some spectra of musical instruments. Here again is an A on my violin, 440 Hz. When you look at the spectrum, let's look at the waveform first. You can see that it repeats, and those gaps are again 1/440 seconds. If you look at the spectrum, we saw in lecture 1 that it had peaks at multiples of 440. Today we're really concentrating on the heights of those peaks; how much of each harmonic are we hearing. Now, when you look at the spectrum, you look at the second harmonic, the one that's at 880 Hz is actually 20 decibels below the first one, the fundamental. That means it's

100 times lower. On the other hand, the fifth harmonic is almost as loud as the fundamental. That's very characteristic of a violin.

Let's look at the spectrum of a trumpet. Again, when we look at the waveform of a trumpet, we see that it's periodic, that it repeats every 1/440 seconds. When we look at the spectrum, what we see is that we see peaks at the multiples of 440, but the heights of those peaks form a very different pattern from what we had when we were looking at the violin. Let's look at a clarinet. A clarinet waveform looks like this. Again, the peak-to-peak distance is 1/440 seconds because it's an A, 440 Hz. The spectrum has something interesting about it. If you notice, all of the odd overtones of the clarinet sound are much louder than the even ones. The fundamental is very loud. The second one is small. The third harmonic is loud. The next one is small. In every case the even ones are much smaller. That has to do with the closed-endedness of the tube in a clarinet.

Now, let's compare all three of these instruments together. Here we have a violin spectrum, a trumpet spectrum, and a clarinet spectrum. These different instruments have different patterns. Let's go back to the question we had. Why should we care about the spectrum or the Fourier Transform? The answer is that our ears do exactly this. It's how we distinguish different instruments and different voices from different timbres. It has to do with the heights of these various peaks. How our ears do it is fascinating and has a mathematical component to it. Let's look at that.

Our ears use something called resonance. This isn't just musical instruments that give you resonance. Violin strings, twirling tubes, singing in the shower. These are all versions of resonance. Sometimes you get beautiful and sometimes even catastrophic things when you have resonance. Bridges sometimes collapse because of resonance. Resonance is most commonly cited as the cause of the Tacoma Narrows bridge collapse. They call it Galloping Gertie. You can see really shocking videos on YouTube of this bridge collapsing. That's maybe because of resonance.

When you drive down a dirt road, we had a lot of dirt roads back in Wisconsin. When you drive down a dirt road, sometimes you hit what's called a washboard section where it's bump-bump-bump; regularly spaced bumps. Interestingly, if you hit that at exactly the right speed, it's horrible. Your car starts to shake and rock and roll. It's because you've hit it when the shocks have their resonant frequency. If you speed up or slow down, either way you'll get away from the resonant frequency of your shocks and you won't have that horrible reaction. It's a little bit ironic because the washboard is caused by previous cars going over that and by their shocks going at a particular rate. That's how you get washboard, and it's also how you avoid it. You go at a different speed than everybody else who is travelling it.

You see resonance when you see a wine glass breaking. If you want to break a wine glass, first you clink the glass to find its resonant frequency. Then you sing or play a very loud noise at exactly that frequency. What it's doing is, it's forcing the glass to vibrate in its resonant frequency where it vibrates a whole lot and then finally breaks. Now, the underlying mathematics here has to do with differential equations. The models that we talked about last time, if you apply those models in all of these cases, you get phenomena that have key vibrational modes. Those are called the resonant frequencies. If you force that system at exactly that frequency, the solutions become very large.

There's a very dramatic example of this up in Canada. The Bay of Fundy has tides that are over 50 feet from top to bottom. When the tide goes out, the water goes down 50 feet. The reason has to do with resonance. The Bay of Fundy has a particular resonant frequency. In fact, it's the same as the tidal frequency. Interestingly, you can think of the Bay of Fundy as more of a clarinet because it's closed at the other end. It's not like a flute open at both ends. Also, if you think about it, if the earth turned a little faster or slower, then the length of the Bay of Fundy would have a resonant frequency that's different from the tides. You wouldn't have these wildly changing tides in the Bay of Fundy. Maybe there's some other bay on earth where you would all of sudden hit its resonant frequency.

The key here is that different-sized objects have different resonant frequencies. If you hit the resonant frequency, it sounds very loud. What does this have to do with your ear? Let's take a trip inside your ear and see how it works. Deep inside your ear on the other side of the ear drum, there's a little organ called the cochlea. It's sort of conical-shaped. It actually looks to me a little bit like a French horn. What happens inside your cochlea is your cochlea is different sizes at different places. What that means is that different places resonate at different frequencies. If a particular sound comes in—if a particular sine wave comes in, there is some place in your cochlea where that resonates very loudly. The basilar membrane is inside the cochlea and it picks up those vibrations, exactly where in your cochlea it's vibrating, and sends that message to your brain. What it's doing is, your ear is figuring out a recipe for that sound.

Let's walk through what happens when you hear a violin playing a note. When I play an A, the sound wave hits your ear. The vibrations hit your ear in terms of a wave front like this. That's the pressure changes that we've seen before. Each overtone on the spectrum, each element in our recipe, each ingredient resonates the cochlea in a different place and with a different amplitude. It's a different force on your basilar membrane. What your ear is doing is exactly what the Fourier Transform is doing. It's separating a complicated wave into simple sine functions and sending those to your brain. It's sending the signal. It's sending the recipe back to your brain.

Let's look at some other instruments. What your brain is doing to tell the difference between say a violin and a clarinet, we've seen both of those spectra now. What your brain is doing is your brain has stored up patterns of spectra from various instruments. Your brain knows that a spectrum of a particular pattern is a violin, and a spectrum of this different pattern is a clarinet. What your brain is doing is pattern matching and telling yourself, oh, I've seen that pattern before. I've heard that spectrum before. That's a violin. Now, I want to be careful. It's a little bit more complicated than I've told you so far.

There's a caveat to all of this. The spectrum changes over time. It turns out that the spectrum of the very beginning of the note, what musically we call the attack, is incredibly key. To illustrate this, we've used a little bit of trickery electronically. What we've done is we've recorded a note on an instrument. Now we've electronically taken off the attack. Gordy has taken the very initial part of the sound off of this. Let's hear it. Here's a note on an instrument. I want you to guess what instrument is it that we're hearing? When I've played this for my students, they think it sounds a little bit like a piano. Something like that. Like some vibrating string like that. Well, here it is when we actually put the attack back.

Here is the full note. You can hear. It's actually a banjo. The pluck on the banjo gives the initial part of the spectrum lots of high overtones, but it turns out that those high overtones die out very quickly. After that period, you're left with just a vibrating string. Just like a vibrating string on a violin or a piano, the piano has a very soft attack. That's why when we take the attack off of the banjo it sounds a lot like a piano. The timbre here is important. The timbre of the attack is particularly important. We can also look at the different timbres that you can create on a single instrument.

Let's go back to my violin. Here are four different ways to play a 440-Hz A on a violin. These are essentially four different recipes using the same ingredients, the same sine waves, just different amounts. We'll play them for you from a recording first of all. Can you tell how I'm playing my As in these four? Here's the first. Here's the second. Here's a third way of playing an A. Here's a fourth. I'll play those so that you can see them. The first one was a pizzicato, like this. The second was just an open A, an A with no fingers on it, like this. The third one was the same note, but on my G string all the way up here. The last one was something called playing ponticello, playing with my bow very near the bridge like this.

Let's look at the spectra of those four sounds, and we're not going to look at the attack. We're going to look at after the attack, the spectrum of the continuous part, the ringing part of those sounds. Let's look first at the pizzicato. Here's the pizzicato again. Here's the spectrum of the open A, and we can listen to it. Here's the spectrum of an A played on my G string. Finally, here is the spectrum of a note played ponticello over near the bridge. What do we see in there? There are differences in these spectra. Let's look at these more closely.

The pizzicato is all about the lowest overtones. The attack would have the higher overtones, but they've died out fairly quickly. The spectrum is now showing us not the attack, but the ringing part which is only the lowest overtones that have come through. The open A has a rich set of overtones in most ranges. You can see all the way through these ranges up to the higher frequencies. You see a lot of all of these. The A on the G string, the higher overtones, are much quieter. The recipe calls for much less of those higher overtones and just more of the initial ones, the lower frequencies. When you play ponticello, I want you to look closely here from about 3000 Hz to 5000 Hz. They're even louder than the open A. That's what's giving the ponticello note the sort of pinched icy, edgy sound to it.

There's another way you can change the timbre of an instrument, and that's called harmonics. Now I know it's a bad word. We've already used the harmonic once, that word once. String harmonics that I'm about to play for you are different from the harmonics that describe the modes of vibrations, the overtones. They're related, but they're not the same. The idea here is that we lightly stop the string from vibrating at a particular point. If I press hard on the string, what I'm doing is I'm shortening the effective length of the string. Only this part is vibrating. What I'm asking you to do now is just press lightly on the string to stop it from vibrating. If you think back to the jump rope demonstration, you can imagine when we have the jump rope going—you can imagine somebody coming in and stopping the string in the middle.

Let's ask ourselves what would happen. That initial, that fundamental frequency—the fundamental mode where the whole string is vibrating— if somebody stops the string in the middle, that's going to be completely disrupted. The string is trying to move in the middle. Contrast that with the second harmonic, the first overtone where we have one loop here and one loop here. There is actually a node right in the middle of the jump rope. If somebody were to stop the string right in the middle, there's no problem with that. The string can continue to vibrate on each side even when somebody has their finger lightly touch the middle.

The third mode, well there's a small loop right in the third mode, but the fourth mode had three nodes. One of the nodes was right in the middle of the string. If somebody were to put their finger and stop the string right there, there would be no problem with that. When you think through all of this, what you come up with—what you realize is that all of the even modes would have nodes in the middle. Those would be allowed. All of the odd modes wouldn't because they are moving in the middle.

We can hear what this sounds like because I can do this on my violin. Here is the original A. Here is the A we get when I slightly touch the string right in the middle. When we look at the spectrum of those two, you see it acts exactly like we just described mathematically. The harmonic is giving you only the even overtones. All of the odd ones are damped out. The person touching the string there is not allowing the string to vibrate at the odd modes, just the even ones. I also want you to notice that we just changed the fundamental. The lowest frequency is no longer 440 Hz. The lowest frequency is actually what musicians call up an octave. We'll talk more about intervals later. The lowest frequency is now 880 Hz. It's double the fundamental frequency of the original.

Now, there's nothing special about 1/2. We could stop the string in lots of different places. If we stop the string 2/3 of the way up, what happens? When we think through the example of the jump rope, 2/3 of the way we would only hear the modes where there's a node at that place. The fundamental doesn't have a node there. The second harmonic doesn't have a node. It's the third one that vibrates in three pieces. That had a node 2/3 of the way up. In fact when you think through it, only the multiples of three will have nodes at 2/3. We should hear only every third overtone. Let's see if that actually happens.

Here again is the full A. Here is a harmonic when I stop the string 2/3 of the way up. You can see in the spectrum that all but the multiples of three are gone. The timbre and the fundamental have changed. The timbre has changed because we've eliminated some of the overtones. The fundamental has changed because the lowest frequency we hear now is three times the original fundamental's frequency. It's the third harmonic, the second overtone, and it's what musicians would call an E.

That was 2/3, but what about 1/3? This was 2/3. One-third is somewhere up here. If you think about the analysis with the jump rope, the mathematics should be exactly the same. Stopping the string 2/3 of the way up the string and 1/3 of the way up the string should give you identical mathematics. Again, only the multiples of three should work. Let's test this. Here again is stopping the string 2/3 of the way up the string. Let's test this and see what happens if I find 1/3 of the way up the string. Let's see what that sounds like.

Again, 2/3; 1/3. Those sound almost exactly the same. If you look at the spectra, you'll see that they are very similar as well. They have the peaks in exactly the same places. That's because we're looking at only the multiples of three in the original overtone series of the A. They have very similar heights of all of the overtones. They have very similar timbres. This is how violinists use fractions to show off. If you're asked to play a note that's exactly this note, you have two options. You could either play the note by hitting it and stopping the string at two-thirds of the way up like this. Or you could play the same note with the same timbre by finding the point way up here and playing up there.

Now, violinists are sort of notorious in the musical world for being cocky and being showoffs. Violinists know that it looks much more impressive to stop the string up here to find this place than it does here. Every violinist is going to try to hit this one just because it looks better. You're asked to play this exact note in the Mendelssohn Violin Concerto in the third movement. I'm going to play it for you the easy way first. I'm going to find this note right here. That was the easy way. The hard way is going to be to find the note way up here at 1/3 instead of 2/3. Here is the Mendelssohn Violin Concerto the way you'll always see it done in concert. Every violinist who's playing this will hit the harmonic that's way up here. That's how you'll see it done in concert.

I want to talk about one other way to change timbre. Instead of the violin, I want to talk about it on the piano. If you're designing a piano, you actually have a choice. The choice you have is where on the string should the hammer come up and hit the string? Different choices will actually give you different timbres. Remember that when we were looking at the overtones, we were looking at the seventh of those. The seventh harmonic was not a note that was on our 12-tone scale.

When we're making a piano, we can choose to put the hammer in a place so that the seventh overtone is less-heard. Using partial differential equations, we can actually predict how much of each overtone we're going to hear for a given hammer position. This program allows us to do exactly that. If we move the hammer, we're going to see how much of each overtone is produced. When we move the hammer a bit, the bars are telling you how much of each one of those overtones are produced. To avoid the seventh one, we make the following decision about the hammer. To avoid the seventh harmonic, the one that's not on our scale, we position the hammer exactly one-seventh of the way up the string.

To understand this, think back to the jump rope. The seventh harmonic is going to have seven loops. It's going to have a node 1/7 of the way up the string. If we hit it there, we're going to disrupt that mode, and so you're not going to hear any of the seventh harmonic. String harmonics we're trying to keep the string from vibrating at particular points, and we're stopping the string at those particular points. We're eliminating those nodes. Here, we're forcing the string to vibrate in a particular place. We're therefore eliminating any of the overtones that have a node there.

Pianos are actually made this way. When I talk to pianists about it, they're always a little bit surprised. I sometimes can almost see them running back to their offices to measure the strings. It turns out not all of the hammers are at 1/7. Sometimes it's a little bit too close. There's not enough room. When they can't fit a hammer at 1/7, they put it at 2/7, but the mathematics is the same. It eliminates the seventh harmonic.

That finishes our discussion on the mathematics of timbre and individual instruments. Let's talk a little bit about how individual composers use timbre in composing music. The primary way that composers use timbre is by choosing different instruments for different parts. Think about a piece like Peter and the Wolf by Prokofiev. The bassoon represents the grandfather, and the oboe with its very different timbre—sort of a pinched sound—represents the duck. The flute, the flighty flute represents the bird. The percussion is actually the hunter. These are different timbres for different instruments because of the storyline.

A more subtle way of doing this is not asking different instruments to play different things because of the difference in timbre, but asking a single instrument to play in different ways. Plucking, bowing, or playing harmonics. That takes us back to the opening music, the Air on the G String. Bach wrote the Orchestral Suite no. 3 around 1731. It was August Wilhelm, a German violinist, who adapted it just for violin and piano. He changed the key to C. He brought it down a little bit. He also decided to have violinists play it entirely on the G string. Now, violinists can tell which string you're playing a note on by the timbre. This is how we get the Air of the G String. Interestingly, this was the first piece of Bach ever recorded back in 1902.

We're going to close with the second half of the piece we started with. This is the second half of the Air on the G String. This is what I want you to think about while we're listening to this. I want you think about the choice of instrument that was made by Bach and Wilhelm. The choice of instrument by Bach was to play it on a stringed instrument. The choice by Wilhelm was to bring it down an octave. Then to not play it like I just played, but play it only on the G string. It gives it a darker quality. How do you perceive this?

You perceive this because your ear hears this. It hears the darker quality via a Fourier Transform. That's what your ear is doing: Breaking down a complicated wave into its constituent pieces, figuring out what the recipe for that particular sound is. That tells us the overtone series that we saw in lecture 1, but the amount of each one of those tells us the timbre. Listen as your ear does a Fourier Transform. Listen to the Air on the G String, which emphasizes the lower, darker parts of this piece.

Thanks for joining us. Next time we're going to talk about auditory illusions. In particular, we're going to go back and see why pitch, high and low, is more complicated than you first might think.

Pitch and Auditory Illusions
Lecture 3

Thus far, we've learned that a note on almost any instrument produces many different frequencies, called overtones or harmonics. We've also learned that how much each overtone is produced is called timbre. And we've learned to break down a wave form into its constituent frequencies, figuring out what recipe goes with a particular sound. The mathematics of that is the Fourier transform. In this lecture, we will see how these ideas lead to our brains being tricked with auditory illusions. We'll also learn why pitch is not as simple as a low-to-high continuum.

Defining Auditory Illusions

- An auditory illusion is similar to an optical illusion, but rather than a visual stimulus, it's a sound that tricks the brain.

- Consider a male voice versus a female voice on a cell phone. A man's voice vibrates at around 100 Hz; a woman's voice is much higher, perhaps 350 Hz. But the speaker on a cell phone has a range of only 350 Hz to 4000 Hz. Your brain thinks you hear the low frequencies of a male voice, but the speaker on the cell phone can't produce frequencies that low. It misses the fundamental in the first couple of overtones.

- Why is your brain tricked? Let's go through exactly what happens when you hear a male voice on a cell phone.
  - Vocal cords, like all the other one-dimensional vibrators we've discussed, vibrate at a particular sequence of overtones. When you hear a male voice at 100 Hz, his vocal cords are also vibrating at 200 Hz, 300 Hz, and so on. When he speaks into his phone, those vibrations are digitally encoded and sent as 0s and 1s, and the wave form is decoded by your phone.

  - At this point, you're still not missing the fundamental on the first few overtones. The entire signal is present, but when it's played back on your phone's speaker, you lose some of the lower overtones.

o   Here's where your brain gets involved. Your ear, first of all, does the Fourier transform and sends the spectrum to the brain. The brain recognizes that if you were hearing a 400-Hz sound, the overtones would be 800, 1200, 1600, and so on. But the sound you're hearing also has 500, 600, 700, 900, and so on. In fact, three-fourths of the sounds that are coming into your brain don't fit the pattern of a 400-Hz sound.

o   The pattern matches closer to what your brain knows as a 100-Hz sound. All that's missing are the first three overtones, 100, 200, and 300.

o   In your brain, the idea of a low G means a particular set of neurons all firing at the same time. When you hear a 100-Hz note, there's actually a neuron firing 100 times per second. When there's something vibrating at 200 times per second, there's another neuron that's firing at exactly 200 times per second. Thus, the idea of a low G is simply a set of neurons firing at the same time. When you remove just three of those, you're still firing the same set of neurons. To your brain, the pitch low G is just a particular pattern of neurons firing together.

o   We need to remember here the difference between pitch and frequency. Both relate to how high or how low a note is. But pitch is the perceptual attribute—the "psychoacoustical attribute" of a sound—whereas frequency is the physical attribute of the wave form.

o   The missing fundamental tells us that pitch and frequency are not the same. When a male speaks at 100 Hz, the pitch is a low G, but the lowest frequency that comes through on the phone is 400 Hz.

Musical Notation

- On a piano keyboard, the higher pitches are to the right and the lower pitches are to the left. The white keys are called A, B, C, D, up through G, and then that pattern repeats. The reference place on a piano is A, 440 Hz. The black keys are the sharps and the flats, the incidentals. For instance, the black key between A and B is A-sharp and B-flat.

- The interval between two notes is the distance in pitch from the lower one to the higher one. The smallest interval on a piano is to go from one key to the next, black or white, or from white to white.
  - Going from A to A-sharp would be a half-step; going from G-flat to G would be a half-step; and going between two white keys, B and C, is also a half-step.

  - Going from one key to the next of the same name is called an octave. Thus, going from an A to another A or going from a D-sharp to the next sharp is an octave.

- If we need to distinguish As, we number them: A^0 is the lowest A on the piano, followed by A^1, A^2, A^3. A^4 is at 440 Hz. There's a bit of an oddity about this: You increase the number not at A but at C. Thus, the bottommost notes are A^0, B^0, and C^1, and if you go up to 440, that's A^4 and then B^4 and C^5.

- A sharp symbol means to go up one half-step. That really means to go up one key on the piano, and a flat symbol means to go down one. Thus, B-sharp is actually the same thing as a C; an F-flat is the same thing as an E. A B-double-sharp is the same thing as a C-sharp, and an F-double-flat is the same thing as an E-flat, at least on a piano.

- An octave is made up of 12 half-steps. If you start at one key and go up 12 keys, you'll get to another key of the same name. How do these notes correspond to frequencies? For example, what are the frequencies of the As in the octaves above and below 440 Hz? Starting at 440 Hz, the next A is at 880, and the next one is at 1760.

We have to double the frequency every time we go up an octave. To go down from an A at 440, we halve it, so we get 220, 110, and 55.

- The key observation here is that octaves are multiplicative. Remember that overtones are additive. This difference between the multiplicative system of intervals and an additive system of overtones has numerous implications, some of which are very surprising.

  o Suppose a piano key sounds at some fundamental frequency x. What are the frequencies of the octaves above and below x? For the octaves above, the answer would be $2x$, $4x$, $8x$, and $16x$. For the octaves below, the answer would be $1/2x$, $1/4x$, and $1/8x$.

  o In general, if we want to go n octaves away from x, the formula would be $2nx$, and that works for both positive and negative n.

  o What about the overtones of x? Those are the multiples $2x$, $3x$, $4x$, $5x$, $6x$, and $7x$. In general, the end-harmonic above x will be nx. Note that this works only for positive n. There are no harmonics below the fundamental, at least in natural sounds. To go from one to the next, we are just adding x again. The general formula here is $n \times x$, and it's multiplication because multiplication is just repeated addition.

Comparing Overtones and Octaves

- Let's compare overtones and octaves played at frequency x. We hear the overtones x, $2x$, $3x$, $4x$, $5x$. The octaves above that are x, $2x$, $4x$, $8x$, $16x$. All of the octaves are in the overtone series, but not all of the notes in the overtone series are octaves.

- What about the notes that aren't octaves? We hear a full G at 200 Hz and then we hear each overtone isolated in turn. The fundamental is a G^3. The first overtone (the second harmonic) at 400 Hz is a G^4. The third harmonic, now at 600 Hz, is no longer a G; it's a D^5. It shouldn't be surprising that the fourth harmonic at 800 Hz is a

G again because we doubled the 400 Hz we just heard. The fifth harmonic at 1000 Hz is a B^5.

- There are many different representations of musical notes: the sound itself, numbers (frequencies), keys on a piano, notes on a staff, and peaks on a spectrum. We see these different representations added as we listen to the first 10 overtones of F^2.

- In all these representations, the octaves fall on the powers of 2, as we've discussed. Note, too, that the third harmonic is a C. That's the first note that isn't an F. It's the first note that isn't in the octave scale, and the C is a fifth above F. In other words, C is the fifth note on the F-major scale; that's how it gets the name "fifth."

- For our purposes, the two most important intervals are the octave, going from one note to the next of the same name, and the fifth, the fifth note on the major scale of the lower note. Another way to think of a fifth is going up seven half-steps.

- A key mathematical observation is that going up an octave is multiplying the frequency by 2. Going down an octave is dividing by 2. Going up a fifth is multiplying the frequency by 3/2; therefore, going down is dividing by 3/2. We can walk through a numerical example with the fundamental 87 Hz.

- In general, we see that this works, but there's an important complicating fact here.
  - The first overtone above an F^2 is an F^3. But the overtone series of an F^3 is not the same as the overtone series of an F^2.

  - The third harmonic above the F^2 is C^4, but when we play a C^4 on the piano, we hear *its* overtone series.

  - Each note comes with its own symphony of overtones. If the overtones of two notes match up, the result is a pleasant sound, what musicians call "consonance." If the overtones don't match up, the result is an unpleasant sound, "dissonance."

- The reason the overtones get closer together as we go up the piano keyboard is that the intervals are multiplicative. If we go from one octave to the next, we're multiplying by 2.
  - The normal number line has equally spaced points; the differences between numbers are the same.

  - But on a keyboard, it's the ratios that are the same, not the differences. It's a logarithmic scale: Every time you go up, you're multiplying, not adding.

Deconstructing the Missing Fundamental

- As we said, when the lower overtones are removed, the brain reconstructs the fundamental and fools you. We can hear this when we progressively remove the overtones from a G^3. The timbre changes, but because of the missing-fundamental illusion, musicians will agree that the fundamental stays at G^3.

- What happens if we add overtones? We get a bigger and more complete picture of the sound, and gradually, we start to actually hear the fundamental.

- Organ makers use this auditory illusion. The lowest note needed in organ music most of the time is incredibly low; it's at 16.4 Hz. To produce a note that low requires a 32-foot pipe, which is too large

The lowest note produced in most organ music is at 16.4 Hz, which requires a 32-foot pipe.

for many churches. The solution is to use the missing-fundamental illusion to make people think the 32-foot pipe is present. This is done by adding smaller pipes with higher frequencies to give the illusion of a lower frequency.

○ A 32-foot pipe vibrates at 16.4 Hz, which we'll call x. The overtones of a correct 32-foot pipe should be $2x$, $3x$, $4x$, $5x$, $6x$, and so on. Which smaller pipes could we use to simulate that 32-foot pipe?

○ The idea here is to produce the first and second overtones of what would be a 32-foot pipe so that listeners will hear the fundamental. What pipe would have a fundamental of $2x$? The answer is a 16-foot pipe, exactly half the length of the 32-foot pipe. The wavelength is half, so the frequency is doubled.

○ However, a 16-foot pipe will produce overtones only at $2x$, $4x$, $6x$, $8x$, $10x$, $12x$. We are missing $3x$, so we need to add another pipe with a fundamental of $3x$. We're trying to triple the frequency, which means we cut the wavelength by a factor of 1/3, and that's the size pipe we need: a pipe that measures 10 2/3 feet.

○ When we put all the overtones from those two pipes together, we're missing only a few, and that gives the illusion of something playing at x Hz.

The Scale Illusion

• Let's begin by listening to the full sound of the scale illusion. If you're like most people, in one ear, you hear the sound go down and up in pitch, and in the other ear, it seems to go up and down.

• In fact, there were no descending or ascending scales at all. The sounds jumped around, but your brain is so used to hearing scales that go up and down that it mixed the sound up and decided you must be hearing a scale.

• Tchaikovsky used this illusion in 1893 in his Sixth Symphony, *Pathétique*. The scale illusion comes in the opening of the last movement. The melody is not really present in the first or second violin parts; instead, the melody emerges from both parts (the first and second violins) coming together with the scale illusion.

Shepard Tones, Falling Bells, and the Tritone Paradox
- Shepard tones are reminiscent of an optical illusion known as the Penrose staircase. They always go up but somehow manage to get back to where they started. How can we make an endlessly rising note? The key is that each note is a symphony of different frequencies.
  - If you sit down at a piano and play A, A-sharp, B, C, and C-sharp, by the time you get to the next A, you will have played all 12 notes and gone up exactly one octave.

  - Now imagine sitting down at a keyboard that goes infinitely low and infinitely high. You play not just one A but every single A on the keyboard, and then every single A-sharp, and then every single B, C, C-sharp. By the time you get up to A, you're playing the same note you started with because you're playing every single A on the piano.

  - At every stage, you're going up one half-step, but you manage to get back to the beginning. In other words, Shepard tones are actually in a circle.

- Related to Shepard tones is an illusion called falling bells. These are notes that seem to rise, but they don't come back to where they started; they fall over time. The idea is to take Shepard tones, again, on an infinite piano, and slowly move the "envelope" of tones downward. From one note to the next, the pitch is definitely going up, but over time, the envelope drags the pitches lower and lower.

- In the tritone paradox, we hear four pairs of notes. Interestingly, people disagree on whether those pairs go from higher notes to lower notes or vice versa.
  - A "tritone" is a musical term for a particular interval of six half-steps. From A to D-sharp or from C to F-sharp would be a tritone.

o   In this paradox, two Shepard tones are played that are six half-steps apart. Two notes that are a distance of six half-steps apart are across from each other on the circle.

o   If you think the intervals go up, that means you're thinking that you are going one way around the circle. If you think the notes are going down, you're thinking that you are going the other way around the circle.

o   When you go from playing every A on an infinite piano to every D-sharp, you might have gone from every A up to D-sharp, or you might have gone from every A down six keys to D-sharp. Because it's every A and then every D-sharp, you cannot distinguish between the two.

o   Each note is made up of many different frequencies. You can compare two individual frequencies, but once we manufacture them and put them into these notes, you cannot compare the entire note.

•   In Lecture 2, we learned that timbre is more complex than pitch because pitch can be represented on a one-dimensional scale of low to high. The Shepard tones and other illusions show that it's not that simple. Here, notes are constructed that cannot be compared in pitch; neither is really higher or lower than the other. Frequency—the physical attribute, not the perceived one—is a one-dimensional scale, but pitch—the perceived attribute—is much more complicated.

Suggested Reading

Benson, *Music: A Mathematical Offering*, chapter 4.

Deutsch, "Diana Deutsch's Audio Illusions."

Loy, *Musimathics*, vol. 1, chapter 6.

1. How does our knowledge of how the ear works explain the missing-fundamental illusion?

2. How did Shepard use the fact that we interpret multiple frequencies (in a harmonic series) as a single note to create an endlessly rising note?

Pitch and Auditory Illusions
Lecture 3—Transcript

Dave: Welcome back. So far we've learned that a note on pretty much any instrument produces many different frequencies. We call these overtones or harmonics. It is a symphony in a single note. We've learned how much each overtone is produced is called timbre. And we've learned to break down a waveform into its constituent frequencies, sort of figuring out what recipe goes with a particular sound. The mathematics of that is the Fourier Transform. And your ear does that. Your bodies actually take a Fourier Transform when you listen to things.

Today we are going to figure out how these ideas lead to our brains being tricked. These are called auditory illusions. We're also going to learn how pitch, how we talk about it, and why it's not so simple as a sort of a low to high continuum. We're going to find out how auditory illusions are used in music.

Oh, I'm sorry, it's the producer, I really have to take this. Hello?

Producer: Hey, Dave, not everyone is familiar with the term auditory illusion. You should define it.

Dave: Oh, that's a really good point, I will get to it. Sorry about that. An auditory illusion is, well, actually you just heard one. You see that was producer. Could you tell if the producer was male or female? Now that's probably really easy for you. It's a male producer. You heard the nice low frequencies of Zach's male voice. Actually, you didn't hear the low frequencies of Zach's voice. It was an auditory illusion. Your brain is tricking you into thinking something is there when it really isn't. An auditory illusion is a lot like an optical illusion. Optical illusions are visual things that trick your brain, auditory illusions are sounds that trick your brain.

The basic conundrum is like this. A man's voice vibrates at maybe around 100 Hz. A woman's voice is much higher, maybe 350 Hz or so. The speaker on the cell phone only has a range of about 350 Hz up to 4000 Hz. You brain thinks you hear the low frequencies of Zach's voice, but the speaker on the cell phone simply can't produce frequencies that low. It's missing the fundamental in the first couple of overtones.

Why is your brain tricked? Why don't you think all callers are women? It's because you have knowledge of overtones and the Fourier Transform and how your ear works, we're going to use that knowledge to figure out exactly what happens.

So let's quickly go through exactly what happens when Zach calls and we talk to him on the phone. Now, this is a bit of a simplification. Well, here's Zach's voice again. "Auditory illusion." When Zach speaks like that the vibrations are not just at 100 Hz, but also overtones. Vocal cords, like all of the other one-dimensional vibrators we've talked about, vibrate at a particular sequence of overtones or harmonic series. So when you hear something at 100 Hz, his vocal cords are also vibrating at 200 Hz, 300 Hz, 400 Hz, 500, 600, 700, on and on up that series. When he speaks, those vibrations are digitally encoded by his phone and then sent zeroes and ones. That message is sent to my phone and the waveform is decoded by my phone.

Now at this point, we're still not missing the fundamental on the first few overtones. The entire signal is there. It's when it's played back on my phone's speaker that we lose some of the lower overtones. The range is from 350 to 4000 Hz, and so the speaker only plays things like 400 Hz, 500, 600, 700, 800. It's missing the lowest, the 100, 200, and 300. Here's where your brain gets involved. Your ear, first of all, does the Fourier Transform and it sends the spectrum to the brain.

We're going to talk a little bit more about how your brain does this in lecture 12. But your brain is essentially in an absolutely fantastic pattern recognition machine. Your brain asks, "Well, is this sound of voice at a high G? Because after all 400 Hz is the lowest frequency that is being transmitted to your ear." And your brain does the following thinking. If it were a 400 Hz sound, then the overtones would be 800, 1200, 1600. It would be multiples of 400, but the sound that you're hearing also has 500, 600, 700. It has the 800, but it also has 900, 1000, 1100. In fact, 3/4 of the sounds that are coming to your brain don't fit the pattern, and so your brain rules out the possibility that it's a 400-Hz note. On the other hand, is the sound of voice at a low G a 100-Hz note? That's actually closer; that pattern matches closer to what your brain knows as a 100 Hz note. A 100-Hz note would vibrate at 100, 200, 300, 400, 500, 600, and all you're missing in that is your first three, 100, 200, 300. This is actually a neurological phenomenon, what's going on in your brain.

In your brain, the idea of a low G means a particular set of neurons all firing at the same time. When you hear 100-Hz note, when something vibrates at 100 Hz, there's actually a neuron. The neuroscientist can tell now that there's a neuron that's vibrating, that's firing 100 times per second. When there's something vibrating at 200 times per second, there's another neuron that's firing at exactly 200 Hz per second, and 300 and 400 and 500 and 600. And so, the idea of a low G is simply a whole set of neurons all firing at the same time. When you remove just three of those, you're still firing merely the same set of neurons. To your brain, the pitch low G is just a particular pattern of neurons firing together. When Zach talks to us on the phone, his phone voice doesn't fit that pattern perfectly, but it fits close enough. You hear a low G, you hear a man's voice, even though the low frequencies aren't there.

Now, we have to remember in this discussion the difference between pitch and frequency. Both relate to how high or how low a note is. The base versus the soprano. But pitch is the perceptual attribute, more particularly you might call it the psychoacoustical attribute of a sound, whereas frequency is the physical attribute of the waveform. The missing fundamental tells us that pitch and frequency are not the same. When Zach speaks at 100 Hz, the pitch is a low G but what comes through on the phone, the lowest frequency is 400 Hz. Now, in most cases, pitch and frequency are really interchangeable, and we think of them as the same thing. In fact, usually, when I'm speaking to a musical audience, I'll talk about pitch and when I'm talking to more of a math or science audience, I'll talk about frequency. But really we should be more particular and when we're talking about perceptual things use the word pitch and when talking about physical vibrations we should use the word frequency.

This distinction between perceptual attributes and physical attributes is actually the source of something you've probably heard before. If a tree falls in the woods and no one is there to hear it, does it make a sound? Well, the definition of sound is that sound is a perceptual attribute, not a physical attribute. Therefore, when a tree falls in the woods, if a tree falls and no one is there to hear it, there is no sound because nobody is perceiving it. The lack of perception means there is no sound.

So, let's dig deeper into this and try to understand what's going on musically. We're going to need a lot more music in later lectures and so we're going to talk about some notation here. Now I know this is going to be review for some of you and this might be a little bit too quick for others. So, if this is too quick for you, you might need to replay this section, especially if you're new to music.

I've found that for most students, the easiest point of entry is a piano keyboard, with its lovely ebony and ivory keys. So let's look at a piano keyboard. On a piano keyboard, the higher pitches are to the right and the lower pitches are to the left. The white keys are named and they're named A, B, C, D, E, all the way through G, and then that pattern repeats, A, B, C, again and again. You need some place to start and the sort of reference place on a piano is 440 Hz and that is A.

Now there's a long story. The reference point has not always been 440 Hz. It's gone back and forth. In fact, modern orchestras typically tune a little bit sharp because it sounds a little bit happier. But for now, the reference point is 440 Hz. So that's the names of the white keys.

The black keys are the sharps and the flats, the incidentals. The black key between A and B is A-sharp and it's also named B-flat. At least on a piano those are the same. We'll find out later that those really shouldn't be the same, but that's for another lecture. The interval between two notes is how far in pitch to go from the lower one to the higher one. The smallest interval we have, the smallest interval on a piano is to go from one key to the next, black or white, or from white to white. A half step is what we call that. Going from A to A-sharp would be a half step. Going from G-flat to G would be a half step. And going between the two white keys, B and C, is also a half step. Going from one key to the next of the same name is called an octave. So going from an A to another A, the next A, or going from a D-sharp to the next D-sharp, that's called an octave.

If we need to distinguish As, as there are many different As, put numbers on them. So A0 is the very lowest A on the piano, and then A1, A2, A3. It's actually A4 that's a 440 Hz. Now there's a bit of an oddity about this. You'd increase the number, not at A that you think you might, but at C. So the bottommost notes are A0, B0, and then C1. And if you'd go up to 440A, that's A4 and then B4 and then C5.

Now, a sharp symbol means to go up one half step. That really means to go up one key on the piano, and a flat symbol means to go down one. So, B-sharp is actually the same thing as a C. An F-flat is the same thing as an E. We can actually do double sharps and double flats. Some composers love to use those. It may get very difficult to read music. But a B-double sharp is the same thing as a C-sharp and an F-double flat is the same thing as an E-flat, at least on a piano.

An octave is made up of 12 half steps. If you start at one name and go up 12 keys you'll get to another key of the same name. So how do these notes correspond to frequencies? If you look at the As, the octaves above and below 440 Hz, you can ask what are the frequencies of those notes? Now going up, you start at 440 Hz and then the next A is at 880 and the next one is at 1760. You have to double the frequency every time you go up an octave. You notice we're not just adding 440 Hz each time. To go down from an A at 440 A, you half it, so you get 220 and then 110 Hz and then 55. To go up an octave, you multiply by 2 and to go down an octave you divide by 2.

The key observation here is that octaves are multiplicative. Remember that overtones are additive. This difference between this multiplicative system of intervals and an additive system of overtones has incredible numbers of implications. Some of them are very surprising. One of them we're going to talk about today, and that's the fact that no piano is ever in tune—more about that later.

I do want to make sure we understand the difference between an additive system and a multiplicative system. So suppose a piano key sounds at some fundamental frequency. Let's just call it x. We can ask, what are the octaves above and below x? What are the frequencies of those? Well, above, you would multiply by 2 and so the octaves above x would be $2x$, $4x$, $8x$, $16x$. Going back down the other way, we would $1/2x$, $1/4x$, and $1/8x$.

In general, if you want to go n octaves away from x, the formula would be $2^n x$ and that actually works for both positive and negative $-n$. To get from one to the next, we multiply. The general formula here is exponential, it's $2^n x$. n is an exponent. Really what we're doing here is repeated multiplication is exactly what exponentiation is.

What above the overtones? Let's go back to the frequency x that we're playing a piano key at. What are the harmonics, the overtones that you would hear? We talked about those before and those exactly are the multiples, $2x$, $3x$, $4x$, $5x$, $6x$, and $7x$. In general, the nth harmonic above x is going to be nx. There is this discrepancy in naming the nth overtone as actually $n + 1 \times x$ because of this discrepancy. We should note that that works only for positive n. There are no harmonics below the fundamental, at least in natural sounds.

To go from one to the next, we are just adding x again. The general formula here has $n \times x$ and its multiplication because multiplication is just repeated addition.

So, let's compare these two. We have the overtones and we have the octaves. We are playing at frequency x. We're also going to hear the overtones x, $2x$, $3x$, $4x$, $5x$. The octaves above that are x, $2x$, $4x$, $8x$, $16x$. All of the octaves are in the overtones series, but not all of the notes in the overtone series are octaves. It's a little bit like the fact that every square is a rectangle, but not every rectangle is a square. When you hear a 100-Hz note, many of the overtones you hear are octave.

What about the overtones that aren't octaves? Now this is going to be necessary for later discussions of scale, so we should get into this now. We're going to use digital technology in order to hear this. So, I'm going to play a G repeatedly. It's not exactly at 200 Hz, but for the simplifications of the calculations, let's call it 200 Hz. And Gordy, our sound engineer, is going to isolate each overtone in turn. So, I'm going to play the full G, like this. And now what he's going to do is he's going to isolate each one of these in turn. So here is just the fundamental. Even though I'm playing it, you're only going to hear the fundamental. And that's a G3. Now here's the first overtone, the second harmonic, $k=2$, if you're working with the formula. It's at 400 Hz.

Now if you find that on the piano, you'll find that that's exactly one octave above the fundamental and so that one is a G4. Here's the third harmonic. We're now at 600 Hz. I'm still playing the G and you're going to hear the third harmonic. You notice that that is not a G anymore. Musically, that's a D and that's a D5. Now, what mode you're hearing is you're hearing the mode where the jump rope is divided to three pieces with two nodes.

Here's the fourth harmonic at 800 Hz. And it shouldn't be surprising that that's a G again because we doubled the 400 Hz we heard a minute ago.

Here's the fifth harmonic. We are now at 1000 Hz. And the note you're hearing now is a B5, if you find it on the piano.

So let's look at multiple representations of these harmonics. Now mathematicians love to look at different representations. Mathematicians have things like algebraic representations, graphical, numerical, verbal representations. I like to think of it sort of like Hokusai's famous woodblock prints, *Thirty-Six Views of Mt. Fuji*. The most famous is probably the *Great Wave off Kamegawa*. Hokusai was looking at the same subject, Mt. Fuji, in this case, from different perspectives. Mathematicians do this. They may take something like a problem, $y=x^2$ and look at it from an algebraic perspective or graphical or even a numerical perspective of the table of numbers. And experts in mathematics effortlessly translate between these two representations, between any one of these. Picking the most useful one for their purposes at a particular kind.

Different representations of a musical note are also important and we have many of them. We have the sound. You could hear musical note, whether it's the original sound or digitally modified like we just heard. There are numbers involved, the frequencies, or, in fact, the wavelength. You could think of these as keys on a piano representing those notes. You could think of them as notes on a staff, how we read music. You could even think of them in terms of the spectrum and look at the spectrum and look at the different peaks, each one of those peaks is a different frequency using the Fourier Transform.

Expert musicians and people who deal with sound a lot effortlessly translate among these different representations.

So, let's look at the harmonics of F2. F2 is about 87 Hz. A full F2 on a piano. It's too low for my violin so I can't play it, but here's an F2 on a piano. And it might be too low for your speakers, but you're still going to hear it because of the missing fundamental illusion.

We're going to play the sequence of overtones of F2, all the first 10 of them, and every time we're going to add a different representation so that you get a sense of how these representations work together. Now, I want to tell you that there's an important thing about sign waves versus notes. If we use just sign waves, then these lowest notes at 87 Hz, your speaker might not be able to play it and you wouldn't hear anything. Instead we're going to use notes with overtones. We're going to generate these with the computer, but we're going to use notes with overtones. And because we do that, even though your speaker can't play at 87 Hz, you're going to hear all of the overtones and you're going to know that we're playing a note at 87 Hz.

So let's begin with sound. Here's an F2 with all of its overtones in turn. And now let's add the frequencies, the numbers, the representation that involves numbers. Here it is again, now with the numbers. If you're quick with numbers, you'll notice that those are just the multiples of 87.

Now let's look at this on a piano keyboard. Let's hear it again. Now you may remember that the seventh one, the seventh harmonic is not on our scale. We're just pointing to a key that's the closest key that we have on that scale. Finally, we can look at notes on the musical staff. So, let's play them again and look at the notes on a musical staff. Again, that seventh one, we don't have a way of representing that on our musical scale, so that's an approximation.

What do we notice in all these representations? Well, we notice that the octaves fall on the powers of two. We've already discussed that 1, 2, 4, 8.

We've noticed that the third harmonic is a C. That's the first note that isn't an F. It's the first note that isn't in the octave scale and the C is a fifth above F. In other words, C is the fifth note on the F major scale, that's how it gets the name of fifth.

For us, the two most important intervals are octave, going from one note to the next of the same name, and the fifth. The fifth note on the major scale of the lower note. Another way to think of a fifth is going up seven half steps. Now, there's a key mathematical observation that going up an octave is multiplying the frequency by two. Going down an octave is dividing by two. Going up a fifth is multiplying the frequency by three halves, therefore, going down is dividing by three halves. Just to see that, let's look through a numerical example to make sure we understand this.

The fundamental we're working with is 87 Hz. The second harmonic is going to be double that, 174. And the third harmonic is going to be another 87 Hz higher, 261. The notes, the fundamental is an F2. The second harmonic is an F3. And the third harmonic is a C4, seven half steps above the F3. To go from one octave to the next, to go from F2 to F3, we're multiplying by 2, 87 Hz times two is equal 174 Hz. To go from the F3 to the C4, that's a fifth again, we're multiplying by three halves. If you take 174 Hz and multiply it by three halves, you get 261 Hz. In general, we see that this works exactly. Octaves are multiplying by two, fifths are multiplying by three halves.

If we were talking about wave lengths instead of frequencies, going up an octave would be dividing by two and going up a fifth would be dividing by three halves. Because remember, there is this reciprocal relationship between frequencies and wavelengths. Now there's an important complicating fact there, especially if we're thinking of playing this on a piano.

If we're looking at the F2, the first overtone, the second harmonic above an F2 is an F3. But if we play an F3 on a piano, we hear its overtones and the overtone series of an F3 is not necessarily the same thing as the overtone series of an F2. The third harmonic above the F2 is C4, but when we play a C4 on the piano we hear its overtone series. Each note comes with its own symphony of overtones. And when we play two notes, if those overtones match up, it sort of gives us a pleasant sound. Musicians call this consonance.

If the overtones don't match up, it gives us a sort of an unpleasant sound and musicians call this dissonance. We're going to talk about much more about this in later lectures.

I want to take us on a quick mathematical tangent though. Did you notice how the overtones kept getting closer together as we went up the piano keyboard? There's a mathematical reason for this. The intervals are multiplicative. If you go from one octave to the next, you're multiplying by two. The normal number line has equally spaced points. You remember normal number line from when you were young? It's 1 to 2, 2 to 3, each one of those have the same space, equally spaced points; the differences were the same.

On a keyboard, equally spaced intervals on a keyboard don't have that. It's the ratios that are the same, not the differences that are the same. Mathematicians hear this and think of a logarithmic scale. Logarithmic scales come up in many different areas. If you look at investments, the proper scale to look at investments is on a logarithmic scale. You can double your money and then double it again. You should be looking at the same thing in terms of investments.

A Richter scale used to measure earthquake severity, that's also a logarithmic scale. If you go from a 6.0 on the Richter scale to an earthquake that 7.0, is actually 10 times worse in terms of the amplitude of vibration. And if you go from a 7.0 to an 8.0, the 8.0 versus 6.0 is now 100 times worse in terms of that vibration.

Decibels are another example of a logarithmic scale. That's something we've seen before. Going up 10 decibels means you increase the intensity of the sound by a factor of 10 and every time you go up 10 decibels, it's another factor of 10. The keyboard here is a physical example of a logarithmic scale, where every time you go up you're multiplying and not adding.

So let's go back and see if we can deconstruct the missing fundamental now that we know some more information about intervals and notes and pitch. The basic idea here is that when you remove the lower overtones, your brain reconstructs the fundamental and it fools you. Let's see if we can hear that musically this time on my violin. So each time I play a G3, right around

200 Hz, Gordy is going to remove the next lowest frequency and as he remove overtones, the timbre is going to change, but because of this missing fundamental illusion, musicians are all going to agree that the fundamental stays at G3, even though there are no frequencies that low anymore. So, I'm just going to play G3, each time Gordy is going to remove the next lower overtone.

Here's the full G3 first of all. And now we're going to start removing overtones. What you can hear, it gets tinier and tinier but the fundamental stays at the same pitch. It's still a G3.

Now instead of removing overtones, let's try to add them. So we're going to add up overtones. Here we're actually making the recipe and putting things in. We're going to start with just the second harmonic. We're going to completely remove the fundamental and all the higher ones, and just let you listen to the second harmonic and that should sound an octave above. For reference the G that I'm going to play—here's the full G. And the pitch of the octave above the second harmonic is an octave above that, and that's a G4. So we're going to start by playing just that second harmonic and then we're going to add the third, add the fourth, and gradually as we add the higher harmonics you get a bigger and a more complete picture of the sound and gradually you're going to actually start to hear the fundamental, which is lower down that G3. So here we go. Again, even though you're not hearing anything vibrating at 200 Hz you gradually start to perceive a note that low. We're adding the higher frequencies and at some point your brain starts reconstructing the lower one.

Let's hear it one more time so you get the sense of this. So how is this used in music? It turns out that organ makers use this auditory illusion. The lowest note needed in an organ music most of the time is a note that is incredibly low, it's at 16.4 Hz and to produce a note that low you have to have a 32-foot pipe. Now the problem is that many churches are simply too small to fit a 32-foot pipe. The solution is to use the missing fundamental illusion to make people think that there is a 32-foot pipe there. We're doing what we just did, we're adding higher frequencies to get the illusion of a lower one. A 32-foot pipe vibrates at 16.4 Hz. Let's just call that x so we don't have to deal with a number.

The overtones of a correct 32-foot pipe should be 2x, 3x, 4x, 5x, 6x, on and on and up. Now you can't fit that 32-foot pipe, but you can fit smaller pipes. Now let's figure out which smaller pipes you should put. The idea here is to produce the first and second overtones of what would be a 32-foot pipe so that listeners will hear the fundamental. So, we need to figure out what pipe would have a fundamental of 2x and when we do that, we figure out that it's a 16-foot pipe, it's exactly half the length. The wavelength is half, so that the frequency is doubled. So we put a 16-foot pipe so the fundamental of the 16-foot pipe is at 2x, but that's only going to produce overtones at 2x, 4x, 6x, 8x, 10, 12. Those are going to be the overtones of a 16-foot pipe. In particular we are missing 3x, so let's put another pipe with a fundamental of 3x.

When you think about that we're trying to triple the frequency and so we should take the wavelength and cut it by a factor of one-third and that's the size pipe you use. You need 32 feet divided by 3, and gives you a 10 and 2/3 foot pipe. When you put a 10-2/3–foot pipe in there, you hear the overtones of that, which are going to be the fundamental at 3x and then its overtones at 6x, 9x, 12x, 15, just the multiples of 3x. When we put all of these together. If we played the 16-foot pipe and the 10-2/3–foot pipe and we listen to all of those overtones, the things that we're hearing are 2x, 3x, 4x, 6x, 8x, 9x, 10x, 12x. We're only missing a few of them. We're missing 7x, 11x, and so we're only missing a few of them and that gives us the illusion of something playing at x Hz.

Now most churches can accommodate 10-foot and 16-foot pipes, and so the problem is solved.

So let's try to hear this effect. We're going to play some organ music in the background and the missing fundamental illusion here is actually happening on two different levels. Now the organ might be tricking you into thinking it has a 32-foot pipe when it doesn't. I'm actually not sure which church and which organ this particular organ music was played on, but it might have not a 32-foot pipe but the 10-2/3 and the 16-foot pipe. So the organ itself might be tricking us. But if you don't have a nice sound system with some big sub-woofer playing the very low frequencies, then your speakers probably can't produce the lowest notes even of the 10-2/3 and 16-foot pipe. It's multiple layers of illusions. Your brain is tricking you into hearing something that I'm telling you is your brain tricking you into hearing a long organ pipe. Oh, that hurt to think about.

Let's move on to another sound illusion. Let's move on to the scale illusion. Now your brain is an amazing pattern recognizer and sometimes it gets fooled because of that. The scale illusion uses stereo sound to fool it. Now this illusion will be better if you have headphones or a good stereo system, but the point will be clear without it. I'll make sure that you understand the point even if you don't have those things. This isn't exactly mathematical but it is a form of pattern recognition, which is very mathematical and this effect is incredibly cool. This is work done by Diana Deutsch who is a pioneer in psychoacoustics. She was British-born and she works at the University of California, San Diego. She has many, many different auditory illusions, and if you look in our website you can hear these.

We're going to listen to the full sound at first and then we'll deconstruct it. Here's the full sound of the scale illusion. What did you hear when we listened to that? If you're like most people, what you heard was that in one ear the sound went down and back up in pitch, umm, bom, bom, bom, bom, bom, bom, bom. In the other ear, it went up and back down, bom, bom, bom, bom, bom bom, bom. What was actually playing? Let's take these apart and listen to the left and right tracks separately. In fact, there were no descending or ascending scales at all. It didn't go up and back down. It jumped around. Your brain was tricked. This is pattern recognition gone-awry. You are so used to hearing scales that go up and back down that your brain mixed the sounds up and said you must be hearing a scale.

Now, Deutsch identified this illusion in 1973, but Tchaikovsky used it in 1893. So let's go and let's hear what Tchaikovsky did with the scale illusion. In the Sixth Symphony, which is titled *Pathétique*, which doesn't mean pathetic, it means something more like sympathetic. The Sixth Symphony is a little bit strange in terms of symphonic structure. It has a triumphant fast third movement. Usually the last movement is fast and triumphant, but the last movement of *Pathétique* is a slow, tragic movement. It was written just before his death, which might have been a suicide. Music historians are a little bit uncertain of this. One very prominent theory is that Tchaikovsky was gay and he was about to be outed and instead of going through that he drank unboiled water and he died of cholera just a few days later.

The *Pathétique* was first performed just nine days before his death, and the scale illusion comes in the opening of the last movement. Here's the opening theme. I'll play it for you on my violin first. It's such an emotive melody. I have vivid memories of the first time I played this symphony. I was at Interlochen Music Camp for the summer and we were playing with Carl St. Clair who conducted the Boston Symphony sometimes. He is now at the Pacific Symphony. And we played it the first time without much emotion at all and St. Clair stopped the orchestra and said, "Tchaikovsky wrote three ballets, 10 operas, six symphonies, wonderful concertos. He wrote some of the best music ever written and these are some of the last notes Tchaikovsky ever wrote. He knew he was going to die. Let's play that again."

And indeed we played that theme with much more emotion or did we? We certainly played with much more emotion and it sounded much better but we didn't actually play the theme. None of us played the theme because the theme is actually an illusion. In order to see that, let's look at the score because this mournful, this disconsolate melody isn't actually there. Now, if you can't read music, it's okay, we'll help you get through this. We'll give you the gist of this.

Here are the first and second violin parts. In an orchestra, the first violin part is a group, probably about 16 violins and they are playing one part. The second violin part is played by maybe 14 violinists. There are separate sections playing different music. So here's what the first violins are playing. That's the first violin part. Here's what the second violins are playing. The mournful melody actually emerges from both parts. It's the scale illusion.

So let me play the melody that you hear and we'll highlight it one note at each time how you're hearing this melody. Now that was just my violin. Let's hear it with the entire symphony, the way it was meant to be heard. So here's the passage with the entire symphony and I hope you could hear the melody as it comes out that's not really there. It's just the individual parts coming together with the scale illusion. Here's Tchaikovsky's Sixth Symphony, the opening. It's such a wonderful piece to listen to. Just to make sure we understand, here again I'll play the individual parts. The part you can't hear because nobody is playing the actual melody. Here's the first violin part. And here's what the second violins are playing. And those two are working together to give us the illusion of this wonderful, beautiful melody.

Finally, we're going to talk about three different, three stranger illusions that really bend the mind a little bit. We're going to talk about Shepard tones, falling bells, and the tri-tone paradox.

Let's look at Shepard tones first. There's actually no better way to introduce you to Shepard tones than just to let you listen. Here's a continuous version of Shepard tones. And here's a discrete, a mathematical word for sort of separate, individual version. These sounds may be reminiscent of an optical illusion, the Penrose staircase. You've probably seen something like this in the work of M.C. Escher, works like *Waterfall* or *Ascending and Descending* use this illusion. Like the staircase, Shepard tones are always going up, but somehow manage to get back where they were started.

So, who is Roger Shepard of the Shepard tone. Roger Shepard was a cognitive scientist with a psychology Ph.D. from Yale. He worked at Bell Labs, Harvard, and Stanford. He is a recipient of the National Medal of Science. He really liked to find ways of tricking the brain. Some of the more optical Shepard drawings are quite famous, but he is actually most famous for his auditory illusion, the endlessly rising tone. So let's see if we can understand what's going on with Shepard tones. How can you make an endlessly rising note? Well, the key is that each note is a symphony of different frequencies.

So here's the basic idea. Imagine that you sit down at a piano and you play— let's do something easy first. Just an A and then A-sharp and then B and C, C-sharp. By the time you get to the next A, you will have played all 12 notes and gotten to the A and you will have definitely gone up exactly one octave. Now let's do something a little crazier. Let's sit down at an infinite keyboard that goes infinitely low and infinitely high. And let's sit down and play, not just one A, but every single A on the keyboard and then every single A-sharp and then every single B, C, C-sharp. By the time we get up to A, you're playing the same note we started with because you're playing every single A on the piano. You're back to the beginning. At every stage you're going up one-half step, but you manage to get back to the beginning. In other words, Shepard tones are actually in a circle.

Now let's refine this just a little bit because there's a problem with this. Because we only perceive notes as low as some particular value and as high as some other particular value, you might actually hear notes jumping into that if we did what I just suggested. There's a solution to this, which is part of the Shepard tones, and that's to play the middle notes very loudly and to play the higher octaves softer and softer, and to play the lower octaves softer and softer. It's to put these sounds in sort of an envelope. Now as we play the notes—bom, bom, bom, bom, bom, bom, bom, instead of jumping into a range of hearing the notes at the bottom creep in so we don't hear something jumping down to our lowest range of hearing, and we don't hear things going out of our range of hearing because of the sort of creeping out of the range.

Now related to Shepard tones is an illusion called falling bells. It is fairly easy to explain once we have this idea of the Shepard tones encased in this sort of envelope. With just a small adjustment, we can understand falling bells. Falling bells are notes that seem to rise, but actually they don't just come back to where they started. They actually fall over time. The idea is to take Shepard tones, again, we're just moving up, bom, bom, bom, bom, on our infinite piano. Now take this envelope in which they are encased and slowly move that envelope downward. Now from one note to the next, your pitch is definitely going up but over time the envelope drags the pitches lower and lower. If you want to hear this, it's on YouTube. It's a wonderful little illusion.

Finally, let's go to the tri-tone paradox. Once again listen to this illusion first. So what you're about to hear is four pairs of notes. For each pair of notes I want you to decide for yourself, is it going from a lower note to higher note, or is it going from a higher note to a lower note? On the piano, are you going from a one note to further to the right or are you going from one note further to the left. If you are with somebody else, you may want to give thumbs up. When I do this for a large crowd, I ask everybody to give a thumbs up if it's going from a lower note to a higher note, and thumbs down if they think it's going from a higher to a lower note. So let's hear that.

It turns out that people disagree on whether those are going from higher notes to lower notes. In fact, well-trained musicians disagree and the funny thing is that each one of them is sure of their answer. I've done this in audiences of 500 people and there's thumbs going up and down all over the place and people were arguing with each other. What's going on?

When you hear these tri-tones—first of all, let me explain what a tri-tone is. A tri-tone is a musical term for a particular interval of six half steps. It goes from A to D-sharp, would be a tri-tone, or from C to F-sharp. I can play them for you on the violin here. Here's a tri-tone. If we add one more note you get a famous theme. You hear that in many places, but probably the most famous are Maria from *West Side Story*. It is also the intro to *The Simpsons* theme on TV.

Now to understand this paradox, all we're doing is we're taking those Shepard tones we had before and we're playing two of them that are six half steps apart. Six half steps is across the circle, from these 12 notes that are on the circle, that are the Shepard tones. Do you think that intervals go up? That means you're thinking you are going one way around that circle. If you think the notes are going down, you're just going down the other way around the circle. Which view is correct? Well, neither one really.

You see, when you go from playing every A on an infinite piano to every D-sharp, you might have gone from everyday A up to D-sharp, or you might have gone from every A down six keys to a D-sharp. Because it's every A and then every D-sharp, those notes you cannot distinguish between those two things. You simply cannot compare these two notes that we've played for you in this tri-tone illusion. Higher or lower, it's not really clear. Each note is made up of many different frequencies. You can compare two individual frequencies, but once we manufacture them and put them into these notes, you cannot compare the entire note.

Let's go back to the definition of timbre we saw before. In lecture 2, we heard that timbre is more complex than pitch because pitch can be represented on a one-dimensional scale low to high. The Shepard tones and Deutsch's work show that it's not so simple. They've constructed notes that cannot be compared in pitch, neither is really higher nor lower than the other. Frequency, the physical, not perceived attribute, is a one-dimensional scale, but pitch, the perceived attribute is much more complicated. We might think that one note is higher than another but in reality they might not be comparable.

I'm sorry, it's Zach again. But now we know something about men's voices on phones. Let's listen. Hey, Zach.

Zach: Dave, I know you love these, but we're out of time. No more auditory illusions.

Dave: Oh, okay, okay. Now they know why they can tell that you're a guy.

Zach: There are easier ways.

Dave: Well, easier, yes, but now you know not only how the missing fundamental illusion tricks your brain when you're on the phone, but you also know how pitch is much more complicated than you might have first thought. You know how you can use overtones to construct sounds that trick your mind. For a musical coda, let's return to a piece of music with all of its frequencies intact. So I'm going to play for you the Arabian Dance from Tchaikovsky's Nutcracker Suite. The Arabian Dance is based on an Arabian scale, not the standard Western scale. And it's a good way to foreshadow what we're going to talk about in the next lecture.

The next lecture's discussion is about the mathematics of different scale.

Thanks for joining us.

How Scales Are Constructed
Lecture 4

V ivaldi's *Spring* and *Lady Meng Jiang* are from two very different musical traditions, Western and Chinese. But what is it that makes them different? Many differences exist between music from different cultures, such as instruments, notations, and so on, but one of the key differences is that they use different musical scales. They make different choices about notes. In this lecture and the next, we'll look at how the harmonic series informs our choice of scales and how we tune those scales.

Defining a Scale

- A scale is a collection of notes, increasing or decreasing in pitch. For our purposes, we can think about them as covering a range of one octave, from one frequency to its double (e.g., from A at 440 Hz to 880 Hz).

- Remember, an octave is from one key on a piano to the next of the same name, 12 half-steps. As we know, the keys on a piano have names—A, B, C-sharp—but when we talk about scales, we also give them numbers—the fundamental, the second up through the seventh, and the octave.

- The number of notes on a scale is key. We talk about the number of notes on a scale as being the number of notes before you get to the next octave. When you play a scale, you usually start on the bottom and go to the next octave, but if you have a seven-note scale, a "heptatonic scale," you actually play eight notes because you include the eighth note on the top end.

- The piano's keys are sort of a fixed reference point; the names of the keys never change. However, the numbers—the fundamental, second, third, and so on—do change. When you're in the key of C, C is where you measure from, and when you're in the key of G, G is where you measure from.

- When we talk about the key of the scale, we're not talking about a piano key. We're talking about the lowest note of the scale, usually the first. When we talk about the key of some composition, that's the note that's most important, and pieces tend to start and end on that particular note.

- An interval is the distance in pitch between one note and another. It's related to scales; in numbers, the relation is as follows: The interval of the fifth is the distance between the fundamental and the fifth note on the major scale when starting on the fundamental.

Constructing Scales

- Scales can have different moods (bright and happy versus darker and sad), but one of the things they all have in common is that they all have the fifth and the octave. Those are the second and third harmonics we hear when we're vibrating just a single note or a single column of air. Nearly every musical tradition on earth contains both the fifth and octave.

One of the key differences between Western music and music from other cultures is that they use different musical scales—they make different choices about notes.

- Let's review what we need to construct scales.
  - o We know that objects vibrate in different modes (overtones), and we know that the wavelengths of the most common overtones are in a ratio of 1/1 to 1/2, 1/3, 1/4. The harmonic series and the frequencies are just multiples, 1, 2, 3, 4; those are arithmetic series.

  - o What we learn from the overtone series is that to go up an octave, we multiply frequencies by 2, and to go down an octave, we divide frequencies by 2. We also learned about a fifth—seven half-notes on a piano is a fifth—and to go up a fifth, we multiply the frequencies by 3/2. To go back down, we divide by 3/2.

- Let's look at a numerical example: How do we go up an octave from a 440 A? We multiply by 2 and get 880 Hz. If we start back at A and want to go up a fifth, that would be the fifth note on the A-major scale, E^5. To figure out what the frequency of that is, we multiply 440 Hz by 3/2 and get 660 Hz. The octaves and the fifths are the key ingredients we need to construct scales.

Choosing Notes on a Scale

- Let's start by building a scale with a 100-Hz note, roughly a G^2. The next octave is 200 Hz, a G^3. We can try building a 5-note scale by putting the notes equally spaced between 100 and 200 Hz (i.e., 100, 120, 140, 160, 180, 200). The resulting scale sounds nonstandard.

- Let's now take this pattern up an octave and go from 200 to 400 Hz (between a G^3 and a G^4). Again, our pattern is that we're going up 20 Hz at a time, which means that this scale has 10 notes, not 5. These notes sound much closer together in pitch.

- Going 20 Hz at a time from 400 to 800 Hz (from a G^4 to a G^5), there are 20 notes in the octave. This would be strange because it would mean that higher voices would have more notes available to them in their octaves. In other words, some of the notes for sopranos might not exist for the tenors or basses.

- The key problem is this: These intervals and octaves have a multiplicative structure. We shouldn't be adding the same number each time; we should be multiplying by the same number each time.
  o Sticking to this multiplicative system puts corresponding notes in each octave for each voice, and it reduces the problem to looking at a single octave.

o If we can figure out where the notes go in a single octave, we can use the multiplicative structure to get the same notes in higher octaves, for sopranos, and in lower octaves, for basses.

Just Tuning

- For our first attempt to choose scale notes for a single octave, we'll try using the overtone series of the bottom note to determine the higher notes. This is called "just tuning." Let's find the notes for an A-major scale.

- We can figure out the overtones and the notes for an A^4 at 440 Hz: A^4, A^5, E^6, A^6, C-sharp^7, E^7, sharp of an F-sharp^7, A^7, and B^7. The problem is that most of those notes are not in the octave we want, which is between A^4 and A^5.

- Instead of working with 440 Hz, let's talk about relative frequency; let's treat the A^4 as 1. We're looking to get relative frequencies between 1 and 2, and to do this, we're going to go down an octave, which is dividing by 2 in frequency.
  o One of the notes we have in the overtone series of the A is an E^6, but that isn't the note we want. We actually want an E^5, and to get from an E^6 to an E^5, we're just going down an octave, which is dividing by 2. An E^6 is the third harmonic above A, so it has a frequency three times A; we divide that in half, and we get our E^5 of 3/2.

  o We can do the same thing with a C-sharp. C-sharp is the fifth harmonic, so it's five times the frequency of A, but it's two octaves too high. We divide by 2 twice, and we get 5/4 for our C-sharp.

  o We can take as many of the overtones of A as we want and bring them down an octave; the result is a just scale.

A Pentatonic Scale

- To get a just-tuned pentatonic scale, we have to do only the notes we just discussed.

o   We have an A (the fundamental), and the second one is also an A. The third one is an E; that's a new note. The fourth is an A again. The fifth is a C-sharp. The sixth is an E again. The seventh is an F-sharp (at least that's the closest note on our scale). Finally, the ninth note, the B, is the fifth note we have.

o   To get a pentatonic just scale, we take harmonics 1 through 9—because of the duplication, we need all of those first nine to get just five notes—and we get those in the right octave by dividing by 2.

•   The nice thing about this just pentatonic scale is that everything is perfectly in tune with the A. The downside of it is that the notes are not necessarily in tune with each other. Let's look at what this means; in particular, let's look at the B versus the F-sharp.

o   In terms of frequency, we arrived at a 495-Hz B. That B has its own overtone series, so when we play the B at 495 Hz, we also hear its first overtone (its second harmonic) at 990, and its second overtone (its third harmonic) at 1485. Roughly, those are a B (the fundamental), the octave (B^5), and the next overtone (F-sharp^6).

o   But the F-sharp that we've decided on for our scale, the F-sharp^5, has its own overtone series. The fundamental frequency for that F-sharp is 770 Hz, and its first overtone is 1540, but its first overtone should be an octave above; it should be F-sharp^6.

o   This is a problem because one of the overtones of the B is an F-sharp^6 at 1485 Hz, and one of the overtones of the F-sharp is an F-sharp^6 at 1549 Hz. Those are very different; the two notes would produce dissonance.

•   Let's look at this B to F-sharp problem a different way. The F-sharp should be the fifth note above B, exactly seven half-steps above B. Therefore, it should have a frequency that is 3/2 times the frequency of B. That's what it means to go up a fifth. The frequency of B is 495; multiplying by 3/2, we get 742.5 Hz. That's very different from 770 Hz.

- This tells us that there's a real problem with tuning in general. We can get the B and F-sharp to be perfectly in tune with A, but we can't get them to be perfectly in tune with each other.

A Heptatonic Scale
- To go from a five-note scale to a seven-note scale, the philosophy is, again, that we're building on the overtones of the fixed reference point of the A and bringing those back into the correct octave by dividing by 2. That way, we'll get an A-major just heptatonic scale.

- However, the two notes we added when we went from a pentatonic to a heptatonic scale are not quite right. The D and the F-sharp can't have come from this process.
  o When we look at the harmonics of an A, we're multiplying by n, and for the octaves below that, we're taking one of those and dividing by 2. That tells us that every note we get in this process has to have the form $n/2^k$. There's no way of getting 4/3 or 5/3 from this process because 4/3 and 5/3 are not of the form $n/2^k$.

  o The trick that's used here to get a just heptatonic scale is the fact that D does not appear on the overtone series of A, but on the overtone series of a D are other As; thus, we can tune the Ds so that the overtone series of the D matches up with the A.

Musical Results of Just Tuning
- Great music is built on this philosophy of just tuning. The key question to ask to determine whether a musical tradition should use just tuning is whether or not modulation (switching keys) is used.
  o If we modulate "Twinkle, Twinkle, Little Star" from A to C, it's still recognizable as the same melody; it just starts on a different note.

o   Remember that the key is the bottom note of the scale, and it's the note that a melody returns to. It's usually the first and last note of the melody; switching keys is just starting on a different note.

o   If you're not going to do any transposing and you're not going to play multiple notes at once—only notes played with the fundamental—then just tuning is wonderful.

o   But if you want to modulate—if you want to be able to switch keys or to play chords with two notes that are not the fundamental—then just tuning leads to problems.

•   Just tuning is used with the bagpipe in Scottish culture. The bagpipe has a drone that is always heard underneath the music. The chanter is a recorder-like part that plays the higher notes, one note at a time. There's no problem like the B and F-sharp that we just saw, because the chanter simply plays one note at a time; it never plays two of those notes. Thus, a bagpipe is properly tuned as just tuned.

•   Indian music, played with such instruments as the sitar and the tabla, also always stays in one key and has a drone that plays a low note throughout an entire piece. The melody is then played on top, one note at a time above the drone. Each scale is matched to different overtones of the fundamental, and different sets of overtones are chosen depending on which scale is being used.

Bootstrapping
•   A second way to choose notes on a scale is bootstrapping, that is, going from one to the next. Here again, we'll use the overtone series 1, 1/2, 1/3, 1/4 and frequencies of 1, 2, 3, 4, 5.

•   The first philosophy was to take A as a fixed reference point and build on the overtones of A. The second philosophy is to take A and use that to get a note, and then to take that as the new reference point and get another note, and so on.

○ The idea is that the overtones of each note should be included in the scale. It's not possible to include all of them, but we're going to try for most audible.

○ The most audible intervals we hear are the octave and the fifth. The second harmonic is the octave and the third harmonic gives us the fifth, so if we want to use this philosophy, we have to include the octave and the fifth.

• We start with A; the third harmonic of an A is an E. E is the fifth note on an A-major scale. We then add the third harmonic of the E, a B. Once we bring that into the correct octave, we have another note. Next, we add the fifth note above B, an F-sharp. Then, the third harmonic of the F-sharp is a C-sharp, which gives us a pentatonic scale.

• The notes in this pentatonic scale sound consonant, but the problem here is that we've ended with a C-sharp. The second overtone above a C-sharp is a G-sharp, and that's not on our pentatonic scale. Still, a pentatonic scale can be used to produce interesting music.

• For example, Chinese music, such as the piece we heard at the beginning of this lecture, *Lady Meng Jiang*, uses a pentatonic scale. In China, this piece would be played on a two-stringed instrument called an *erhu*.

• A melody in the second movement of Dvořák's *New World Symphony* is based on a D-flat major pentatonic scale. Dvořák chose the English horn to play this melody, the instrument in an orchestra whose spectrum is closest to a human voice.

Why Pianos Are Never in Tune
• The bottom note on a piano is A^0. The idea is that we will start there and bootstrap up a fifth repeatedly, tuning the fifths exactly, until we reach A^7. To go up a fifth, we multiply the frequency by 3/2.

- A^7 is seven octaves above A^0, and we know that to go up an octave, we multiply the frequency by 2. Checking our work, we find that the fifths we got were $27.5 \times 3/2^{12}$ and the octaves were 27.5×2^7. Obviously, those are not the same numbers.

- How should we tune this top A^7? Should we put it in tune with all the other fifths, or should we put it in tune with the octaves? The fact that we can't do both explains why no piano is ever in tune.

Suggested Reading

Benson, *Music: A Mathematical Offering*, chapters 4–6.

Forster, *Musical Mathematics*, chapters 9–11.

Harkleroad, *The Math behind the Music*, chapter 3.

Loy, *Musimathics*, vol. 1, chapter 3.

Wright, *Mathematics and Music*, chapters 4–6, 11–12.

Questions to Consider

1. How can you use the harmonic series of a single note to create a scale with as many notes as you wish?

2. What makes a 12-note scale a natural choice?

3. Why is a piano never in tune?

How Scales Are Constructed
Lecture 4—Transcript

Welcome back. Here are two pieces from two very different musical traditions and I want you to think about this: What makes them different?

That was Vivaldi. That was Vivaldi's "Spring" from 1723. Here's a piece from a very different musical tradition. What makes these pieces so different? How can we so quickly distinguish Western music from Chinese music? That was a piece called *Lady Meng Jiang*. Why is it that mathematics plays a role in this difference?

Now there are, of course, many differences between music from different cultures, instruments, notations, and things like that, but one of the key differences is that they use different musical scales. They make different choices about notes.

What is a scale? A scale is a collection of notes, increasing or decreasing in pitch and for us, we are thinking about them covering a range of one octave, from one frequency to its double, say from A at 440 Hz to 880 Hz. Remember an octave is from one key on a piano to the next of the same name, 12 half steps. You need to know that the names here, the scale notes, are numbered as well as named. The keys on the piano have names. They're A, B, C-sharp; those are the keys on the piano.

But when we talk about scales, we also give them the numbers. We talk about the bottom one, the fundamental, and then second, the third, the fourth, the fifth, on and on through the seventh and finally, the octave. Now some of those are major, some of those minor, sometimes we call the fourth and the fifth perfect, but they're numbered. We also have the system called the Solfège system which is Do Re Mi Fa So La Ti Do. You of course know that from *The Sound of Music*.

Now the number of notes on a scale is key. We talk about the number of notes on a scale as being the number of notes before you get to the next octave. When you play a scale, you usually start on the bottom and get to the next octave, but if we have a seven-note scale, what we call a heptatonic scale, there will actually be eight notes when you play it because you also include the eighth note on the top end.

Now here's a really important fact about the names on the scale. The piano's keys are fixed. They're sort of a fixed reference point. You never change the names of the piano keys. However, the numbers that we talked about, the fundamental, the second, the third, fourth, those are sort of measurements that keep changing. When you're in the key of C, C is where you measure it from, and when you're in the key of G, G is where you measure it from.

Solfège works the same way. The "Do" changes. It's always called Do but the note name, if we're on a piano, the name of the note Do might stand for an A if we're in the key of A and then Do Re Mi Fa So from there, or maybe if we're in the key of D-flat, then the Do is D-flat and the Re is higher than that, on and on.

When we talk about the key of the scale, we're not talking about a piano key. We're talking about the lowest note of the scale, usually first. When we get to compositions, when we talk about the key of some piece, that's the note that's most important and pieces usually tend to start and end on that particular note.

Now an interval is the distance in pitch between one note and another. It's certainly related to scales and in numbers, it's the following relation. The fifth, the interval of the fifth is the distance between the fundamental and the fifth note on the major scale when starting on that fundamental.

So let me play you an example of a scale. Here's a seven-note, a heptatonic E-major scale. I'm going to play it starting on my open E. That's the basis for Vivaldi's "Spring" and here's a different scale. Here's a five-note pentatonic G-major scale. That scale is the basis for *Lady Meng Jiang*, the Chinese piece that I played at the beginning. Now major versus minor, that's a matter of mood and we're going to hear the difference between those in a minute.

First I want to make the mathematical connection between these. Remember, the overall goal, the central question in this entire course, is how does mathematics inform the musical experience? The main point of this lecture and the next is the following: How do the harmonic series, how does the harmonic series inform our choice of scales, how we tune these scales, and the implications of those choices of which notes we put in and how exactly we tune those. These next two lectures, this and the next, are each in three parts.

Today's lecture, we're going to start by answering the question why doesn't the obvious solution work for constructing a scale? The key idea here is that octaves and intervals are multiplicative whereas overtones are additive. Then we're going to look at two methods of constructing scales that do work in different ways. The first method is going to be to choose scale notes based on the fundamental. So whatever that fundamental note is, we're going to choose scale notes based on that. The second method is to choose one scale note based on the previous and then to use that to choose the next one, and to use that to choose the next one. This is some sort of bootstrapping idea. And when we choose how many notes and which ones in different ways, those actually give rise to different moods and those are adopted by different cultures.

A bonus today is we're going to find out why pianos are never in tune. Now if you're like me, you might know somebody who has the title piano tuner and you might think that this is–you're going to be really depressing when you tell that person. No, piano tuners know this all very well and in fact, they're very good at avoiding the problems that we're going to talk about today and in later lectures.

In the following lecture, we're going to talk more about scales and that's also going to be in three parts. First, we're going to talk about how exactly to tune a scale. So for instance, where exactly should I put my fingers on the string to get a beautiful sounding E-major scale like the one I just played? Secondly, we're going to talk about the mathematical reasons why 12 is a really good number of keys to put in an octave. On a piano, we have 12 different half steps before we get to the next octave and there's a mathematical reason why 12 was chosen. The third thing we're going to talk about next time is how changes in tuning mirror changes in composition, how math made modern music mad or at least irrational.

So let's play examples of a bunch of different scales and I just want you to listen to these six different scales. I'm going to play them both up and back down. Now these are all based on the harmonic overtones and I'm going to play all of these in A. Here's an A major scale, a standard Western scale, sometimes called a diatonic scale. It's major. It's bright and happy. And here's an A minor scale, also heptatonic, seven notes before you get to the octave and this has a mood that's more dark, a little bit sadder. Here's an A major pentatonic scale. Chinese music might be based on something like this. And here's an A-minor pentatonic scale. If we add a single note to that, we get something like a blues scale where the note we're adding is the augmented fourth that you've heard in "Maria" and *The Simpsons* theme. And here's an Arabian scale. We heard this at the last lecture when I played a piece of Tchaikovsky for you.

Now all the scales have sort of a different feel, a different mood to them, but one of the things they all have in common is they all have the fifth and the octave. Now remember those are the second and third harmonics that we hear when we're vibrating just a single note or a single column of air and then fifth and the octave are almost universal. Nearly every single musical tradition we have on earth contains both the fifth and the octave.

I did want to talk about one musical tradition that doesn't have those. In Indonesia, they use an instrument called the gamelan, and they play scales that are not based on the harmonic overtones that we're used to. Here's an example of a scale on a gamelan played by Mike Simpson, director of Inspire Works.

One of the things you might notice about it is, if you compare it to one of the scales we heard before, there is no perfect fifth in the gamelan scale and there's no perfect fifths used in Indonesian music. There's actually a mathematical reason for this cultural fact. You see, when you look at vibrations of bars, they don't vibrate in the same modes that strings and tubes of air do. They have a different overtone series, sort of like the timpani had a different series, and when you look at that series, since the music of Indonesia is based on the gamelan, there scales are based on the overtones of the gamelan. So because the bars do not vibrate with the fifth, Indonesian scales don't have a fifth in them.

Let's go back to Western scales and review what we need to construct these scales. We know that objects vibrate in different modes, overtones, and we know that the most common, the wavelengths of those overtones, are in a ratio of 1 to 1/2, 1/3, 1/4, the harmonic sequence and the frequencies are just multiples, 1, 2, 3, 4, those are arithmetic sequence.

What we learn from the overtone series is that to go up an octave, you're multiplying frequencies by two and to go down an octave, you're dividing frequencies by two. Also, we learned about a fifth, seven half-steps on a piano is a fifth and to go up a fifth, you're multiplying the frequencies by 3/2. To go back down, you're dividing by 3/2.

Let's look at a numerical example, just to make sure that we understand this. If I play an A, a 440 A, what is it to go up an octave? We have to multiply by two and we get 880 Hz. If we start back at the A and want to go up a fifth, seven keys on a piano, going up a fifth, that would the fifth note on the A major scale and going up a fifth gets us to the note E, E5, and to figure out what the frequency of that is we take 440 Hz and we multiply be 3/2 and we get 660 Hz.

If instead we wanted to go down from an A4, a 440 Hz A, to go down seven keys, we're asking A4 is the fifth note on what major scale? The answer to that would be it's the fifth on a D scale, a D4, and to figure out the frequency of that, we take 440 Hz of our A and we divide by 3/2, which is the same thing as multiplying by 2/3, and we get 293 1/3 Hz. The octaves and the fifths are the key ingredients we need in order to construct our scales.

Now different cultures have different music and I think you've heard the different moods they create and they have those in part because they choose different scales, they choose different notes, and those choices are at least partly mathematical. And so today, one of the questions we're asking is how might we choose notes on a scale?

First, we're going to talk about why the obvious solution to that fails and then we're going to look at two different methods that actually succeed. So let's go about building a scale starting with 100-Hz note, roughly a G2. Now the next octave is 200 Hz, a G3 so we could ask ourselves if we're trying to build say a five-note, why not put the notes equally spaced between 100 and 200. What you get is a five-note scale and those weak frequencies, if you want to evenly space them, it should be 100, and then 120, 140, 160, 180, and finally 200, and that would be a five-note scale. Again, it has six notes because we're including the octave. Let's listen to that scale.

That sounded a little nonstandard but let's keep going with this. Let's take this pattern up an octave and go from 200 Hz to 400 Hz. Every time, again, our pattern was that we're going up 20 Hz at a time. Now between 200 Hz and 400 Hz, that's between a G3 and a G4, that's more of a tenor voice, not so much a bass voice. If we go up 20 Hz at a time, we go 200, 220, 240, 260, all the way to 380, and finally 400 and there are actually 10 notes in there, not five. Let's listen to that part.

Those notes are sounding a lot closer together in pitch but let's keep going. If we go from 400 to 800, we've now moved on to female voices and we've moved on to those female voices, we're going from a G4 to a G5. This is maybe a mezzo-soprano voice and if we continue doing up 20 Hz at a time, well, we're going 400, 420, 440, 460, 480; we have to go a long time before we get to 780 and 800. There are actually 20 notes in the octave between 400 and 800 if we do things this way, not five or 10.

Now this would be very strange. Higher the voices would have more notes available to them in their octaves. You know it really should be the same number of notes. It would be very weird if you wrote a song for a soprano but then tenors couldn't sing it because some of the notes weren't included in the they scale that they were using. Think about trying to sing a song like "Happy Birthday" with everybody together. You couldn't do it because some of the notes for the sopranos might not exist for the tenors or for the basses.

The key problem is this: these intervals and octaves have a multiplicative structure that we've talked about before. You shouldn't be adding the same number each time; you should be multiplying by the same number each time. If we go back to 100 Hz, roughly a bass voice, if you put a 150-Hz note on the scale, think about that. That's exactly halfway between 100 and 200 at least additively but if you put a note there, then you see that 150

Hz, we shouldn't think of it as 50 Hz more than 100. We should think of it multiplicatively. 150 is 3/2 times 100. It's a multiplicative structure.

Where should we put the corresponding note for tenors? In between the 200 and the 400? Well, we can use the same multiplicative structure. If the note we added was 3/2 of the fundamental, let's take 3/2 times the new fundamental, which is at 200 so for tenors, let's take 200 times 3/2 and we get 300 Hz for the note in the tenor octave.

Now we note that this is going to work really well. See the note that we gave to the basses was 150 Hz and the new note that we have for the tenors is at 300 Hz. That's a doubling and so those are exactly in octaves again. Where would the corresponding note go for a female voice between 400 and 800 Hz? Let's do the same thing again. Let's take 400 and multiply it by 3/2. That gets us to 600 Hz. Again the notes we've added now, we've added a 150-Hz note for the bases, we added a 300-Hz note for tenors, and now we have a 600-Hz note—those are all in octaves. It's a doubling to get from one to the next.

Sticking to this multiplicative system works. It puts corresponding notes in each octave and it actually does something that mathematicians love to do. It reduces the problem to looking at a single octave. If we can figure out where the notes go in a single octave, we can use the multiplicative structure to get those same notes in octaves higher, for sopranos, or in octaves lower, for the bass and the male voices. This is a very mathematical trick to do that instead of solving one problem, you reduce it into a simpler problem and then you solve that.

With our reduced problem, we're trying to determine the sale notes for a single octave and then we're going to use the multiple structure, multiplicative structure, multiplying by two and dividing by two to get the rest of the notes. Remember that the fundamental underlying problem here is that all these intervals have to be multiplicative, even though the overtones that we saw earlier were additive. In terms of intervals, we want to use the multiplicative structure. Remember that a piano is actually a logarithmic scale, equal spacing on a piano, those are ratios not differences.

So how should we go about choosing the scale notes for a single octave? Our first idea and the first way we're going to go about this is to use the overtone series of the bottom note to determine the higher notes and this is something called just tuning. Things are justified in some sense by the lowest note.

Let's find the notes for an A major scale. If we play an A4 at 440 Hz, we know that we can figure out what the overtones are and which notes those are. We worked on that last time. The problem is most of these notes are in the wrong octave. We have the A4 and then we have the A5, that's the second harmonic, and then an E6, A6, C-sharp7, an E7, this mysterious seventh note, which is close to an F-sharp7, an A7, and finally an E7. Most of those notes are not in the octave we want, which is between A4 and A5.

Now instead of working with 440 Hz, let's talk about relative frequency and so let's just treat the A4 as one. If we do that, we're looking to get relative frequencies between one and two and to do this, we're going to make use of going down an octave, which is dividing by two in frequency. So one of the notes we have on the overtone series of the A is an E6 and E6 isn't the note we want. We actually want an E5 that's in the correct octave, but to get from an E6 to an E5, we're just going down an octave, which is dividing by two. An E6 is the third harmonic above A and so it has a frequency three times the A, so we're going to divide that in half and we get our E5 of 3/2. Again, that's three because that's the third harmonic of A that's in the wrong octave. We divide by two to get 3/2.

We can use the same thing with a C-sharp. C-sharp is the fifth harmonic, so it's five times the frequency of A but it's two octaves too high. We divide by two twice and we get five divided by four, 5/4, for our C-sharp.

For our B, we have to go way out to the very end of the notes that I've talked about, the ninth harmonic is a B and we have to bring that down three full octaves and so we take nine divided by two three times and you get 9/8.

You can do this as many times as you want and you can get, take as many of the overtones of A and bring them down into an octave and you get what's called a just scale. So let's look at a just tuned pentatonic scale. To get five notes, we have to do just the notes we've talked about in the last section. We have to take, let's see, an A, that's the fundamental, but then the second one is also an A; we already have that. The third one is an E, that's a new note. The fourth is an A again. The fifth is a C-sharp. The sixth is an E again. The seventh is an F-sharp sort of, at least that's the closest note on our scale. Finally, the ninth note, the B, is the fifth note that we have and so to get a pentatonic just scale, we have to take harmonics one through nine because of the duplication of those, we need all of those first nine to get just five notes in a just pentatonic scale and we're going to get those in the right octave by dividing by two.

Now on this chart, you can see both the frequencies and the wavelengths and we put the wavelengths up here because you can actually do a little detective work with their wavelengths. Given the relative wavelengths, you can tell exactly where each note is coming from.

Let's look at B on this chart. It's 8/9 so the wavelength of a B is 8/9 compared to the wavelength of the A. From the denominator, you can tell it was the ninth harmonic, that was 1/9, and the numerator is eight, which is multiplying by two three times, and so that tells you we took the ninth harmonic and moved it down three octaves.

So let's look at the just pentatonic scale. What wrong with this just pentatonic scale? Well, let's play it for you. Here again is A, B, C-sharp, E, and then something like an F-sharp, and A. If you have a musical ear, you'll notice that the F-sharp is very sharp compared with the standard Western scale. That's because it's not one of the notes on our piano and that's why we had to put the piano hammers in a particular place.

Now the nice thing about this just pentatonic scale is everything is perfectly in tune with the A. The downside of this is that these notes are not necessarily in tune with each other. Let's look at what this means, in particular let's look at the B versus the F-sharp.

Now remember that the B that we've arrived at, in terms of frequency we've arrived at a 495 Hz B, that B has its own overtone series and so when we play the B at 495 Hz, we also hear its first overtone, its second harmonic at 990, and its second overtone, it's third harmonic at 1485. Now roughly those are a B and then the octave, the fundamental is a B, the octave is B5 and then the next overtone is an F-sharp6.

But the F-sharp that we've decided on for our scale, the F-sharp5 has its own overtone series. Now we've decided on the fundamental frequency for that F-sharp of 770 Hz, its first overtone is going to be 1540 and its first overtone should be an octave above. It should be an F-sharp6. Now we have a real problem because one of the overtones of the B is an F-sharp6 at 1485 Hz and one of the overtones of the F-sharp is an F-sharp6 at 1549 Hz. Those are very different. Those two notes would sound bad together. We're going to talk about this later. They would produce what's called dissonance. We're going to talk about that in lecture 6.

The overtones of the F-sharp6 should match up, but they don't. Let's say there's a different way, this B to F-sharp problem. You see the F-sharp should be the fifth note above B. It should be a fifth above B, exactly seven half steps above B. The F-sharp should have a frequency therefore which is 3/2 times the frequency of B. That's what it means to go up a fifth. We know what the frequency of B is. We've pegged it at 495. We can multiply by 3/2 and we get 742 and a half Hz. That's very different from 770 Hz.

This tells you that there's a real problem with tuning in general. The B and F-sharp, you can tune them to be perfectly in tune with A, but you can't tune them to be perfectly in tune with each other. Now this just tuned pentatonic scale that we've created, it's great if you're only playing each note with a fundamental because those are perfectly in tune. It's a very bad scale if you want to play notes with each other.

Let's move up and add a couple of notes and move up to a seven-note scale. If we go from a five-note pentatonic scale to a seven-note heptatonic scale again, the philosophy here is that we're building on the overtones of this fixed reference point of the A and then we're bringing those back into the correct octave by dividing by two. We get here a just heptatonic scale, an A major just heptatonic scale, and you see the frequencies have these nice fractions.

Now the Pythagoreans thought that sound sounded really nice when the ratio of their frequencies was a fraction with a nice small denominator, and you can see that most of the fractions in this just heptatonic scale are nice fractions with small denominators. These are pleasing sounds. We're going to talk more about the Pythagoreans next time. The two notes that I added to this however, when we went from a pentatonic to a heptatonic scale, are actually not quite right. I'm not telling the full story and in fact, the numbers are giving away that I'm not telling the full story.

You see mathematically, we can look at the D and the F-sharp and they can't have come from this process. Just think about the relative frequencies here. When you look at the harmonics of an A, you're multiplying by n, we're repeatedly adding and that's multiplying by n. And then the octaves below that, we're taking one of those and dividing by two. That tells us that every note we get through in this process has to have the form n divided by 2^k. There's no way of getting 4/3 or 5/3 from this process because 4/3 and 5/3 are not of the form n divided by 2^k.

The trick that's used here to get a heptatonic just scale is the fact that D does not appear on the overtone series of A, but on the overtone series of a D, are other As and so we can tune the Ds so that the overtone series of the D match up with the A. There's actually great music built on this philosophy of just tuning. It's not what we used standardly on pianos–we'll talk about that later–but it is really good for wonderful music and so I want you to hear some of that. The key question in order to figure out if your musical tradition should use just tuning or not is whether or not you should transpose, whether or not you should modulate, and this is switching keys. And I want to demonstrate that by playing probably the first piece that I ever played.

Now when I was four years old, I learned how to play "Twinkle" and here's "Twinkle" played on an A. We could modulate that up to the key of C. What we're doing is we're just shifting up and instead of starting out with an A, we're going to start out with a C. Now that's easily recognizable as the same melody, it's just starting on a different note.

Switching keys, remember that the key is the bottom note of scale and it's the note that a melody keeps coming back to. It's usually the first and last note of the melody so switching keys is just saying, oh instead of starting on this note, I want to start in this other note. If you're not going to do any transposing and if you're not going to play multiple notes at once, just notes played with the fundamental, then just tuning is really wonderful. On the other hand, if you want to modulate, if you want to be able to switch keys or if you want to play chords where you're going to play two notes that are not the fundamental together, then just tuning is not the way to go. It leads to awful problems like the B and the F-sharp that we were talking about a minute ago.

But there are cultures where they have used just tuning and one of them is the bagpipe in Scottish culture. The bagpipe always stays in one key. It has a drone. It plays this fundamental and possibly the fifth and that fundamental, that drone goes on and on. It just keeps going and you always hear that under a bagpipe. It's the chanter, it's the recorder-like part that gives you the higher notes, the one note at a time. There's no problem with this, there's no problem like the B and the F-sharp that we had a minute ago, because the chanter is simply playing one note at a time and it's never playing two of those notes. And therefore, a bagpipe is properly tuned as just tuned, where the higher notes are exactly tuned to the overtones of the drone. So in theory, all bagpipe notes are perfectly in tune with the drone.

Now if you're like me, I've always thought that when I hear bagpipes, I feel like they're never quite in tune with themselves. It's a little bit strange but in theory, they're always perfectly in tune. There's a problem if you're a modern bagpipe player and that's the electronic tuners you use to tune the instruments, those don't use just tuning. They use an equal tempered system. We're going to talk about what that system is later.

Let's hear an example of a bagpipe tone and I want you to listen for the low drone notes that never change and how the higher melody is tuned to those overtones exactly, the overtones of the drone. Those are the Scottish bagpipes.

I want to talk about another musical tradition where just tuning is exactly the right thing to do. In Indian music, they play with instruments like the sitar and the tabla, and Indian music always stays in one key and it also has a drone that's playing a low note and it's playing that note throughout the entire piece. The melody is then played on top, one note at a time above the drone. And each scale they're using, they call them ragas, each scale has its own particular tuning. Each scale is matched to different overtones of the fundamental and they have different sets of overtones to choose depending on which raga they're using.

If you're interested in this, one of the recommended readings by Forster has an in-depth section on Indian tunings. So depending on the mood you're going for in a particular Indian piece, you may have a sunrise raga and you might tune the particular notes to some of the overtones. Or you might play a spring raga, which might tune to different overtones, but always tuning to the overtones of the fundamental, overtones of the drone. Or if you played a winter raga, you might make a different choice. But in all these cases, just tuning is used. You're always tuning the higher notes exactly to the overtone of the bottom note. It's a different mood depending on which ones you choose.

Let's hear an example of Indian music and I want you to notice that all of the notes being played appear in the overtone series of the drone or they are octaves below notes that appear in that series. These notes might not be in tune with each other, but that's okay because they're never played at the same time. The piece stays in the same key the entire time and that key is established by the drone. So let's listen to a sitar and tabla piece from the Indian tradition.

And again in Indian music, it's always staying in one key with one fundamental and no modulation. You're not changing keys. You're always using just tuning where each note appears on the overtone series of the fundamental and you're dividing by two to get into the correct octave.

So that's one way to choose notes on a scale. Let's talk about a second way and that's bootstrapping, to go from one to the next. Again, we're going to use the overtone series, 1, 1/2, 1/3, 1/4, and frequencies, that's of course 1, 2, 3, 4, 5. The old philosophy was just to take A as a fixed reference point and build on the overtones of A. The second philosophy is going to be to take the A and use that to get a note and then to take that as the new reference point and get another note, and take that as the new reference point to get another note, bootstrapping from one note to the next. The idea is that the overtones of each note should be included in the scale and it's not possible to include all of them, but we're going to try for most audible.

So remember that the most audible intervals that you hear are the octave and the fifth. The second harmonic is the octave and the third harmonic gives you the fifth so if we want to do, use this philosophy, we're going to have to include the octave and the fifth. Let's start with A and try to apply this new philosophy, adding overtone notes. Now we start with A and the third harmonic of an A is an E. We're going from A to E. E is the fifth note on A major scale. Here's an A. Here's an E, and you note that it's the fifth note on a major scale.

Okay now we've added a note, here's our scale so far. You can't make really interesting music with just those notes so let's add another one. Let's look at the E and look at its third harmonic. If we look at the second harmonic, that's just another E an octave above, but if we look at the third harmonic, the third harmonic above an E is a B, and so once we bring that into the correct octave, that gives us another note.

It's still not enough for interesting music so let's keep going. Now let's look at the B bootstrapping along. The fifth note above E, a fifth above B is an F-sharp. Let's put that into our scale.

There's still a gap in there and so let's add one more note. For music folks, if you know this, we're just walking around the circle of fifths. We're going to talk more about that next time. So the third harmonic of the F-sharp is the C-sharp and now I think we might have enough notes to play interesting music. What do we have? We have a pentatonic scale. Let's hear the pentatonic scale.

That's a nice pentatonic scale. We heard some Chinese music based on a pentatonic scale like that earlier. In the Western tradition, some composers really like the pentatonic scale. Carl Orff, who composed *Carmina Burana* in 1937, he thought it was a really wonderful scale for children, in part because it's a very simple scale and you can improvise in a pentatonic scale and everything sounds quite good. It's simpler and there are fewer choices to make and fewer of those choices sound bad. The nice thing about this scale, about the pentatonic scale is that notes sound consonant. You've matched overtones from one to the next.

One of the problems is that while we've gone from one to the next, we've ended with a C-sharp. The second overtone above a C-sharp is a G-sharp and that's not on our pentatonic scale. But still a pentatonic scale is good enough for producing interesting music so let's look at some of that music.

Chinese music uses a pentatonic scale and the piece I played at the beginning is exactly an example of that. The piece was called *Lady Meng Jiang*. In Mandarin, it's called Mèng Jiāng nǚ and it's a folk tale about the Great Wall. Lady Meng Jiang was a woman whose husband was sent off to help build the Great Wall and he died while he was doing that. And when she found out about it, she went to the Great Wall and she cried and her crying brought down a whole section of the Great Wall. That's the story behind *Lady Meng Jiang*.

Now at the beginning, we heard it on violin. I played it for you. Now I want you to hear it on the traditional instrument it would be played on in China, which was called erhu. It's a two-stringed Chinese instrument and the timbre is very different from a violin. The box on an erhu is very much smaller and it's different from the wooden box of my violin, and because of that, those two things have different resonances and it gives it different timbres. But the key here is a G major pentatonic scale and that's the scale that's used in *Lady Meng Jiang*.

Now as you listen to this, I want you to think about a few things. I want you to think about the philosophy that led to this particular pentatonic scale, how the overtones of each note gave you the next note and we bootstrapped our way until we had five notes. It's such a beautiful piece played on its original instrument, the erhu, and I also want you to think about that, how the distinctive timbre of the erhu is something you can hear because your ears are doing a Fourier Transform. So let's listen to the *Lady Meng Jiang*.

Pentatonic scales aren't just used in Chinese music or other cultures, they're actually used in Western music as well and I wanted you to have a chance to listen to an example of that. So let's look at Dvořák's 9th Symphony. Now this is called the New World Symphony. Dvořák composed this after he had spent some time in Iowa and he was drawing on Native American and African-American musical traditions, some of which included pentatonic scales. I want to listen to the second movement. It's a lush, beautiful, it's a very famous movement in classical music and what I want you to hear is that this melody is based on a D-flat major pentatonic scale. I want you to ponder the choices in choosing the next note based on the previous one leading to a pentatonic scale and the mood set by those choices. So let's hear the main melody from Dvořák's New World Symphony, the second movement.

Oh, it's such a wonderful, beautiful melody. Dvořák chooses a different timbre rather than the violin to play this, the difference, pattern of overtones, think about the spectrum. The instrument he chooses in order to play this melody is actually the English horn. Now the English horn is probably is the instrument in the orchestra whose spectrum is closest to a human voice and he chooses the English horn for the statement of the theme, giving this really soulful, melancholy sound to it. It's maybe one of the most beautiful melodies in all of classical music. So let's listen to that. Let's listen to the English horn playing this melody from Dvořák's 9th Symphony.

Oh, that's such wonderful music. So that concludes our discussion of these pentatonic scales. I want to last talk about why pianos are never in tune and why this bootstrapping idea, getting from one fifth to the next, actually proves that.

Let's think about a piano. We have a piano right here and let's think about trying to tune it. So we're going to start on the bottom note. The bottom note on the piano is here. It's A0 and the idea is we're going to bootstrap up a fifth every time, tuning the fifths exactly. Remember, to go up a fifth, we're multiplying the frequency by 3/2. Every time we go up a fifth, we're going up seven keys on our piano. You take the frequency of the previous note and multiply it by 3/2.

We have an A down here on the bottom and then the fifth above that is an E, and then a B, and then an F-sharp, and we can talk about it. We can calculate the frequencies that these should be at. The A0 should be at 27.5 Hz. The E1 should be at 3/2 times that. You get 41 and a quarter Hz. The B1 should be at 3/2 times that. You get 61.875. At some point you realize we should be little bit smarter about this and use the tools of mathematics, and use exponential notation. So let's call the F2, the F-sharp2 here should be 27.5 times $3/2^3$ and you get 92.8125 Hz. The C-sharp3, that's the next one should be $27.5 \ 3/2^3$, and the next one is a G-sharp, and that's 27.5 times $3/2^5$, all the way on until you get up here to an A7. And the A7, according to our calculations, should be 27.5 Hz times $3/2^{12}$.

But again, like any good math students, we should check our work. So let's see. See we started down at the A0 and we ended up here at an A7. That's seven octaves above A0 and we know how to go up an octave. To go up an octave, we should be multiplying frequencies times two. And so we have 27.5 Hz, that's for A0. A1 should then be 27.5 times two. A2 should be multiplied that times two again, 27.5 times 2^2, all the way one until we get to A7 which should be 27.5 Hz times 2^7. And now, we've checked our work except the answers we got, the fifths were 27.5 times $3/2^{12}$ and the octaves were 27.5 times 2^7. The problem is that those are not the same numbers. That's the problem when we try to do this.

If you think about it in terms of number theory, the left side of this equation, $3/2^{12}$, has powers of three over powers of two. There's no cancelling in that fraction whereas the right side is an integer, 2^7. When we pull out a calculator and get numbers, $3/2^{12}$ is 129.74 about, 2^7 is 128. Those are simply different frequencies.

The question is how should you tune this top A7? Should you in tune it, make it in tune with all the other fifths or should you put it in tune with the octaves? The important point here is you can't do both. You either tune your fifths in tune or your octaves in tune, but you can't have both of them perfectly in tune. No piano is ever in tune, and we're going to talk about that more next time.

Now this is a really well-studied problem and the history of mathematics includes parts where people are dealing with exactly this problem. Marin Mersenne, a French mathematician in the 1600s wrote about this problem. Hermann von Helmholtz wrote a large tome in German in the 1800s about this and both of them are essentially saying we can't have everything in tune so what are we going to do to get close? That's what we're going to talk about next time. How, exactly, do we tune the notes on our scale?

To close, I want to return to Dvořák because it's such a beautiful piece and let's listen to Dvořák's 9th Symphony again. This is later in piece where the orchestra is reduced to a string quartet and eventually just three instruments: a single violin, a viola, and a cello on a stage with many other instruments who are quiet at that point. This is one of my favorite pieces to play in an orchestra.

I want you to think about how every musical tradition chooses scales differently for their particular music and how those choices are very mathematical in nature. So here again is Dvořák's 9th Symphony, the second movement. Thanks for joining us.

How Scale Tunings and Composition Coevolved
Lecture 5

The main point of the last lecture was that mathematics, especially the math of the harmonic sequence, informs which notes to include in a scale. In this lecture, we will continue to discuss scales, in particular, how mathematics informs the tuning of those notes—exactly which frequencies we choose to put on a particular scale. We'll also discuss the profound impact these small changes have on composition, because this lecture also relates to the coevolution of scale tunings and musical composition in Western classical music.

Brief Review
- In the last lecture, we used math in the overtone series to inform our choice of notes on a scale. We used two key methods for choosing notes: First, we talked about choosing notes based on the overtones of a single fundamental, a fixed reference point. The second method was using overtones of one note to inform the next note and then using the overtones of that note to get the next—bootstrapping.

- Remember that objects vibrate in different modes, and we now know very well that those frequencies are in a ratio of 1 to 2, to 3, to 4, to 5, and the wavelengths are in a ratio of 1, 1/2, 1/3, 1/4. What we learned from the overtone series is that to go up an octave, we multiply the frequencies by 2, and to go down an octave, we divide by 2. We also know that to go up a fifth, we multiply the frequencies by 3/2.

Just Tuning Revisited
- Let's start by finding the frequencies in A-major scale. Where exactly should you put your fingers on the strings to play in A-major scale? We're going to come up with three different answers, two of which we discussed in the last lecture: just tuning and Pythagorean tuning, which is the bootstrapping idea. The third answer is equal-tempered tuning, which is modern piano tuning.

- As we said, just tuning is great for some instruments, such as bagpipes and sitars. It's used in some musical traditions where there were no modulations, no key changes. Pianos are never in tune, in part because we try to modulate. Essentially, bootstrapping is modulation. We start at the low A and we take the fifth of that, and then we modulate into that key to find the fifth note in that.

- The problems with tuning pianos gave rise to a slow evolution of tunings that mirror changes in composition. But if we use just tuning, no evolution of tunings is needed. We can always just tune things exactly with the fundamental.

- We can calculate the exact frequencies on a just scale using the overtones. As we've seen, we can generate as many notes as we want by taking the overtones and bringing them into the correct octave. In this way, we generate a seven-note scale. The problem with this scale is that although the notes are in tune with A (the fundamental), they aren't in tune with each other.

- Let's look at the F-sharp. If you remember, the F-sharp we got originally for a pentatonic scale was a different F-sharp; it was not in our 12-note scale. This F-sharp is in our 12-note scale.
  o The just-tuned F-sharp is related to the ratio of 5/3. The frequency should be 5/3 multiplied by the fundamental. That's about 1.667.

  o The overtones of B include an F-sharp, and we've figured out the frequency for B. B is related to the ratio 9/8; the first overtone of B will be $2 \times 9/8$, which is 9/4. The second overtone will be an F-sharp. It's actually an F-sharp[6], and that is 3 times the fundamental B, or $3 \times 9/8$, or 27/8.

  o To get an F-sharp[5], we divide the F-sharp[6] by 2 and get 27/16, or about 1.688.

- This is why playing in an ensemble is difficult. If you see an F-sharp on your page, then you actually need to play a different note if everyone around you is in the key of A (F-sharp at 1.667) than if everyone is in the key of B (F-sharp at 1.688).

- What's going on here is a fundamental problem. We can't create the scale so that the overtones of one note exactly match up with the other notes. Even with only three notes, the additive structure of the overtones conflicts with the multiplicative structure of intervals.

- This isn't just a problem with pianos or other fixed-tuned instruments. The mathematics tells us that no instrument can play A, B, and F-sharp so that they're all in tune with each other.

Pythagorean Tuning
- Of course, Pythagorean tuning is named after Pythagoras of Samos. Followers of his belief system thought that all numbers could be written as fractions (rational numbers). They didn't believe in the existence of such numbers as $\sqrt{2}$, which cannot be written as a fraction. The Pythagoreans further believed that musical notes were pleasing together if the ratio of frequencies was a fraction with small numbers. Thus, they prized the octave, with its 2:1 ratio, and the fifth, with its 2:3 ratio. The fifth is the key in Pythagorean tuning.

- The goal in Pythagorean tuning is to keep the fifths exactly in tune. When we tune Pythagorean scales, what we're doing is walking around the "circle of fifths." From one note to the next, we're going up a fifth, which is seven half-steps or seven keys on a piano. That's also going from the fundamental to the fifth note on the major scale.

- Let's take a trip around the circle of fifths: We start on A, and the fifth note on the A-major scale is E; the fifth note on that scale is B, then F-sharp, and then C-sharp. We can also go backwards. The fifth below A is D; in other words, an A is the fifth note on the D-major scale.

- Again, to go up an octave is multiplying by 2, down an octave is dividing by 2, and up a fifth is multiplying by 3/2. If we start out on A^4 at 440 Hz, let's think of that as 1 and work in relation to that frequency. We're looking to put scale notes in between A^4 and A^5 to tune our scale. Really, that's between 440 Hz and 880 Hz, which is the octave above an A^4, but in terms of our fundamental at 1, we're thinking of getting numbers between 1 and 2.

o As an example, let's see if we can find the C-sharp on our scale. To get a C-sharp, it looks on our scale as if we have to go up 4/5. To do that, we need to multiply by $3/2^4$. That doesn't get us to the correct C-sharp; it gets us to C-sharp^7.

o We have to go back two octaves to get down to C-sharp^5, the one we want. That's dividing by 2 each time. Now that we've found our C-sharp, we should multiply by $3/2^4$ and then divide by 2^2. The answer comes out to about 1.266.

• If we work through all the details, we can come up with an A-major scale where the fifths are tuned exactly perfectly. For comparison, the C-sharp on the just scale was 4/5, or 0.8, whereas the C-sharp on the Pythagorean scale is 64/81, or about 0.79. Those are quite different.

• If we think about this on a piano, we could start tuning at A and go up to 12/5. As we saw in the last lecture, the problem with piano tuning was that going up 12/5 was different from going up seven octaves, although it ended up at the same key: $3/2^{12}$ was not the same as 2^7. That gap between 12/5 and seven octaves is called the "Pythagorean comma." Even though the gap is small, it has led to significant changes in composition.

"Tempering" the Gap
• There are multiple ways to "fix" the gap, although there are no exact solutions. We can, for example, put the entire gap in the last fifth. We can spread the gap out among more of the fifths so that they're not perfect 3/2 ratios but the last fifth doesn't have such a large gap.

• When we spread the gap out more, keyboards will sound good in a greater number of different keys. Spreading the gap out gave composers more flexibility, resulting in an evolution in music—from the Baroque, to the Romantic, to 20th-century music.

- By 1900, modern tuning on a piano spread the gap out completely evenly. Every fifth on a modern-tuned piano, or an equal-tempered piano, is equally out of tune. Remember, though, the problem here is that $3/2^{12}$ is not the same as 2^7.

- Mathematically, we can solve this by finding a solution to $r^{12} = 2^7$. We take the 12th roots of both sides to get an answer of $r = 2^{7/12}$. When we plug that into a calculator, we get about 1.4983, close to 1.5. That value of r is irrational; it cannot be written as a fraction. The Pythagoreans didn't think that such numbers existed.

- Let's look at another perspective: If we divide the octave into 12 equal half-steps (multiplicatively, not additively), then each one should have a ratio of $2^{1/12}$. If each half-step had a ratio of $2^{1/12}$, then seven of them will have a ratio of $2^{7/12}$, which is the number we just got.

- Let's use this number to construct the scale. Again, we start with a 440-Hz A. If we want to find C-sharp, that's up four fifths and down two octaves. We go up four fifths from the 440-Hz A—that's our key number r^4—and then we divide by 4 to go down two octaves. When we do that calculation, we get roughly 554.36 Hz. Remember that a just C-sharp was at 5/4 of the fundamental, and that gives us a 550-Hz note.

  o How different are the just C-sharp, the Pythagorean C-sharp, and the equal-tempered C-sharp?

  o With the A at 440, the just C-sharp was 550 Hz exactly. The Pythagorean C-sharp was roughly 556.89, and the equal-temperament C-sharp was 554.36. The Pythagorean C-sharp sounds sharper and higher in pitch. The equal-tempered C-sharp is in between the just and the Pythagorean.

Why 12 Keys per Octave?

- Why does the equal-temperament system use 12 notes and not a different number? Would another number work better?

- Let's build a scale with equal spacing, which gives us maximum flexibility. If we have equal spacing, we can modulate into any key we want. The notes that we definitely want in our scale include the octave, the fifth, the fourth, and the major third.

- Suppose the fundamental is at 100 Hz. In just tuning, which sounds best, the octave will be double that, the fifth will 3/2 of that, the fourth will be 4/3, and the major third will be 5/4. Those are the notes that are perfectly in tune with the overtones, and those are the key fractions that we need to look at: 3/2 is 1.5, 4/3 is $1.\overline{3}$, and 5/4 is 1.25. For what values of n will a scale with n equally spaced notes include notes that are close to these key fractions?
  - Let's work by trial and error. If we want to add a note between the fundamental and the octave, that note needs to be exactly halfway in between. If we do the calculation, we get a "tritone," the augmented fourth.

  - If we want to add two notes between the fundamental and the octave, we get close to the major third, but we don't get close to the fourth or fifth. In fact, as we continue to add notes, we get close to some of the key ratios but not all three.

  - It's not until we reach 12 notes that we get very close to the three key ratios we want to hit. If we want equally spaced notes and we want to match up with the most prominent overtones (the major third, the fourth, and the fifth), we need at least 12 notes.

What about n-Note Scales?

- Let's try to resolve this in a different way, using some mathematical theory. If we were to place n equally spaced notes (multiplicatively spaced), they would have relative frequency of 1 (the fundamental) and then $2^{1/n}$, $2^{2/n}$, $2^{3/n}$, up to $2^{n/n}$, which is 2, and we would be at the octave. Remember for our 12-note scale that each half-step was $2^{1/12}$; this is just a generalization of that for n notes.

- Let's say that the kth one of those is close to the fifth: $2^{k/n} \approx 3/2$. We can multiply both sides of that equation by 2, then we take the $\log_2$ (log base 2), and what we get is that the $\log_2$ of 3 needs to be very close to $k/n + 1$. In other words, we need a fraction k/n that is very close to $\log_2(3) - 1$. We're looking for a rational approximation of the $\log_2(3)$.

  ○ Here, "rational" means "ratio" or "fraction," and "rational approximation" means that we're trying to get close to an irrational number using just rationals (fractions). There's a sort of astonishing connection here to something called "continued fractions" that we'll discuss more in a later lecture.

  ○ The $\log_2(3)$ is about 1.58496. To get an approximation of this, we can find the continued fraction. Then we ask the question: Where should we cut off this fraction?

The most famous continued fraction is the "golden ratio," which appears in art and architecture and throughout nature.

- If we stop after two layers, we get 3/2 (1.5), which is not a very good approximation of 1.58496. If we stop after three layers, we get 1.6, which is a little bit better. When we stop after four layers, the value of the continued fraction is 19/12, or 1.5833..., quite close to the actual value of the $\log_2(3)$.

- What would it mean musically to take this as a rational approximation?
  - It would mean that we are approximating $\log_2(3)$ with 19/12, and when we invert the log, we're taking exponentials, so that would mean $2^{19/12}$, or approximately 3. We can divide both sides of that equation by 2, and we get $2^{7/12}$, or approximately 3/2.

  - That's saying that one way to approximate 3/2 is to use $2^{7/12}$. That was the equal-tempered fifth. In other words, this continued fraction just gave us the equal-tempered 12-note system of Western music today.

- What would our musical system look like if we had taken one more layer of fractions? When we do that, we get 65/41, and that gives us $2^{24/41} \approx 3/2$. Musically, we would need 41 keys between one octave and the next, and the 24th of those would be very close to a perfect fifth.

- Here's what the mathematics is telling us: If we want to get a better and better approximation—if we want a note that is closer and closer to the pure fifth of 3/2—we need to keep taking more layers in our continued fraction. As we do that, the advantage is that some notes are much better in tune; the disadvantage is that we have too many notes in each octave.

Why Do Tunings Matter?
- Just tuning, Pythagorean tuning, and equal-tempered tuning aren't actually very different, so why do we care? The answer is that tunings matter because composers use keyboards to compose music, and what sounds good on a keyboard depends on the tuning. Before we had equal-tempered tuning, composers chose different

keys for different moods, because when the gap wasn't spread out evenly, different keys actually sounded different.

- In Western music, from about 1500 to 1900, the Pythagorean comma was spread out more and more equally. Tuning systems included the meantone and quarter-comma meantone, Werckmeister III, Kirnberger III, well-tempered, quasi-equal tempered, and finally, equal tempered. Pianos were tuned equal tempered by the late 1800s.

- Interestingly, the fact that guitars have frets that go across all of the strings made it necessary to use equal-tempered tuning back in 1500, when guitars were first made. There is almost no piano-and-guitar music in the period 1500–1900, partially because a guitar and piano used different tuning systems and would have been out of tune with each other.

- A quick tour of the history of Western classical music shows a coevolution of tunings and composition. Tunings moved from not spreading out the Pythagorean comma at all to evenly spreading it out. As that happened, composers gained access to increasing numbers of keys that sounded good, and over time, they lost the devotion to a single key and moved toward all keys being equal. Understanding Western classical music requires understanding the mathematics of the tunings that underpin the compositions.

Suggested Reading

Barbour, *Tuning and Temperament.*

Benson, *Music: A Mathematical Offering*, chapters 4–6.

Duffin, *How Equal Temperament Ruined Harmony.*

Dunne and McConnell, "Pianos and Continued Fractions."

Forster, *Musical Mathematics*, chapters 9–11.

Harkleroad, *The Math behind the Music.*

Loy, *Musimathics*, vol. 1, chapter 3.

Wright, *Mathematics and Music*, chapters 4–6, 11–12.

1. How do subtle changes in tuning mirror changes in compositional styles, and how does mathematics inform those changes?

2. Explain the choices a piano tuner has to make when tuning the fifths on a piano.

How Scale Tunings and Composition Coevolved
Lecture 5—Transcript

Welcome back. Last time, the main point was that mathematics and especially, the math of the harmonic sequence informs which notes you might want to include in a scale. Today, we're continuing talking about scales. Today, were going to talk about how mathematics informs the tuning of those notes, very small changes in tuning. We're talking about exactly which frequencies we choose to put on a particular scale. We're also going to talk about what a profound impact those small changes have on composition, because one of the main points today is about the co-evolution of scale tunings and musical composition in Western classical music.

Let's start with a little bit of music. I want to play two pieces here at the beginning. Now these are both from Western classical music tradition. The first is the Allemande from Partita no. 2. This was composed in about 1720. This is the first movement of the Partita. The last movement is the Chaconne that I was asked about in my interview at St. Mary's College. This other piece I want to talk about is David Froom. It's from his Sonata for Violin Solo. It was composed in 2004.

I want you to think about what makes these so different? How did we get from the Baroque style music to 20th-century music like the Froom? How does mathematics plays a role in this change? First, let's hear a little Bach. That's Bach and now let's move forward a couple of centuries to Froom. This is the Sonata for Violin Solo, 2004.

What makes those pieces so very different? How did we get from this Bach style, this Baroque style, where we start in one key, we modulate to another related key, and then we come back. And then we get to Froom, the 20th-century music. There's seemingly no tonal center. There's no reference note. It's not based on a single scale. It's not Sonata in A minor or D major, it's just a sonata because there's no tonal center. How does mathematics plays a role in this change and I think it's surprising that it's important exactly how you tune the scales, that small changes in scale tunings makes a such a big difference.

Let's quickly review what we talked about last time. We were choosing notes on a scale and we were using math in the overtone series to inform a choice of those notes, how many notes, which ones, and how those choices give different moods and styles. We saw toward the end how a piano is never in tune.

Now there were two key methods we talked about last time. We talked about choosing notes based on the overtones of a single fundamental. That was the idea of having a fixed reference point and basing everything on that. And the second method was having overtones of one note inform the next note and then using the overtones of that note to get the next, bootstrapping.

Today's lecture is again in three parts. The first part we're going to talk about calculating the exact pitches. These are called tunings and temperaments, exactly what frequency should we put these notes at. This is essentially the question where exactly should I put my fingers on the strings in order to play a major scale. It's also the same thing as where you should put the holes on a flute or how long should the pipes be on a xylophone, things like that.

The second thing we're going to talk about is why are there 12 keys per octave on Western music and on our piano and not some other number? Why 12? And the third thing we're going to talk about is how subtle changes in tunings mirror the changes in composition over the last few hundred years of Western music. We really want to understand this mathematical difference between Baroque music and 20th-century music.

We're also going to get a couple of fascinating little asides. Along the way, we're going to find out why playing in a music ensemble is so hard. We're also going to find out there's so little classical music written for guitar and piano, and finally, we're going to figure out how piano tuners get around the fact that they can't tune a piano perfectly. This is really foreshadowing of the next lecture, which is on dissonance and piano tuning.

Now remember that objects vibrate in different modes and remember, we know now very well that those frequencies are in a ratio of 1 to 2, to 3, to 4, to 5 and the wavelengths are in a ratio of 1, 1/2, 1/3, 1/4. What we learned from the overtone series is that to go up an octave, you multiply the frequencies by two and to go down an octave, you divide by two.

You can see that in the chart of the overtones, looking from the first to the second, the first harmonic to the second harmonic, or from the second harmonic to the fourth harmonic. We also see that to go up a fifth, you multiple the frequencies by 3/2. A fifth, remember, is seven keys on a piano it's the fifth note on the major scale of the bottom note, and you can see that in the chart of the harmonics looking from the second to the third harmonic, or from the fourth to the sixth harmonic.

Now before we dig into these tunings, a word of warning about this, and this is from J. Murray Barbour. He wrote a 1967 tome on the topic of tunings. This is what he said: "Explanations of the tuning of the musical scale are usually so full of figures that the non-mathematician shies away from them in terror. This is unfortunate, for the subject is not only of interest to the musicologist and theorist, but of immediate and practical concern to the performer." That's quite the warning, but we're going to do our best to make this challenging topic as simple and clear as possible.

So let's start by finding the frequencies in an A major scale. Where exactly should I put my fingers on the strings to play an A major scale. We're going to come up with actually three different answers. We talked about two of them last time: just tuning, where you're using the overtones of the fundamental. We're going to talk about why it matters when you're playing music this, just tuning; we're also going to talk about Pythagorean tuning which is using this bootstrapping idea from getting from one to the next; and finally, we're going to talk about equal tempered tuning, which is modern piano tuning.

Let's go back to just tuning, which we talked about last time. Remember, this was really great for some instruments, bagpipes, sitars. It was good for some musical traditions where there was no modulations, no key change like Indian music. Now, pianos are never in tune, in part because we try to modulate. Essentially, bootstrapping is modulation. You're starting at the low A and you're taking the fifth of that and then you're modulating into that key to find the fifth note in that.

What we'll see is that the problems with tuning pianos gave rise to a slow evolution of tunings and those mirror these changes in composition. Now if you're using just tuning, there's really no problem. There's no evolution of tunings needed. You can always just tune things exactly in tune with the fundamental. There are no companion changes in composition because of that.

So let's calculate the exact frequencies on a just scale. In order to do that, we're going to use the overtones to get frequencies of the scale. We're going to take overtones and they're in the wrong octave, and we're going to bring them down into the correct octave. We're going to generate as many notes as we want and we've seen the solutions. This is what we get if we take a seven-note scale.

Now the problem with this scale is that while the notes were in tune with A, with the fundamental, they weren't in tune with each other. And let's look at the F-sharp. If you remember the F-sharp we got originally for a pentatonic scale, that was a different F-sharp. That was not in our 12-note scale. This F-sharp is in our 12-note scale. It's not the seventh harmonic.

So just tuned F-sharp is related to the ratio of five-thirds. The frequency should be five-thirds times whatever the fundamental is. That's about 1.667. The overtones of B include an F-sharp and we've figured out the frequency for B. B is related to the ratio nine-eighths and so the overtones of B, well the first overtone is going to be two times that. That's going to be eighteen-eighths or nine-fourths, and the second one is going to be an F-sharp. It's actually an F-sharp6 and that is going to be three times the fundamental B and so we're going to get nine-eighths times three or 27/8. Now an F-sharp5, if we want to get an F-sharp5, we take the F-sharp6 and we divide by two and we get 27/16 or about 1.688.

This is why playing in an ensemble is hard. You see the F-sharp that's written on your page, I remember it was my high school music teacher, Mrs. Wotruba, who always said you have to listen to everybody around you and at the time I sort of thought that what she meant was to keep rhythm with everybody, you have to listen to everything around you. It's more than just that. You see if there's an F-sharp on my page then I actually need to play a different note if everybody around me is in the key of A than if everybody around me is in the key of B. If everybody around me is in the key of A, my F-sharp should be at 1.667. If everybody around me is in the key of B, I should play a different note, 1.688, roughly.

What's going on here is that there's a fundamental problem. You can't create the scale so that the overtones of one note exactly match up with the other notes. Even just with three notes, the additive structure of the overtones really conflicts with the multiplicative structure of intervals.

You might think this is just a problem with pianos or other fixed-tuned instruments like organs and xylophones, but that's actually not the case. What the mathematics is telling us is that no instrument can play A, B and F-sharp so that they're all in tune with each other. This isn't a problem with implementation. It's not a problem of a particular instrument. It's actually a problem of theory. It's a problem of the mathematics. No instrument can make it work.

In fact, string quartets know this. Despite having a lot of tonal freedom, you can adjust the note a lot. You can adjust it very slightly on a string instrument but they do tune their open strings and when you hear a string quartet tuning up, everybody matches their As and then the violins tune up a fifth to an E and the cello and viola tune down fifths to a D, G, and finally C. And the next thing a string quartet will do is they'll check the low C against the high E and if they've been tuning perfect fifths, they'll find out the low C and the high E are not in tune. This is the fundamental problem that we're dealing with.

So let's move on from just tuning and let's talk about Pythagorean tuning. Now this is of course named after Pythagoras of Samos. He founded Pythagoreanism, a religion, and his life is really shrouded in mystery. We don't have a whole lot of historical records about exactly who Pythagoras was and what he did. His followers tended to attribute many, many things to him, and whether or not those are true, it's really not known.

The Pythagoreans believe that all numbers can be written as fractions, as rational numbers. They didn't think that there existed numbers like the $\sqrt{2}$. $\sqrt{2}$ is not written as a fraction. You cannot do that. Now there's really no evidence that Pythagoras actually proved what he's most famous for today, the Pythagorean Theorem. Of course, like a lot of mathematical theorems there's a lot of evidence that other people knew the Pythagorean Theorem long before Pythagoras was ever born. The musical ideas of the Pythagoreans were that notes were pleasing together if the ratio of frequencies is a fraction with really small numbers. So they prized things like the octave with its two-to-one ratio and the fifth with its three-to-two ratio, but especially the fifth and that's what's the key in Pythagorean tuning.

The goal in Pythagorean tuning is to keep the fifths exactly in tune and what we're doing when we tune Pythagorean scales is we're walking around what's called the circle of fifths. From one note to the next we're going to go up a fifth. Remember that was seven half steps or seven keys on a piano. That's also going from the fundamental to the fifth note on that major scale. A natural question you should ask is: Why is the circle of fifths a circle? In the western tradition, we have 12 notes on that circle of fifths. We start at A and finally we go back to A 12 notes later. We're going to talk more why it's 12 later, but first let's take a trip around the circle of fifths.

Let's start on A and the fifth note on the A major scale is E and the fifth note on that scale is B, and then F-sharp, and then C-sharp and you see we're just walking around the circle. We can also go backwards. To go backwards, we're asking what's the fifth below A? And we get D. In other words, an A is the fifth note on the D major scale.

Now recall to go up an octave was multiplying by two, down an octave was dividing by two, and up a fifth was multiplying by 3/2. So if we start out on A4 at 440 Hz let's think of that as just one and work in relation to that frequency. We're looking for notes between A4 and A5. We're looking to put scales notes in between A4 and A5 to tune our scale, really that's between 440 Hz and 880 Hz, which is the octave above an A4. But in terms are our fundamental at one, we're thinking of just getting numbers between one and two so that in relation to the A at 440, the numbers are just between one and two.

So we can do that with our circle of fifths and I just want to work through an example. A C-sharp, let's see if we can find the C-sharp on our scale. Now to get a C-sharp, it looks on our scale like we have to go up four-fifths. To go up four-fifths, we would be multiplying by 3/2 four times so that's multiplying by 3/2 to the fourth. Now that doesn't get us to the correct C-sharp. That gets us to C-sharp7. We have to go back two octaves to get down to C-sharp5, the one that we want. That's dividing by two each time. And so now we found our C-sharp, we should multiply by 3/2 to the fourth and then divide by two squared. We can simplify that. It's three to the fourth over two to the sixth and with the calculator that comes out about 1.266.

We can do exactly that and we can work through the details and we can come up with an A major scale where the fifths are tuned exactly perfectly and when we do that, we get this. I love the G-sharp sitting there at 128/243. Now for comparison, the C-sharp on the just scale was four-fifths or 0.8 whereas the C-sharp in our Pythagorean scale is 64/81, which is about 0.79. Those are quite different.

So we can do that. We can start tuning at the A and if we think about it on piano, we could start tuning at A and we can go up 12/5. If you remember last time the problem with piano tuning was that going up 12/5 was different from going up seven octaves, although it ended you up at the same key. And that was the problem last time, $3/2^{12}$ was not the same thing as 2^7. That gap is actually called the Pythagorean comma, the gap between 12/5 and seven octaves and we now know where it gets its name. If you tune a scale in a Pythagorean way, that's the gap you're left with at the end. Is that a big problem? Is that gap noticeable? Let's hear it.

So musicians measure the space between two notes not only in half steps and things like that, but when we're talking about fine distinctions, we actually measure them in what are called cents. One half step, just going from one key to the next on a piano is 100 cents and therefore to go up an octave, you have to go up 1200 cents.

Now remember that everything has to be multiplicative because we are talking about intervals, and these cents have to be multiplicative. So one cent is actually equivalent to the ratio two raised to the 1/1200 and if we do that then we go up 1200 cents, we're multiplying that number times itself 1200 times, the 1200s cancel and we just get two. We just get an octave.

And if you think about it this way, 100 cents is then going to be two to the 1/12 power and that's going to be a half step and we'll see that number again in a bit. The Pythagorean comma, if you do the calculation, turns out to be about 23 cents. So that's about quarter of a step between one note and the next on a piano.

What does that sound like? Let's put that gap of 23 cents at an A 440 and let's play it with sine waves. So the traditional A4 is a 440-Hz A, let's hear that, and then this gap, if we put that gap there, we would get 446.39 Hz roughly. Let's hear that. Now you might think that that sounds small. It turns out that even though that's small it's incredibly important. Just to see how important it is, let's play them at exactly the same time. There we hear beats again and we've heard those before and we'll talk about those more later. That gap has actually led to big changes in composition and we're going to talk about that.

So how would we fix that, this big problem with this gap? There are actually many different solutions. I should put that in quotes, "solutions" because there no exact solutions but there are many different ways of what's called tempering the gap and that's how we get the name temperaments. Pythagorean tuning, you take that entire gap and you put it in 1/5, you take that last fifth and that has the entire gap. Other tunings and temperaments, we use these words interchangeably mostly, other tunings and temperaments spread that gap out among more of the fifths so other fifths are not perfect 3/2 ratios, but that means you don't have such a big gap at the end for your last one.

What you're doing when you spread that gap out more is that keyboards are going to sound good in more different keys. You could play a piece in A or C or F-sharp, lots more keys, and it would still sound fairly good. Spreading that gap out more gave composers more flexibility and you can already sense the sort of progression, this evolution, when composers have more flexibility, they're going to move. Think about the progression from Baroque music all the way through Romantic to 20th-century music.

So what's a modern solution to this tuning problem? Modern tuning starting a little bit before but by 1900 on piano spread that gap out completely evenly. Every fifth on a modern-tuned piano or an equal tempered piano is equally out of tune. Now remember the big problem here was that $3/2^{12}$ was not the same thing as 2^7.

Mathematically, we can solve this by replacing $3/2$ with some number, let's call it r and the equation we would want to be true is that r to the 12th. If we take the fifth and we replace that $3/2$ with r, 12 of those, we want that to exactly equal to 2^7. We want to hit that octave exactly. Well, $r^{12} = 2^7$, that's a fairly easy equation to solve. We just have to take 12th roots of both sides and we get an answer of $r = 2^{7/12}$. When you plug that into a calculator you get about 1.4983. Notice that that's really close to 1.5.

It's a little bit less than 1.5, but also if you think about it, that value of r is irrational and that's why I talk about this as being math, not making modern music mad, but math making modern music irrational. That value of r cannot be written as a fraction. The Pythagoreans didn't think that numbers like these existed.

Let's take this in another perspective. If we divide the octave into 12 equal half steps, remember multiplicatively not additively, then each one should have a ratio of $2^{1/12}$. Remember that was exactly 100 cents. And if each half step had a ratio of $2^{1/12}$ then seven of them will have a ratio of $2^{7/12}$, which is the number that we just got.

So let's use this number to construct the scale. We're going to start again with 440-Hz A and now we're going to find the other notes. I'll just walk through one example. If we want to find our C-sharp, remember that's up 4/5 and then down two octaves and so we would take our 440-Hz A and we would go up 4/5, that's our key number r^4 and then down two octaves would mean dividing by four. And when we do that calculation we get 554.36 Hz, roughly. Now remember that a just C-sharp was at 5/4 of the fundamental and that gives us a 550-Hz note.

So let's compare the three different C-sharps that we have. We have a just C-sharp, we have the Pythagorean C-sharp and we have an equal tempered C-sharp. How different are they? With the A at 440 the just C-sharp was 550 Hz exactly. The Pythagorean C-sharp was 556.89, roughly, and when you talk about Pythagorean scales, you talk about impossibly high major thirds and this is a very sharp note to the ear. And the equal temperament C-sharp is going to be at 554.36 Hz.

Now let's listen to these. First, here's a just C-sharp at 550 Hz. Next let's listen to Pythagorean, the highest of these, and you can probably tell that it's sharper. It's higher in pitch. And finally the equal tempered C-sharp is in between. Let's compare the just and Pythagorean. That's how we get this impossibly high major third note. And when we play those together, you hear the beats. You hear the dissonance, the unpleasant pitches. There's tension in there and that dissonance is going to be the subject of the next lecture.

So now that we've tuned our scales, we have three different ways, but we've tuned our scales and now we've settled at least in modern times on an equal tempered system. Now let's move on and ask: Why is it 12 notes on our equal tempered system and not a different number of notes? These 12 notes that we have on our equal tempered scale are equally spaced. We can ask the very mathematical question: Would another number work better?

Now there might be lots of cultural reasons why we ended up at 12, but let's think about this mathematically and let's just start from scratch with no culture involved. Let's just build a scale and see where we get, and let's build a scale with equal spacing that gives us maximum flexibility. If we have equal spacing, then we can modulate into any key we want and that's a really nice feature of Western music.

Now there are notes that we definitely want in our scale, and that's because when we hear anything vibrating, we hear its first few overtones very clearly. We hear the octave. We hear the fifth and then the difference between the fifth and the octave, that gap is a fourth and we also hear up to the fifth harmonic, which is a major third and so those intervals are really important.

So suppose the fundamental is at 100 Hz, in just tuning which sounds best, the octave is going to be double that. The fifth is going to be 3/2 that. The fourth is going to be 4/3, and the major third is going to be 5/4. Those are the notes that sound best. Those are the just notes. Those are when we're tuning perfectly in tune with the overtones and those are the key fractions we're going to look at. 3/2 is 1.5, 4/3 is 1.333 repeating, and 5/4 at 1.25.

This is a mathematical question. For what values of *n* will a scale with *n* equally spaced notes include notes that are really close to these key fractions? So let's work by trial and error and see. Now if we have two notes, that's the fundamental, and the octave and if we add a second note to our scale so we get a fundamental, one note in between, and then the octave, that note needs to be exactly halfway in between. And if we do the calculation, we get, it's what we call on our scale a tritone, the augmented fourth. We heard about this, it's the beginning of "Maria" or *The Simpsons*. It's actually also originally called the Devil's Interval.

If we have three notes then we're going to put the fundamental in two notes before we get to the octave and when we look at those, and we get close to the major third but we don't get close to the fourth or fifth. Let's listen to those. If we have four notes on our scale, nothing is close to the key notes that we're looking for. If we have five notes you can see that we get close to the fourth and the fifth, but we don't get very close to the major third. If we have six notes, seven notes, eight notes, you see that we can get close to some of these ratios that we are really looking for, but we can't get close to all three of this with any of one of these systems.

Let's keep adding notes, nine notes, 10 notes, 11 notes, still nothing close, 12 notes. With 12 notes, look how close we are. We're actually very close to all three of the key things that we want to hit. The fifth of the 12 notes is very close to the major third. It's 1.2599 approximately. Remember that's very close to the 1.25 we were aiming for. The sixth of the 12 notes is near the fourth. That's 1.3348, that's what you get. The just value is 1.333 repeating. The eighth of the 12 notes is really close to the fifth. The eighth of those notes is about 1.4983. Remember the value we are aiming for is 1.5. With 12 equally spaced notes we get very close to all of the important ones we want.

What is it that we learned from this? We learned that if you want equally spaced notes, and that allows for modulation and key changes, and if you want to match up with the most prominent overtones, the major third, the fourth, and the fifth, you need at least 12 notes and that was, we figured that out by going from the beginning with trial and error.

136

Let's try to resolve this in a different way using some mathematical theory not trial and error. Now this is really cool, but slightly complicated math. It's really worth it to listen to this and you should try to understand. Remember a true, a just fifth is the ratio of 3/2 and we want to figure out an equally spaced system that we get really close to that fifth. If we were to place n equally spaced notes, remember these are multiplicatively spaced, they would have relative frequency, the fundamental, one and then $2^{1/n}$, $2^{2/n}$, $2^{3/n}$, all the way up so that when we had n of those, we would get $2^{n/n}$, which is just two and we would be at the octave. Remember for our 12-note scale, each half step was $2^{1/12}$ and so this is just a generalization of that for n notes.

Now if we got close to the fifth, it would mean, say the kth one of those was really close to the fifth. In other words, $2^{k/n}$ was very close to the 3/2. Now we can multiply both sides of that equation by two, and then we can do what is called taking the $\log_2$ and what we get is that the $\log_2$ of three needs to be very close to $k/n + 1$. In other words, we need a fraction k/n, which is very close to $\log_{2(3)-1}$. We're looking for really a rational approximation of the $\log_{2(3)}$. Now there's lots of mathematics that's been built up to do things like rational approximations. So let's look at some of that.

Here rational means ratio of fraction and rational approximation means we're trying to get close to an irrational number using just rationals, using just fractions. There's sort of an astonishing connection here to something called continued fractions. Now a continued fraction is a fraction that has a denominator, and that denominator includes a fraction that has a denominator, and that denominator includes a fraction that has a denomin— it keeps going again and again. It's actually sort of self-referential. We'll talk more about that in lecture 9.

Now the most famous continued fraction is one called the Golden Ratio. It comes up in the strangest places. It comes up in Fibonacci numbers, art, architecture. It actually comes up in pinecones, sunflowers, pineapples. It's really an amazing thing, and the Golden Ratio when you usually see it written, you see it written as Φ and it's equal to $1 + \sqrt{\Phi}/2$. If we write that as a continued fraction, it's all 1s. You just get 1s down, down, down to infinity in this continued fraction.

Let's look at some other continued fractions. Probably the easiest irrational number to get is the $\sqrt{2}$, which is approximately 1.414. If we write $\sqrt{2}$ as a continued fraction, here's what we get. It starts with a 1 and then we get a bunch of 2s all the way down. It's actually a nice algebraic exercise that I invite you to take on to prove that this formula is equal to $\sqrt{2}$ and that the last formula is actually equal to 5.

Now if we want an approximation of $\sqrt{2}$, we can use this continued fraction and the idea is that all we have to do is stop the fraction at some point, just cut off the rest. If we stop after two layers of our fraction, we get 1.4. That's not too bad. If we stop after three layers, we get 1.417, that's getting closer. Remember $\sqrt{2}$ is 1.414 on and on and on. If we stop after four layers, we get 1.4138, we're getting very close and you can see that as we take more and more layers of our continued fraction, we're approximating the $\sqrt{2}$. That's the whole point of continued fractions, that they give us a nice rational approximation.

So back to music, we wanted to get close to the fifth, which was 3/2, and to do that we needed a fraction which was close to the $\log_{2(3)}$. Now the $\log_{2(3)}$ if you plug it in to a calculator is about 1.58496. One solution to get to this to get a rational approximation of that number would be to simply take 1 and then 1.5/10, that's 15 tenths, or 1.58/100, that's 158 hundredths. Now when mathematicians look at that sequence, it does actually approximate the $\log_{2(3)}$ but it converges much too slowly. You don't get close very quickly.

To get a better approximation, we use the continued fraction. So let's find the continued fraction of $\log_{2(3)}$ and here, this is what we get. You can see it's not quite as simple as the other two continued fractions that we've seen, but it works the same way and if we want a rational approximation, we're really just asking the question: Where should we cut off this fraction?

If we stop after two layers the number we get is 3/2. That's not a very good approximation of 1.58496. If we stop after three layers, we get 8.5, which is 1.6. That's a little bit better. Let's see what happens when we take one more. When we take four layers, this is what the continued fraction looks like, and the value of it is 19/12. It's 1.583. That's getting quite close to the actual value of the $\log_{2(3)}$ so let's stop there for a second.

What would it mean musically to take this as a rational approximation? Well, it would mean that we are approximating $\log_{2(3)}$ with 19/12 and when we invert the log, we're taking exponentials and so that would mean $2^{19/12}$ is approximately three. We can divide both sides of that equation by two and we get that $2^{7/12}$ is approximately 3/2. That's familiar, isn't it? That's saying that one way to approximate 3/2, remember that's the perfect for the just tuned fifth, is to use $2^{7/12}$. That was the equal tempered fifth. In other words, this continued fraction just gave us the equal tempered 12-note system that we have in Western music today.

Now you can ask the question: What would have happened if we had taken one more layer of fractions? Isn't that sort of curious? What would our musical system look like if we just added one more layer? When we do that in the continued fraction, we end up getting 65/41 and that gives us the approximation that $2^{24/41}$ is approximately 3/2. Think about that musically. We would need 41 keys between one octave and the next and the 24th of those would be very close to a perfect fifth. How close would it be? Well our equal tempered fifth, the $2^{7/12}$ is about 1.498. That's quite close to 1.5. If we had chosen 41 keys per octave, if you had taken another layer in our continued fraction, then the 24th one would be at 1.500419 approximately. That would be incredibly close to 1.5. That difference is almost inaudible.

What would this mean for music? Think about what keyboards would look like, 41 keys in between octaves. On a piano you can reach an octave, you couldn't really reach 41 keys. Think about what harps would look like or xylophones, everything would be much bigger. Wind instruments would have to have many, many holes everywhere. It would be very difficult to make them. There are even implications for music theory.

Let's think about what the circle of fifths would look like. Remember, the circle of fifths was going up a fifth 12 times and that got you back to A. If we had 41 notes per octave, you would have to go up 41/5 to get you back. If you want to do the math, you should think about it. Going to the 24th note and then the 24th note after that when do you get back really close to the original and that would be after 41 times. What you would come back to would be much closer to hitting to some octave above A than with our 12-note system but you would have to go 41 things all the way around your circle.

Now some people actually do some work with these non-standard systems and it leads to some really strange looking instruments. If you want to see one of those, one is called the tonal plexus. It has 211 keys per octave and it looks very strange and it's very difficult. It's interesting to listen to.

Now I want to wrap up this little mathematical excursion into rational approximation because that was really complicated so let's make sure we really understand what we just did. We just took a little excursion into a world with more than 12 notes per octave and the mathematics says this: if you want to get a better and better approximation, if you want a note that is closer and closer to the pure fifth of 3/2 what you should do is keep taking more layers in your continued fraction and as you do that, the advantage is that some notes are much better in tune, you're getting closer to the just system, which is perfect. The disadvantage is that you have too many notes in each octave. Instead of 12 notes, you have 41 notes. Take your pick: 12 notes per octave or 41 notes? I'll stick with 12. You know I can honestly barely hear the difference between two neighboring notes on a 41-note octave.

Now the last point I want to get to you is why do tunings matter? And to address that, let's go back to the 12-note scales and the different tunings we talked about, the just tuning, the Pythagorean tuning, and equal tempered tuning. Now those weren't actually very different so really, why should we care so much? You see different tunings sound a little bit different. Those differences are subtle and if you want to hear those, there are recordings out there that will play you piano pieces on a piano tuned in different systems. You need a nice hi-fi system in a quiet room to hear those but you can hear the differences but they are subtle. Concert pianists sometimes request particular temperaments because they're playing a particular piece that sounds best in a particular temperament, but there are much more important reasons to care about these small differences.

Tunings matter because composers use keyboards to compose music. That's the instrument of choice for composers. What sounds good on a keyboard depends on the tuning and therefore, the tunings are affecting the compositions that we have. Before we get to equal tempered tuning, composers choose different keys for different moods because when you didn't have that gap spread out completely evenly, different keys actually sounded different.

Just for an example, C-sharp minor is the key that had a particularly interesting sound. It was described in this way, "a leering key degenerating into grief and rapture. It cannot laugh but it can smile. It cannot howl but it can at least grimace, it's crying. Consequently, only unusual characters and feelings can be brought out in this key." Think about that. That C-sharp minor on a modern tuned piano, that key sounds exactly the same as others but on some of these older tunings, it had a particular quality and that's how people described that quality.

Now as tunings changed, so did composition, and some of us see the mathematics as affecting the composition. Ross Dauphin wrote a 2007 book called *How Equal Temperament Ruined Harmony and Why You Should Care*. For me, I think of this question of the tunings changing and the compositions changing as sort of a chicken-and-egg problem. Did the tunings change first prompting the compositions to change, or was it the other way around? I think they've really co-evolved .

And so let's take a quick tour on the History of Tunings, and then we'll talk about the History of Music as well. Think about tunings, keyboards, but before pianos it was harpsichords and things like that, and we can look at Western music from say 1500 all the way to 1900. And as we look at the tunings that they used, they were spreading out the Pythagorean comma more and more equally. They had names like mean tone and quarter comma mean tone, Werckmeister III, Hernberg III. They had a well-tempered system that was made famous by a piece of Bach, the Well-Tempered Clavier. There was Victorian well-tempered, quasi-equal tempered, and finally, equal tempered, and pianos were tuned equal tempered by the late1800s, around 1900.

Interestingly guitars, because they have frets that go across all of the strings, that makes it necessary to tune things in an equal temperament manner way back in 1500 when guitars were first made. Now interestingly, there is no piano and guitar music in this period, 1500 to 1900, almost none and one of the reasons was that a guitar and piano would have been really out of tune with each other because a guitar was tuned to a different system than a piano until finally in 1900, pianos joined guitars in being equal tempered.

Let's look at compositions through this time period in Western classical music. If we look at early music, Pre-Renaissance, it was a single voice. We're thinking about plain song music, Gregorian chant, very few notes were used. If we move ahead to Renaissance music, it might be two simple voices together. You've got early versions of major and minor scales.

In Baroque music, Bach until he died in 1750, we had multiple voices, more complex harmonies, and modulations into other keys. Classical music up until 1820 had modulations into other keys and those were becoming increasingly important. Early Romantic music, tonality was becoming less and less prominent. Think about the opening of the Beethoven's Fifth, that opening motif, what key is he in? There are a lot of keys that have those two particular notes. The tonality is becoming less and less important. If we move ahead to Romantic music, think about Brahms and Tchaikovsky, they were starting to break away from old traditions.

In the visual arts, think about the Impressionist painters who at the same time were moving away from Realism. The composers were moving away from tonality, and finally you get to the 20th century, you get to Stravinsky, Schoenberg, and tonality is largely and sometimes completely abandoned. Some compositions ignore any sense of sort of a tonal center, a fundamental note to base things on. Looking at the tunings and the compositions, you can see this co-evolution . Tunings are moving from where the Pythagorean comma was not spread out at all to evenly spreading it out and as that happens, composers are moving. They have access to increasing numbers of keys that sound fairly good, and over time they lose the devotion toward a single key and they move towards all keys being equal.

Now I want to illustrate this transition with music and I want to go back to the two pieces we heard at the beginning. In the 1700s, Bach was composing his music and the key of C sounded very good and related keys sounded quite good. Now some intervals in some keys sounded pretty awful, even in his new well-tempered system. Composers at that time would choose a key for its particular qualities and Bach with his well-tempered system composed the Well-Tempered Clavier. It's a piece in which you have a single piece in every one of the keys, the 12 major and the 12 minor keys. When you play the Well-Tempered Clavier on an equal-tempered piano, on a modern one, you're missing a little bit of the brilliance of Bach. You see for Bach on his equal-tempered system, in some of the keys far away from C, he had to avoid certain intervals because those intervals still sounded bad. On a modern tuned piano, all of those intervals sound exactly the same and so you're missing some of the brilliance that Bach had in composing the Well-Tempered Clavier if you hear it playing on a modern tuned equal-tempered piano.

Fast forward to the 20th century, now David Froom is composing 20th-century style music. For him on his piano, all keys are equivalent. Each interval in every key sounds identical. There is no preference for any key. Keys don't have particular moods. They all sound essentially the same and the tuning was using irrational numbers where the half-step is tuned to the $2^{1/12}$.

So let's hear these two pieces that we started this lecture off with again. Let's start with the David Froom first. Here again is the Sonata for Violin. Here's the opening from 2004.

And now let's turn to Bach. Now Bach was born in 1685 and he lived till 1750, and this is the Allemande from Partita no. 2. And while I'm playing this, I want you to think about how Western scales can be tuned in different ways, none of them perfect, but these different tunings match with different music. I think that understanding Western classical music really requires understanding the mathematics of the tunings that underpin all these pieces.

Now my hope is that after listening to this lecture, you'll listen to classical music differently; that you hear the mathematics of tunings when you're listening to your favorite works; that you hear how all of the great composers and the works they wrote are actually affected by mathematics and the mathematics that their tuners used and how they chose to spread out that Pythagorean comma.

So here's the Bach Allemande from Partita no. 2.

Next time, we'll talk about controlling dissonance and how to tune a piano. Thanks for joining us.

Dissonance and Piano Tuning
Lecture 6

W e now understand a single note and how it vibrates, and we understand the sequence of notes called a scale. In this lecture, we'll talk about two or more notes played at the same time—a chord—such as some of the chords we hear in Bach's Chaconne. Not all combinations of notes sound good, and that's also the topic of this lecture: dissonance, the rough, slightly unpleasant sound we hear when music is played out of tune. We'll look in particular at the mathematics of dissonance.

Defining Dissonance

- Dissonance is a discordant sound that's produced by two or more notes played together that sound displeasing or rough. It's a sort of tonal tension. Sometimes, composers will build in dissonance for a tense moment and then release it by finding consonance.

- Dissonance has both a physical and a cultural component, and what's considered dissonant changes over time. The Pythagoreans thought that notes in consonance had a ratio of frequencies with small numbers and that dissonance was anything but that.

- Herman von Helmholtz, a German mathematician and physicist, gave a mathematical description of dissonance. For him, it involved the overtones, as well as the fundamental notes. His explanation was that dissonance was "beats."
  - The *Grove Dictionary of Music* calls this kind of beats "an acoustical phenomenon useful in tuning instruments, resulting from the interference of two sound waves of slightly different frequencies."

  - What we mean by that is a throbbing sound produced when two notes are played slightly out of tune with each other.

o   We hear an example in two Ds, one played on an open D-string and one played on a G-string. The timing of the throbbing sound can be changed by moving the notes closer to each other. As the notes get closer, the beats slow down. As the notes get further apart, the beats speed up. If the notes are exactly the same or very far apart, we hear no beats at all—either just one note or two separate notes.

The Beat Equation

- The beat equation is a trigonometric identity:

$$\sin(a) + \sin(b) = 2\sin\left(\frac{a+b}{2}\right)\cos\left(\frac{a-b}{2}\right)$$

- Let's look at an example to make sure we understand this equation. We'll let a be $5t$ and b be $3t$. Now the equation is:

$$\sin(5t) + \sin(3t) = 2\sin(4t)\cos(t)$$

o   Looking at a graphical representation of this equation, notice that we use point-wise addition to solve the left side. We pick some x value and look at the height of $\sin(5t)$, and then for the same x value, we look at the height of $\sin(3t)$. Adding those two heights gives us the solution for $\sin(5t) + \sin(3t)$.

o   For the right side of the equation, we do point-by-point multiplication. For a particular value of x, we look for the height of $\sin(4t)$ and the height of $\cos(t)$, and we multiply those values. If either of those functions is 0, then when we multiply, the product will be 0. The last thing we have to do on the right side of the beat equation is multiply by 2 to get the solution for $2\sin(4t)\cos(t)$.

o   The graphs for the left and right sides of the equation are exactly the same.

- We can also explore a musical example. Here, let's take a to be $(450 \times 2\pi \times t)$ and b to be $(440 \times 2\pi \times t)$. These represent a 450-Hz sine wave and a 440-Hz sine wave.
  - According to the beat equation:

$$\sin(450 \times 2\pi \times t) + \sin(440 \times 2\pi \times t) = 2\sin(445t \times 2\pi) + \cos(5t \times 2\pi)$$

  - For any particular x, when we add the value of the 450-Hz wave and the value of the 440-Hz wave and we listen to the result, we can hear dissonance.

  - If we zoom out from the graph, we can see the beats in the wave form.

  - On the right side of the equation, when we multiply $\sin(445t \times 2\pi)$ and $\cos(5t \times 2\pi)$, it seems almost as if the cosine becomes an envelope into which the sine wave fits.

  - The sine wave is going back and forth between $+1$ and -1. When it gets to $+1$ and we multiply by the cosine, we simply get the value of the cosine. When it gets to -1 and we multiply by the cosine, we get the negative value of the cosine. That's why this function appears to be wavering back and forth inside the cosine envelope. The cosine term is producing the beats and telling us how fast the beats are.

- The beat equation tells us that if we have a and b, where a is slightly larger than b, we should get $a - b$ beats per second. But from the formula, it looks like we should get $(a - b)/2$ beats per second. Why the difference?
  - It's true that the cosine has a frequency of $(a - b)/2$. But every full wavelength of the cosine has to go down and back up, and when it does that, that single wave form of the cosine produces two beats.

  - The sound is beating twice during one full cycle of the cosine. That tells us that our conjecture was correct. It's not $(a - b)/2$

beats per second, as the cosine would indicate. It's double that, giving us a beat frequency of $a - b$.

- What happens when $a = b$? When we solve the equation, we find that the cosine term disappears, and there are no beats.

- In the last lecture, we learned that subtle changes in pitches have led to big changes in composition. In practice, how exactly do we make subtle changes in pitch? The answer is by using beats. A demonstration of piano tuning helps us understand.
  - When you tune a piano, you need to adjust the tension on the strings. As we know, adjusting the tension affects the frequency at which the strings vibrate.

  - As you bring two strings into tune—as the two frequencies get closer—the beats slow down. When the two frequencies are equal ($a = b$), we're left with two copies of the sine, and the beats disappear. This process is called "tuning a unison."

A Question about Beats
- If you hear two notes played that are close in frequency, your brain hears the right side of the beat equation. If you hear two notes played that are far apart, your brain hears the left side of the equation; it hears two notes, but you actually can hear beats when an octave is played out of tune.

- We originally thought that when the frequencies were far apart, we wouldn't hear beats, but we do, and it seems as if the beat equation doesn't explain this.
  - If we played an A at, say, 442 Hz and another at 220, the beat equation tells us that we should hear the difference between them. We should hear 222 beats per second if we're hearing the right side of the equation. But we're not hearing the right side; we're hearing the left side. We're hearing two notes, so why are we hearing beats?

o To answer this question, we have to go back to the overtone series. If we're playing one note at 220 Hz, we're hearing its overtones, that is, all the multiples of 220: 440, 660, 880, and so on. If we're playing the higher note, 442, we're hearing its overtones: 884, 1226, and so on.

o The beats aren't coming from the fundamentals, which are 200-some Hz apart. The beats are coming from one of the harmonics of the lower A (440 Hz) and the fundamental of the higher A (442 Hz).

o We're hearing both of those frequencies, which are very close together, and because of those frequencies, we hear beats.

• This problem of beats with notes played far apart doesn't appear only with octaves; it also happens with other intervals. The key observation is that if two of the overtones of two notes are close, we will hear beats.

• Let's look at a fifth: an A at 440 Hz and a note at 293 Hz that is close to a D. The A is the fifth note on the D-major scale, and that's why it's an interval of a fifth. If we play A 440, we hear the fundamental at 440; we hear the second harmonic at 880, and then 1320, and 1760. For the note that's close to the D, we hear the fundamental at 293; we hear the second harmonic at 586 and the next one at 879, which is close to the 880 in the first overtone of the 440 A. Listening to those notes, we could hear beats.

• At what frequency should we put the D in order to completely eliminate the beats?
  o Let's put the D at x Hz. If we play something at x, we know its overtones will be $2x$, $3x$, $4x$, and so on. It's the $3x$ that we want to try to match up with the 880, the first overtone of the A. That gives us an equation to work with: $3x = 880$. Solving, we find that we should put the frequency of this D at 279 1/3 Hz.

o   We know that a perfect fifth should have a ratio of 3/2. If we divide 440 Hz by the lower frequency, which is 293 1/3, we get 3/2.

Tuning Fifths

•   What we just calculated was this: If we want a Pythagorean or a just-tuned tuning system—if we want the fifth to be perfect—we should aim the D for 293 1/3 Hz. But on a modern piano, we don't want the fifths to be perfectly in tune; we need them to be slightly narrower. Instead of 3/2, the ratio needs to be $2^{7/12}$.

•   We need to determine the correct frequency for the D, and then, we use that and the beat equation to figure out how fast the beats should be when we play that D with a 440 A. We then use that answer to tune the D.

•   The first step is to find the frequency for a correctly tuned equal-tempered D. That means adjusting the fifths so that the octaves will work out when we get to the top—spreading that Pythagorean comma completely evenly around all the fifths.
   o   Remember, the half-steps were tuned to $2^{1/12}$, and the fifths were tuned to a ratio of $2^{7/12}$. If the A is tuned to 440, then the D should be tuned to some frequency z so that $z(2^{7/12}) = 440$.

   o   Solving, we find that the D should be tuned approximately to 293.66 Hz.

•   The next step is to figure out how fast the beats will be if we tune the D exactly to that value.
   o   If we play the 440 A, we'll hear all of its overtones, including the pure 880. If we play the equal-tempered D at 293.66 Hz, its second overtone (third harmonic) will be at approximately 880.99 Hz.

   o   The beat equation told us that the difference between those two would give us the frequency of the beats. That difference is about 0.99, just slightly under 1 beat per second.

- The math tells us that if we want equal-tempered fifths, we should tune the fifths so that they're not perfect, but they're just narrow enough that we hear 1 beat per second.

- Essentially, we now know everything we need to know in order to tune a piano. Of course, many piano tuners today use electronic tuners, and in fact, some of them don't tune in an equal-tempered manner because some performers don't want equal-tempered tuning for particular pieces.

Piano tuning is an art, and the truly great tuners work by ear, not with an electronic tuner.

- The octave, the fifth, and the fourth are called perfect intervals, and greater precision is required in playing them. If they are played a little bit out of tune, the beats can be heard.
  - This becomes important in some music. For example, much of the music of Aaron Copland invokes an open American spirit. The way he achieved that open feeling was by using open chords—these perfect intervals.

  - An excellent example can be heard in a piece written by Copland called the *Fanfare for the Common Man*.

A Mathematical Coda
- Virtually everything we've done in this lecture relies on a single equation, the beat equation. We can walk through a proof of this equation that requires just a few trigonometric facts and some basic geometry.

- The proof implies that when two notes are just slightly out of tune, we should get dissonance. From this, we know why musicians have to be more careful with some intervals than with others and why piano tuners use dissonance to tune in an equal-tempered system.

Suggested Reading

Benson, *Music: A Mathematical Offering*, chapter 1.

Fischer, *Piano Tuning*.

Forster, *Musical Mathematics*, chapters 2, 5 (on the subtleties of vibrating piano strings).

Loy, *Musimathics*, vol. 1, chapter 6.

Questions to Consider

1. How does mathematics explain the "beating" phenomenon we hear when two notes of similar frequencies are played?

2. Why is it more important for musicians to play octaves, fifths, and fourths in tune than other intervals?

Dissonance and Piano Tuning
Lecture 6—Transcript

Welcome back. That was probably the calmest section of the Bach Chaconne. It's easier in some ways, there aren't that many notes, but it's much harder in other ways. If you play it a little out of tune; some of those notes are played—were just a little out of tune, and when you play some of those notes out of tune people notice. That's because you hear dissonance and that's what today's lecture's about, dissonance, that sort of rough slightly unpleasant sound especially when things are a little out of tune.

First, let's review. We now understand that a single note and its vibrations, and we understand the sequence of notes called a scale. Today we're going to talk about two or more notes played at the same time, a chord, like some of the chords you just heard on the Chaconne. Now not all combinations of notes sound good, and today we're going to talk about the mathematics of dissonance when they don't sound so good and the musical implications of that.

Let's look a little closer at this opening music. You see, not all intervals are created equal. Musicians work really hard to get some intervals perfect and don't have to work so hard, don't have to care so much about others. Let's hear a particular line in the opening music.

So there's four chords in there. That first interval is a minor third. It's not that important to get that exactly in tune. And then we have a major sixth. And a major seventh. Also not that important, and then we hit the octave.

When I miss it a little bit, it sounds horrible. It's very important to get your octaves exactly in tune. Violinists practice octaves for hours to get them exactly in tune. If I miss some of the other intervals, the minor third, the major seventh, you're not going to notice. But if I miss the octave a little bit, you're going to hear the dissonance. That's what we're going to talk about today.

So what is dissonance? Dissonance is a discordant sound that's produced by two or more notes sounding displeasing or rough. It's a sort of tonal tension. It's the opposite of consonance. Sometimes it's intentional. Sometimes composers will build dissonance for a tense moment and then release it by finding consonance.

Today we're going to talk mostly about the dissonance of being out of tune. Now, as we know from the last lecture, being out of tune is sort of a complicated idea but whatever your scale is, there is a sense of out of tune. Now, dissonance has a physical component that we're going to talk about mostly but it also has a cultural component. I want to talk really quickly about the cultural component.

What Bach considered beautiful, medieval composers might have called dissonant. Here's a chord from earlier in the Chaconne. Medieval composers might have thought of that as incredibly dissonant, but Bach wrote it into the piece. What Stravinsky wrote when we fast-forward to 1913 when he wrote *The Rite of Spring*, he asked the violins to play this chord. Now that might have been considered very dissonant by Bach but Stravinsky wrote it into his piece. What's considered dissonant changes over time. Now, mathematically, the Pythagoreans thought that consonance, nice-sounding notes together, had a ratio of frequencies with small numbers and dissonance was anything but that.

Herman von Helmholtz, the German mathematician and physicist, gave a mathematical description of dissonance. For him, it involved the overtones as well as the fundamental notes and we'll see that a little bit later. His explanation was that dissonance was beats. Now, beats are a phenomenon produced by two frequencies being played when the two frequencies are very close to each other.

I want to clarify here because beat is a word with many different meanings. Now, I don't want you to confuse the term I'm using with things like what you do on drums or keeping time or what a conductor does, beating out rhythm, beating out the time signature.

The *Grove Dictionary of Music* calls this kind of beats "an acoustical phenomenon useful in tuning instruments resulting from the interference of two sound waves of slightly different frequencies." What we mean by that is a throbbing sound produced when two notes are played slightly out of tune with each other and it's useful in tuning instruments. So, let's hear what beats sound like. Now you heard them last time, we heard them electronically. We were playing sine waves.

I want you to hear beats on an actual instrument and so I'm going to play two Ds. I'm going to play one on my open D-string here. I'm also going to play another one on my G-string here. If I play them a little bit out of tune, you should hear beats, it's a throbbing sound. And one of the things I can do is I can change how frequently that throbbing sound is going by getting the notes closer and closer to each other. And what you'll notice is as the notes get closer, the beats slow down. If the notes get further apart, the beats speed up. And finally, if the notes are exactly the same, you get no beats at all, you just hear one note.

You'll also note that if I play the notes very far apart, you don't hear beats at all, you just hear two separate notes. That's sort of clearly the—and the other note. Today, we're going to understand the mathematics of dissonance and these beats. And we're going to look at the implications of these for musical performance and for piano tuning.

There's a really important equation that we're going to refer to again and again today and we're going to call that the Beat Equation. Now this is actually just a trigonometric identity that you might have seen in a trigonometry class back in high school but it's this,

$$\sin(a) + \sin(b) = 2 \sin ((a + b)/2) \cos ((a-b)/2)$$

Now, when two notes are played at the same time, that's the left side of the equation,

$$\sin(a) + \sin(b)$$

The cool thing is that sometimes when two notes are played at the same time, you hear the left side, you hear those two notes. But actually, sometimes you hear the right side of this equation and so your mind is going back and forth depending on which notes of it you're hearing. You're sometimes hearing the left side and sometimes hearing the right.

Let's look at an example to make sure we understand this equation. Let's let a be $5t$ and let's let b be $3t$. So now this equation looks like,

$$\sin(5t) + \sin(3t) = 2\sin(4t)\cos(t)$$

Now, for the math lovers out there, we're going to actually go through a proof of this later. It's not too hard to get a proof of this but for now, we're going to just take that this Beat Equation is actually true.

But let's look and see if we can see this in another representation. You remember that mathematicians love to look at different representations. So now let's look at and see if we can see this equation graphically with this example of $5t$ and $3t$.

We can graph sine of $5t$ and it looks like this. And now we can graph the sine of $3t$ and we can—look at what happens when we add those. When we're doing addition, the left side of the equation, we're actually doing point-wise addition.

We find whatever—we pick some x-value and look how high the sine of $5t$ is and of that same x-value, we look how high the sine of $3t$ is, we add those two heights and that's what we get for the value of

$$\sin(5t) + \sin(3t)$$

And so that's how we get the left side of this equation graphically.

Now, let's look at the right side of the equation. The sine of $4t$ has a graph that looks like this. The cosine of t has a graph that looks like this. And now when we multiply, we're actually doing point-by-point multiplication. So now at a particular value of x, we're looking for the height of the sine of $4t$ and the height of the cosine of t, and we're looking to multiply those. And that's going to give us the sine of $4t$ times the cosine of t.

Now, you should notice that if either one of these functions is zero, then when we multiply them we're going to get zero for the product. The last thing we have to do on the right side of this equation is multiply by two to get

$$2 \sin(4t) \cos(t)$$

And that's what this function is here.

Now, let's compare that. We can compare that to what we got on the left side of the equation that look like this, and here's what we got on the right side of the equation that look like this. They look exactly the same.

Let's zoom out just to see if we're being fooled by the scale of this. When we zoom out, we see that even when we zoom out those two graphs are exactly the same. We're confirming that it is an equation, that the left side really does equal the right side.

So that was a graphical representation. Let's see if we can take this to a musical example and in order to do that, let's change a and b a little bit. Let's take a to be $450*2\pi*t$ and b to be $440*2\pi*t$. These represent a 450-Hz sine wave and a 440-Hz sine wave. If you're wondering, the 2π comes because the natural period of sine and cosine is 2π.

Now,

$$\sin(450*2\pi*t) + \sin(440*2\pi*t)$$

should be equal to, according to the Beat Equation,

$$2 \sin(445t*2\pi) + \sin(5t*2\pi)$$

Now, let's look both graphically and musically at this. First, let's look at

$$\sin(440*t*2\pi)$$

When we listen to that, here's what it sounds like.

And you can see the graph of that and if we look at the graph and listen to 450-Hz note, that's

$$\sin(450t*2\pi)$$

Here's what that sounds like.

Now, of course, the notes that we just played, those were pure sine waves. If you were to hear it on a violin, you would hear a 440 A and its overtones. And that's going to become important later. For now, let's see if we can add these functions and see what the sounds sound like when we add these functions.

So here's the 440-Hz A and this is what it looks like. And here's the 450-Hz A and you can notice that it's slightly sharp. When we add them, we again do this point-by-point addition and so we're adding, at any particular x, the value of the 440-Hz plus the value of the 450-Hz and we get this function right here. And when we listen to it, you can hear the dissonance. Those are the beats that we're hearing.

But when we look at it, it looks like just another sine wave. It looks maybe just two times as tall but it looks like just a sine wave. But let's zoom out and it's when we zoom out that we all of a sudden start to see what we were hearing before. You can see the beats now in the waveform, those are the throbbing, waving, those are the acoustic phenomenon that we're talking about. That's the dissonance. So let's find out how the math explains what it is we're hearing.

In order to see that, let's look at the right side. Now the right side of the equation has

$$\sin(445t*2\pi)$$

And that looks like this. But

$$\cos(5t*2\pi)$$

has a much longer wavelength that looks like this. Now, let's think about what happens when we multiply them.

You see when we multiply them, it's almost like the cosine becomes an envelope and the sine wave fits into that envelope. If you think about it, the sine wave is going back and forth between plus and minus one and when it gets to plus one and we multiply by the cosine, we're just getting the value of the cosine. And when it goes to minus one and we multiply by the cosine, we're just getting the negative of the value of the cosine. And that's why this function appears to be just wavering back and forth inside the cosine envelope.

The cosine term is the one producing the beats and that's telling us how fast the beats are. So let's look closer at that. On the right side, we have

$$2 \sin(445) \cos(5)$$

and it's the

$$\cos(5t*2\pi)$$

that's giving us these beats. Let's listen to that in this particular case.

And if we look at the waveform and if we look closely at the scale, we see that in every second there's 10 beats. It's 10 beats per second. Now, if we change the notes a little bit, let's take a 444-Hz and a 440-Hz tone and let's hear what those sound like.

And you could actually count it with your watch or you could look at this waveform and look at one second of that and what you can see is there are four beats per second in that. So, once we've seen a couple of these examples, I think we're ready to make a conjecture, that's the mathematician's term for a good solid educated guess.

When we had 450 and 440, we had 10 beats per second. When we were at 444 and 440, we got four beats per second. So the conjecture should be, that if we have a and b, where a is a little bit bigger than b, we should get $a-b$ beats per second. Why? Because of the Beat Equation.

So—but if we look at that Beat Equation, the right side has

$$\cos(((a-b)/2)*2\pi)$$

So you might ask yourself, why are we hearing a minus b beats per second. The frequency we just guessed was a minus b but it looks from the formula like it should be $(a-b)/2$. So why the difference here?

To understand this, we have to look back at that cosine. You see the cosine has a frequency of $(a-b)/2$, that's true, and it goes down and back up just like this. Every full wavelength of the cosine has to go down and back up, but when it does that, that single waveform, that single wavelength of the cosine, produces two beats.

And so the sound is beating twice during one full cycle of the cosine and so that tells us that our conjecture was correct. It's not $(a-b)/2$ like the cosine would indicate. It's double that and so we can—our conjecture is correct and we get a beat frequency of $a-b$.

Now, let's also look at what happens when a is equal to b. Let's suppose that a and b are exactly the same and they're equal to some frequency f. Then on the right side of the equation, we have two times the sine of the average, well, the average of f and f is just f, times the cosine of half the difference. But the difference is zero. And if you remember from your trigonometry class, the cosine of zero is just one. Remember the cosine is the x-coordinate on the unit circle. So if the angle is zero, the point on the unit circle is $(1, 0)$ and the x-coordinate is 1.

And so,

$$\cos(0) = 1$$

The cosine just disappears and what we get is

$$2 \sin(ft*2\pi)$$

It's just the original sine wave doubled and in fact, if you look at the Beat Equation, that's what we get on the left side as well. We get,

$$\sin(f) + \sin(f)$$

we just get

$$2 \sin(f)$$

Well, enough about this math theory and all of these theories of beats. It's not just a mathematical exercise. It turns out these beats are really useful. So let's see how they're used.

Now, we know from last lecture, lecture 5, that subtle changes in pitches have led to big changes in composition. In practice, how exactly do you make subtle changes in pitch?

Well, the modern way to do it is to have an electronic tuner that tells you how you're making these small changes. But historically, we didn't have those tuners. How do they make these subtle changes? The answer is using beats.

In order to see this, we have to go over to the piano and do a little bit of piano tuning. So in order to tune a piano, we need some tools here. Here's my tuning lever and we also need some things called mutes. Let's see if we have some of these. Let's see.

There's two, I think I'm going to need two more. So here we have four mutes and these are going to be used to dampen some of the vibrations that we're going to see.

Now, let's look at this. Let's look at A. Here's the 440 A. Let's look at the 220 A that's right here.

That sounds pretty bad. Now, if you look really closely inside the piano here, there's actually three strings that we have on a lot of these notes. Down here there's two strings, and down here there's one string, but on this particular A there's three strings. And I don't want to hear all three of them. I want to hear just two of them. So let's hear these two.

Now those two are definitely out of tune and in fact, if you listen closely, you can hear that it's beating.

Those beats are pretty fast and what you do when you tune a piano is you put this lever on the end of a string and you slowly tighten or loosen it. If you remember back to lecture 1, in lecture 1 we talked about how the tension on a string affects the frequency. So if I adjust this lever, I'm pulling it a little bit tighter and letting go, I'm changing the tension and that's changing exactly the frequency it's vibrating at.

Now, these two notes, these two strings that we have here are a little bit out of tune, and as I adjust the lever, you can actually hear the beats and just like on the violin, as the two frequencies get closer the beats slow down. And when I finally get these two exactly in tune, the beats go completely away.

So again, we have three strings here and I'm only hearing the left two, because I muted the one on the right and here's what it sounds like. And now I'll try to tune this from out of tune to in tune. If you listen closely, you can hear wawawawawa. Those are the beats, it still has beats. When I finally get it in tune, then the two frequencies are equal $a = b$ and then all of a sudden our equation simplifies. We just get two copies of the sine.

That's what we're looking for when we tune the piano. We're looking to get notes that exactly match up. These are called tuning a unison, when we have two strings that are supposed to be at exactly the same frequency and that's what we're hearing. We're hearing tuning a unison and we're using beats to do it. And as those notes get closer and closer, the beats slow down and finally when they match up, the beats are gone.

Let's see if we can hear this on a violin because one of the surprising things is, so far we've heard that if you play two notes that are really close in frequency, your brain is hearing the right side of this equation. You hear these beats and we've also heard that if a and b are far apart, your brain hears the left side. It hears two notes but actually, you can hear beats when you play the octave out of tune.

Let's hear these, I'm going to play an octave. Here's a G, and here's a G an octave above it, and if I play those, I'm going to play those a little bit out of tune. Listen closely and you'll hear the beats. And again, as I get them closer and closer to in tune, you can hear the beats slow down. And when I get them exactly in tune it sounds almost like it's a single note even though I'm playing octave.

Let's hear these beats on a piano. So on the piano, I'm going to play an A here at 440, and another A down here at 220. In order to hear this really clearly, we want to hear just one of the strings of each of them. So on the 440 A, I'm going to use this mutes to dampen the outside strings and now when I play the A we're only hearing the middle of these three strings.

I'm going to do the same thing down here on this a. So now I've damped the outside ones and we're only hearing the middle string here. I'm going to move my tuning lever so that I'm turning and tightening and loosening the middle string on the lower octave. And now let's play the octave. That sounds fairly good. If we pull this out of tune, let's hear what it sounds like.

You can hear the beats, wawawawawawa. Let's hear it again. And now I'm going to slowly increase the frequency by increasing the tension on the lower one and you're going to hear the beats slow down and finally disappear. And if I go too far, we get beats again. You can really hear the frequency of those well, wawawawawa. Let me bring that back down to in tune.

When they're in tune, the beats disappear. So why are we hearing beats? Remember we thought that when the frequencies were really close we would hear beats. We would hear the right side of the equation but when we are playing two notes that were further apart we wouldn't hear beats.

We're playing notes that are very far apart. In fact, they're octaves, they're about double. One frequency is double the other. So why is it that we're hearing beats?

Somehow it seems like the beat equation doesn't really explain this. You see, if we played the note that was, say, at 442 Hz and another note at 220, now those are both an A but the A is a little sharp. The 440 would be the correct one so that's an A4, which is a little sharp, and the 220 is the correct A3. If we play those together, the Beat Equation tells us that we should hear the difference between them. We should hear 222 beats per second if we were hearing the right side of the equation.

Now, we're not hearing the right side of the equation, we're hearing the left side of the equation. We're hearing two notes so why is it that we're hearing beats? We definitely did not count out 222 beats per second, we counted out something much slower than that. In order to understand this, we have to go back to the overtone series. You see, if you're playing one note at 220 Hz, you're hearing its overtones, all the multiples of 220—440, 660, 880. If you're playing the higher note, 442, you're hearing its overtones, 884, 1326, all the multiples of 442.

The beats aren't coming from the fundamentals, which are of 200 some Hz apart. The beats are coming from one of the harmonics of the lower A and the fundamental of the higher A. One of the harmonics of the lower A is at 440 Hz. The fundamental of the higher A is at 442. You're hearing both of those frequencies and so you are actually hearing two frequencies that are very close together and because of those frequencies, you're hearing beats. How frequently are those beats? Well, let's go back to the Beat Equation.

If it's 440 and 442, you should hear two beats per second. And so if I tuned the piano strings exactly to 220 and 442, you should hear two beats per second. Now, this problem of beats when you play notes far apart, it doesn't just happen with octaves. It also happens with other intervals. The key observation is that if two of the overtones of two notes are close, we're going to hear beats.

Let's look at a fifth. So at 440-Hz A, that's a correctly tuned A in the modern times, and a note at 293 Hz is pretty close to a D. Remember D here, the A is the fifth note on the D major scale and that's why it's an interval of a fifth. Let's look at the overtones that we're going to hear, the harmonics, and the overtones of these notes. If we play a 440, we're going to hear the fundamental at 440, we're going to hear the second harmonic, the first overtone at 880, and then 1320 and then 1760.

For the note that's really close to the D, the 293, we're going to hear its multiples as well. Its second harmonic, its first overtone it's going to be 586. The next one is going to be 879. The 879 is going to be very close to the 880 that we had as the first overtone of the 440 A.

So if we were to play these two notes, you would hear both of these overtones, these harmonics, and you would produce beats through them. We can ask a mathematical question here, what frequency should we put the D at in order to completely eliminate these beats? So let's see if we can solve that problem. Let's suppose we put that D, instead of a 290 Hz, let's put it just at x Hz and now let's figure out what x should be in order to get a nice consonant sound and eliminate the beats.

Now, if we play something at x, we know its overtones are going to be multiples, $2x$, $3x$, $4x$, and it's the $3x$ that we want to try to match up with the 880, the first overtone of the A. That gives us an equation to work with. It tells us that $3x$ should equal 880. That's an equation we could have solved a long time ago, probably in middle school. We divide both sides by three and we get that we should put x, we should put the frequency of this D at 279 1/3 Hz.

Let's just check our work. We remember that a fifth, a perfect fifth, should have a ratio of three to two. So if we take 440 Hz and divide by the lower frequency, which is 293 1/3. If we do that math, we do indeed get 3/2. That is a perfect fifth.

Let's see if we can hear these on a violin. Now, as we get to these other intervals, the effect becomes much more subtle, but it is a sort of a familiar sound. When you hear somebody tuning up, the violin gets an A from the oboe or maybe the piano if it's just a violin and piano piece. And gets the A and tunes that, and the next thing a violinist will do is tune the D. Remember the A and the D, that's a fifth. So now I'm going to play my A and my D string. One of the things a violinist is doing is listening for the dissonance between those until it's gone. Really, you're listening for the beats in there until they're gone.

Now, most notes on a violin can be adjusted on the fly so it's really no problem if I'm playing this note, I can change it while I'm playing it but these open strings, these have to be tuned fixed. And remember that tuning problems weren't just for pianos and so violinists should actually tune their fifths to be slightly tighter just like they were on a piano.

Let's see what it's like tuning fifths on a piano.

Good, we have the A set at a nice 440 and now we're going to look at tuning the D. Now here is the D. Again, the D has three strings and so I'm going to take mutes to dampen the outside ones and now the D should just be the middle string. And when I play those together, we get this. And now I'm going to tune the D and I'm going to tune it up and down and let's listen to the beats that we should be getting.

You can definitely hear the dissonance on this. You might be able to hear the beats. Let's see if we can hear this a little clearer. When I'm doing is exercise with students. One of the things I have them do is I have them come over and touch the piano. When I play this, you can actually feel the beats, a little bit better than you can hear them. And in fact, if we show you the waveform, you can see sort of a little bit of those bits. It looks sort of wavery like that. Those are the beats coming through visually in the graphics.

Now what we just calculated is that if we want a Pythagorean or a just tuned—tuning system, if we want this fifth to be perfect, we should aim the D for 293 1/3 Hz. And that means aiming it for perfect fifths so that there are no beats at all. Let's listen, see if we can do that. You can hear I went too far. Let's bring it back down a little bit.

That sounds pretty good. Now that was a Pythagorean or a just tuned system. But this is a modern piano, we don't want the fifths to be perfectly in tune. Remember, we needed the fifths to be slightly narrower. We needed the ratio to not be 3/2, but this irrational number that we came up with, $2^{7/12}$. So how should we tune this?

Well, what we're going to do is we're going to use math to figure out the frequency for the D, what it should be, and then we're going to use that and the Beat Equation to figure out how fast the beats should be when we play that D with a 440 A and then we're going to use that to tune the D. So let's do that.

The first step is to find the frequency for a correctly tuned equal tempered D. That means adjusting the fifths so that the octaves will work out when we get to the top, spreading that Pythagorean comma completely evenly around all of the fifths.

Remember the half steps were tuned to $2^{1/12}$ and the fifths, that's seven half steps, were tuned to a ratio of $2^{7/12}$. So if the A is tuned to 440, then the D should be tuned to some number z, some frequency z, so that z times $2^{7/12}$ is exactly 440.

We can solve that equation, we divide both sides by $2^{7/12}$ and then we can use a calculator and what you get is that the D should be tuned approximately to 293.66 Hz. So the next step is for us to figure out how fast the beats will be if we tune it exactly that.

If we play the 440 A we'll hear all of its overtones including the pure 880. If we play a note, the D, the equal tempered D at 293.66 Hz, then we know its overtones are just going to be multiples of it. And the second overtone, the third harmonic, is going to be at approximately 880.99 Hz.

Now we can use the Beat Equation to tell us how frequently the beats should be. Remember the Beat Equation told us that the difference between those was going to give the frequency of the beats. And so the difference between 880.99 and the 880 first overtone of the A, is going to be about .99, just a hair under one beat per second.

So all of this is telling us, if we want equal-tempered fifths, we should tune the fifths so that they're not perfect, but they're narrow just enough so that we hear one beat per second. So let's go hear it on the piano and see if we could tune the D in this equal-tempered way.

So here's the A at 440 Hz, and here's the D that we tuned perfectly at 293 1/3 Hz. Now in order to tune this piano, this particular interval in an equal-tempered way, we're going to have to make the D a little bit sharp. How much sharp? Enough so that we hear just about one beat per second. Let's listen.

Can you hear those beats? Wawawawawawa. That's definitely faster than one beat per second.

That sounds about like one beat per second. One of the things that piano tuners do, a really classically trained, probably an older piano tuner, they could tune a piano with just an old school watch and they could just watch the seconds beat and they would count beats like that.

But essentially, you now know everything you need to know in order to tune a piano. You tune the fifths in this way. Now you have to be careful. It's not that every fifth has just one beat per second. You actually have to go back and do the calculations and figure out how many beats for each one of the fifths because it changes as you go from the bottom to the top, again, because it's multiplicative.

But you do this process, you can tune the fifths by calculating them, figuring out how many beats and tuning them exactly like that and then you tune the octaves perfectly. It's a little bit more complicated because you have this multiple strings and once you tune one string you have to remove the mutes and make sure the other strings on that particular key are tuned exactly the same. You have to tune what's called the unisons again.

Now, I have to give you some disclaimers about this. This isn't exactly how piano tuners do this. Among other things, they don't go on the side and figure out the math every time and then come back and tune a fifth. Many of them use electronic tuners and in fact, some of them don't tune in equal-tempered manner. Some performers don't want their pianos tuned in equal-tempered way if they're playing a particular piece.

Piano tuners also have this really interesting rules of thumb. For instance, the one that I find really funny is if they're listening for something that's seven beats per second instead of using a watch and counting out wawawawa, counting out seven per second, some of them will use the phrase "from Chicago to New York." And if you say the phrase "from Chicago to New York" in a single sentence, in a single second, then that's telling you how fast the beat should be because "from Chicago to New York" has seven syllables in it.

A lot of piano tuners, instead of tuning the fifths, will actually have a very specific sequence of intervals to check and it's not just fifths. A lot of times they'll tune something and they'll tune it with another interval and they'll be checking to make sure that one beats slightly faster than the other or one beats slightly slower. That's another thing that piano tuners will do, instead of actually counting the beats per second, they'll just compare them with other ones that they've already tuned so that they would know that one interval should have beats just a little bit faster or just a little bit slower than another interval.

Also, I want to admit that the mathematics we've talked about here is a little bit off and it's off for a very interesting reason. See, the widths of these strings, these strings inside the piano are actually coiled and that changes things. The coiling of the strings actually takes the overtones slightly sharp.

If you remember back to the mathematical models we were talking about in lecture 1, when we talked about those models we assumed that the strings were infinitely thin and it—only under those conditions were the overtones exactly at multiples. When you take into effect that these strings are coiled then for instance, if you play a 400-Hz fundamental note, the first harmonic is the second harmonic, the first overtone, is not at 800 Hz, it's a little bit higher than 800 Hz. Piano tuners have to take into account this effect and they do it in a really subtle way.

You see, because the overtones are a little bit high, piano tuners have to do the following, and you can sort of think about it on the piano here. You see, in the middle of this, in the middle of the piano here, they're tuning things just fine but then say the overtone of this note is going to be a little bit too high, higher than the math would first predict. And so when they get into these higher notes they have to take those frequencies up a little bit and this is called the stretching.

And when you go back down the other way, you want to make sure that the frequencies that you hear when you play a lower note exactly match up here. But the overtones of the lower note are stretched, they're a little bit too high and so you bring the frequencies on the left side a little bit down.

Tuning this gives you what's called the stretch of a piano and this tells you that really, piano tuning is really an incredible art. It's not so much of a science although science certainly goes into it. The really great piano tuners are tuning by ear, not by electronic tuner, and it's not just about tuning. It actually matters when you play the music and so let's go and let's listen to some music and talk about the implications of all these beats and this tuning on music.

So remember that the overtones included things like the octave, the fifth, the fourth, musicians call these perfect intervals. When you play these intervals, it requires greater precision. If you play them a little bit out of tune, you're going to hear beats.

Think back to the opening music when I was playing the slower parts of the Chaconne. Some of the intervals, the tuning wasn't as crucial. It was the octaves, I played an octave and it was very crucial that I get those exactly in tune. The same is true of the other open intervals, the fourths and the fifths, and this happens on almost all instruments. You want to make sure that your octaves, your fourths, and your fifths, are exactly in tune because if they're not quite in tune, you're going to hear beats because the overtones of those should exactly match up and if they don't, you're going to hear beats.

This becomes really important in some music, so let's hear an example on brass instruments. Aaron Copland was an American composer. He lived from 1900 to 1990. He was born in Brooklyn. His parents were Lithuanian Polish Jews and he wrote a lot of music invoking the American spirit, the wide-open American Western landscape, and one of the ways he got that sort of open feeling was by using open chords, these octaves, the fourths, the fifths, the perfect intervals that we were just talking about.

A great example of this comes from 1942. He wrote a piece called *The Fanfare for the Common Man*. He wrote it for the Cincinnati Symphony and it premiered in March of 1943. It was inspired by Vice President Henry Wallace's speech *Century for the Common Man* and when you listen to this, you're going to hear many perfect intervals. You're going to hear a lot of these fourths, fifths, octaves, these open chords and we hoped that the musicians who were playing this practiced for hours to get those exactly in tune because if they're not exactly in tuned, you're going to hear dissonance. You're going to hear beats and one of the things they're practicing to do is to avoid that dissonance. Let's listen to the Copland.

That almost makes me want to go over and join in, play the timpani part. So let's see what we've learned to this point in this talk. When you play two frequencies that are very close, but not equal, you hear dissonance, you hear these beats. These are predicted by mathematics, it's trigonometry, and we can use this phenomenon in piano tuning and we try to avoid this phenomenon in performance.

Now, usually we're ending these talks with a musical coda. Today, we're going to end this with a mathematical coda. Now, virtually everything we've done today relies on a single equation, the Beat Equation. In most lectures that we're talking about, the mathematics would take far too long to derive, think about the Fourier Transform, it would take semesters. Today is the exception. All you need to understand this trigonometry is—this trigonometric formula—is some of the trigonometry you probably saw in high school.

Now, if you were turned off by the abstractness of trigonometry back then, then you weren't alone. Now's your chance to really appreciate the meaning of trig in the context of music. So let's take these last few minutes and prove the Beat Equation.

Here's the Beat Equation and the things we need to remember in order to prove this are that the sine is equal to the opposite over the hypotenuse of the right triangle. And if you happen to be on the circle of radius one, called the unit circle, then the hypotenuse is one and then the sine is just the opposite, the length of the opposite, the y-value. And the cosine is just the length of the adjacent, the x-value.

We also have to remember that cosine is an even function that tells us that cosine of negative x is equal to cosine of x, and sine is an odd function that tells us that the sine of negative x is equal to the negative sine of x. The last thing we have to remember is that the sum of the angles in a triangle is 180 degrees. So let's see if we can do the proof of this Beat Formula.

Before we get to the actual proof, let's simplify the formula we're trying to prove with a little bit of algebra. You see, on the right side we have the average of a and b and we also have half the difference. Let's change variables to simplify that. Let's let $u = (a+b)/2$, the average and let $v =(a-b)/2$, half the difference.

When we do this, then when we add u and v, the $b/2$s cancel and we just get a and when we subtract, when we take $u-v$, the $a/2$s cancel and we just get b. And when we plug those into our formula, the Beat Formula is equivalent to, in u and v,

$$\sin(u+v) + \sin(u-v) = 2 \sin(u) \cos(v)$$

We're actually first going to prove a formula for this left side. We're going to prove what's called the Sine of the Sum Formula,

$$\sin(u+v) = \sin(u) \cos(v) + \cos(u) \sin(v)$$

After we prove it, we're going to use it twice. Let's just use it now and we'll come back and prove it later. We use it twice on the left side, we have $\sin(u+v)$. We can use this formula and write out what it equals. We have the $\sin(u-v)$. We can use the formula and see what it equals. And now we can use the even and odd formulas for cosine and sine to simplify the right side.

When we do that, we see that these two terms cancel. The other two terms are identical and just add and so we see that we just get $2*\sin(u)*\cos(v)$ and that's what we were trying to get.

Now, let's see if we can prove the Sine of the Sum Formula. That's the last thing. If we prove that, we've proven the Beat Equation. To do that, we need an angle u and an angle v. So let's put the angle u at the bottom and put the angle v on top of that. And let's measure out one unit on the top ray. Let's call that point b.

Now, the $\sin(u+b)$ should be the y-coordinate of B because the hypotenuse is one here. So we're really looking now to figure out how far is b away from the x-axis, that's the y-coordinate of B.

In order to see this, we need to draw a few lines. Let's draw the perpendicular to the middle ray from B and we'll call that C. And now at C, we'll draw a vertical line through C and we'll also look at B and draw a horizontal line through B. That vertical and horizontal line, they intersect, let's call that E. And the vertical line hits the axis, let's call that D. And now let's examine this picture.

Remember that what we're looking for is the y-value of B, the distance from B to the axis. And that is just the length of ED. You can see that ED is split into two pieces. The bottom part is DC and the top part is CE. In order to figure out those lengths, let's first look at the right triangle ABC.

Now, the right angle here is at C and the hypotenuse is AB, that's just one. And therefore AC has length $\cos(v)$, it's the adjacent. And BC has length $\sin(v)$. Now, let's look at triangle ADC. The angle there is u and the $\sin(u)$ is going to be the length CD, the opposite, over the hypotenuse AC.

We figured out that AC was the $\cos(v)$ and now we can multiply both sides by $\cos(v)$ and we've solved for CD, it's $\sin(u) \cos(v)$. We're halfway there, we got the bottom part of the line segment and now we have to get the top part EC.

To get EC, first we want to figure out what angle is at BCE. To see that, there are three angles meeting right here at C. One of them is 90 degrees, which tells you the other two must add to 90, we call those complementary angles.

Now we know another pair of complementary angles, it's these two. With the right angle at D, the three of these angles have to add to 180 but the right angle is at D and so these two angles also have to add to 90. Well, if this pair adds to 90 and this pair also adds to 90, these two must be the same. And that tells you that the angle right here at BCE is actually equal to u.

Let's use that to get CE. Now we know the length of BC, that's $\sin(v)$, and we know the angle right here so let's look at that triangle. The $\cos(u)$ should be the adjacent EC over BC, that's EC over the $\sin(v)$ and when we multiply both sides by $\sin(v)$, we get EC. We get EC is the $\cos(u) \sin(v)$.

And that really completes it. You see, the $\sin(u+v)$ should be the y-coordinate of B, that's the length ED that's split into two pieces and now we've solved for the lengths of both of those. So let's finish this.

With just a few trigonometric facts and some basic geometry, we finished the Beat Formula, we've proved it. Now, even if you didn't follow the proof, you can see what it shows.

It implies that when two notes are just slightly out of tune, we should get this discordant sound. We should get dissonance, we should get beats. It tells us why musicians have to be more careful with some of the intervals than others like the slow part of the Chaconne that I played at the beginning.

It shows us how piano tuners use this dissonance, finding ways to tune pianos in an equal-tempered system, that system that solved the piano tuning problem. Now, next time we're going to look at probably the most obvious connection between math and music: rhythm.

Thanks for joining us.

Rhythm—From Numbers to Patterns
Lecture 7

In all of our lectures so far, we've talked about a single topic, pitch. In this lecture, we will turn to rhythm. The term is difficult to define, but we can think of it as a regularly ordered pattern of durations and strengths of notes. Imagine music without rhythm or, more precisely, music without any change in rhythm. There would be no drama, no suspense, no life to the music! At the other end of the spectrum, American composer Steve Reich's work *Clapping Music* shows that it's possible to have music with only rhythm. In this lecture, we'll see how composers use rhythm as a musical tool to add interest and emotion to their work.

Rhythm in Poetry

- Rhythm plays a role not only in music but also in poetry because words form a rhythm. Indian poetry, for example, provides some interesting connections between rhythm and mathematics.

- Indian poetry was traditionally written in Sanskrit, and it has two types of words: those with short syllables and those with long syllables that are exactly twice as long as the short ones.

- Pingala was an Indian poet who lived several centuries before the Common Era. He asked an interesting question: How many different ways are there to put short and long syllables together to get a line of a given length? If we're thinking musically, we could ask: How many different ways can we put one- and two-beat notes together to get a rhythm n beats long?

- Interestingly, the answer to this question follows the pattern of the Fibonacci numbers. For a one-beat rhythm, there is just 1 choice; for two beats, 2 choices; for three beats, 3 choices; followed by 5, 8, 13, and so on. Why is it that the next number in the pattern is the sum of the two previous numbers?

- Here's another question: To get the answer for n beats, do you have to figure out all the choices before it? The answer is no. Binet's formula gives us the number of ways of using short and long syllables to form an n-beat phrase.

Western Musical Notation

- In Western musical notation, a whole note represents four beats; a half note is two beats; a quarter note is one beat; an eighth note is half a beat; a sixteenth note is a quarter of a beat; and so on. Music also uses rests for silences of the same length of any of these notes. Further, there is notation for notes that aren't fractions with a power of 2, such as triplets or quintuplets. A dot added after a note or a rest symbol adds half the length of the note or rest.

- The time signature, which looks suspiciously like a fraction, tells us how many notes are in a particular measure. For example, with 3/4 time, each measure has three beats (the top number), and each beat is one quarter note long. The time signature 4/4 is called "common time." It's four beats per bar, and each beat is a quarter note long.

- There are many standard time signatures: 3/4, 2/4, 2/2, 6/8, and so on. Notice that the top number can be any natural number, but the bottom number must be a power of 2. Modern composers sometimes make use of stranger options, such as 7/16.

Hemiolas

- The time signatures that involve groups of six, such as 6/8 time, are mathematically interesting. The number 6 is the product of two prime numbers, 2 and 3. We can think of 6 as two groups of 3 or three groups of 2.

- Musically, 6/8 sometimes feels like triplets (1-2-3, 1-2-3) and sometimes feels like three 2s, (1-2, 1-2, 1-2). The song "I Like to Be in America" from Leonard Bernstein's *West Side Story* groups the beats in both ways.

- A "hemiola" is a particular musical figure heard in a piece in which every six beats are usually grouped into two groups of 3, and then the hemiola comes when those six beats are grouped into three groups of 2. Hemiola means "one and a half," and that's the ratio of the length of the groups, groups of 3 to groups of 2.

- The hemiola is used extensively in Western classical music, especially by Handel but also by Brahms and Dvořák. The effect of using a hemiola is that it interrupts the normal flow, catching the listener a bit off guard. We hear an example from Handel's *Water Music* of 1717.

Polyrhythms
- Polyrhythms occur when two parts are playing in different rhythms. Chopin's *Fantasie Impromptu*, which we heard at the beginning of this lecture, uses polyrhythms to give the music an agitated, unsettled feeling.

- We hear a polyrhythm of four versus two written in 4/4 time. We can think of this as four quarter notes in one part and two half notes in the other. With an example of three versus two, we hear that the two parts don't quite fit together. This is sort of like a hemiola, except instead of being played sequentially, the notes are played simultaneously.

- One of the more famous examples of polyrhythm comes in the third movement of Tchaikovsky's Piano Concerto No. 3. The time signature is 3/4, three quarter notes per bar. The piano part is played in 3s (1-2-3, 1-2-3, 1-2-3), but the part for the strings is played in 2s (1-2, 1-2).

Polyrhythms are used throughout Western music and in African drumming.

- Why do composers use polyrhythms? They lend a sense of instability to music. Listeners get the feeling of turning around or being unsettled before the music resolves back into a normal rhythm. The two rhythms act as two competing forces, introducing rhythmic tension to the music. Finally, that rhythmic tension is released when the rhythms fall back into line.

Calculating Polyrhythms

- Calculating polyrhythms is similar to adding fractions. With a rhythm of three versus two, what we're doing in one part is dividing something into three equal parts. In the other part, we're dividing the same thing into two equal parts. To do this, we need a sort of common denominator. We need some sort of equal-spaced piece that we can divide the measure into.

- With two versus three, we divide the bar into six equal parts. That's the right-sized piece that allows us to split the bar into groups of three and groups of two. With a rhythm of p versus q, we need to divide the time into the least common multiple of p and q. That's exactly what we would do if we were adding the fractions $1/p$ and $1/q$.

- Let's consider a rhythm of three versus four. The easiest time signature to use for this rhythm would be 12/8, but we could also write the same pattern in 6/8. We could even use triplet notation to write it in 4/4 or 2/4.

- Chopin's *Fantasie Impromptu* is written in 4/4 time. There are four quarter notes in each bar. The right hand in this piece plays sixteenth notes (1-2-3-4, 1-2-3-4, 1-2-3-4 in every beat), and the left hand plays triplets (1-2-3, 1-2-3, 1-2-3, 1-2-3 in every beat). The tempo marking for this piece is *allegro agitato*, and we can hear the agitation caused by this polyrhythm.

Complicated Polyrhythms

- Why and how would you play such rhythms as three versus five or four versus seven? For three versus five, you would need 15 divisions. For four versus seven, you would need 28 divisions.

- Chopin used some of these more exotic polyrhythms. In a span of just five bars in his Nocturne Opus No. 3, he uses three versus five, three versus seven, three versus eight, three versus one, and more.

- Another extreme example comes from the Grieg Piano Concerto, composed by Edvard Grieg. This example is in the first movement, in the cadenza, where the orchestra drops out and leaves just the solo pianist. In this section, the left hand is making runs of seven notes per beat, and the right hand is playing a melody plus eight notes per beat. If we wanted to do this exactly, we would have to divide each beat into 56 pieces.

- The second movement of Charles Ives's Fourth Symphony takes polyrhythms to their logical extreme: Two different parts of the orchestra are in two completely different rhythms. In fact, two conductors are usually used to perform this piece.

Combining Rhythm and Pitch
- So far, we've heard rhythmic patterns, but if we add pitch, we can do more interesting things. Let's return to a single instrument and think about playing a rhythmical pattern that is five notes long.

- We could add to those notes a pattern of three pitches. Notice that the notes and the pitches don't match up. As these patterns are played together, the music sort of turns around and takes a while to get back to the beginning, almost like two gears of different sizes turning together. We know that the pattern repeats every 15 notes (three measures) because 15 is the least common multiple of 3 and 5.

- George Gershwin's piece *Rhapsody in Blue* makes use of these repetitious phrases. We can hear the sense of turning and instability, followed by a resolution when the rhythms and pitches line up again.
  - Another example from *Rhapsody in Blue* has six notes per bar with an eight-note scale; the pattern repeats every 24 notes (four measures).

o   Notice that Gershwin builds up rhythmic tension with this pattern of unmatched rhythms and pitches; he then pauses and hits listeners with a chord full of dissonance.

- There are many examples in music where we can pull out these kinds of rhythmic patterns. For example, in the opening of *Till Eulenspiegel's Merry Pranks* by Richard Strauss, there's a seven-beat phrase played by the horn, but the piece is in 6/8 time; the phrase doesn't repeat for 42 notes. In Olivier Messiaen's *Quartet for the End of Time* is an extreme example, with competing patterns that are 17 and 29 notes long.

A Musical Proof

- Let's close by looking at a mathematical question we can answer with musical notation. Does the following sum go to infinity: $1/2 + 1/4 + 1/8 + 1/16 + 1/32...$? The answer is no. If we keep adding numbers like this forever, we get 1. We can prove this answer with rhythms.

- Let's think about writing a measure of music in 4/4 time; that's four quarter notes per measure. We start with a whole note, which takes four beats, so we have one measure. Mathematically, we have one note that has four beats that equals one measure, so that's $1 = 1$.

- We replace that whole note with two half notes, which are two beats each. We still have one whole measure, but now, mathematically, we're looking at two half notes equals one measure: $1/2 + 1/2 = 1$.

- Next, we replace the second half note with two quarter notes, which are one beat each. We still have one whole measure, but now mathematically, we have $1/2 + 1/4 + 1/4 = 1$.

- The pattern here is as follows: Each time, we replace the last note with two notes, each of which is half as long as the one we replaced. That leaves the total length of the rhythm exactly the same—one measure long. If we continued this process mathematically into infinity, we would prove $1/2 + 1/4 + 1/8 + 1/16 + 1/32 + ... = 1$.

- Mathematically, this is called a "geometric series." Each term is equal to the previous one multiplied by a fixed constant, in this case, 1/2.

Suggested Reading

Magadini, *Polyrhythms*.

Wright, *Mathematics and Music*, chapters 2, 8.

Questions to Consider

1. How is the mathematics of adding fractions (common denominators) related to the musical idea of polyrhythms?

2. How do composers use the idea of least common multiples to create a sense of instability or turning?

Rhythm—From Numbers to Patterns
Lecture 7—Transcript

That beautiful music was Chopin's *Fantasie Impromptu* and I hope today's lecture will help us understand that a little bit better. So far, all the lectures we've talked about have been really about a single topic and that's pitch. Today, we're going to talk about rhythm. Imagine music without rhythm or more precisely, music without any change in rhythm. Think about what that would be like.

It's one of the most famous melodies in all of classical music. It's Beethoven's Fifth but the character is completely lost because there's no rhythm. This motif, this repeated pattern, the falling of a major third. It's supposed to represent fate. Without rhythm, there's like no drama. There's no suspense. There's no life to it.

When you put rhythm in, even just on a violin, oh, it's like fate is knocking on your door. Well, that was music without rhythm and that's why it's so important.

What is music with only rhythm? Can rhythm alone be music? Well, certainly percussion instruments, they alone can play music, but nearly all percussion instruments have different pitches—tympani, xylophones, drums—or at least different timbres. Think of a bongo or a bass drum. And they all have, at least, volume.

Can pure rhythm with no pitch, no recognizable overtone series, can that be music? Think of clapping. Or maybe if you're thinking of percussion instruments think about a rim shot where a percussionist will hit the stick on the edge of the drum instead of the head. There's actually a famous modern piece that answers this question with an emphatic "Yes!" More on that in a minute.

First, I want to see if we can find the definition of rhythm. Now, definitions in math and music—you know, some words just sort of defy definitions, but we use them all the time anyway. And somehow, we're comfortable using them even though we don't have a good definition.

In mathematics, you know what points, lines, and planes are but mathematicians have really struggled to give those good definitions. And sometimes, we just take those as axioms, sort of undefinable primaries. We agree what they are without definition, and we all sort of assume that everybody around us is using the same implicit definition. Mathematicians also, for centuries, use things like dimension, function, all of these without definition. Infinitesimal, convergence, infinity.

In music, we've actually already seen one sort of undefinable or very difficult to define term, timbre. Remember, one definition was actually negative, what it's not. And the other definitions just told us what it allowed us to do, to tell a flute from a violin.

Today, we're going to talk about another musical undefinable and that's rhythm. Now, you might think you know what rhythm is, but if you look to the *Grove Music Dictionary*, it actually quotes Curt Sachs from Rhythm and Tempo. This is what he said, "What is rhythm? The answer, I am afraid, is, so far, just – a word: a word without generally accepted meaning. Everybody believes himself entitled to usurp it for an arbitrary definition of his own. The confusion is terrifying indeed."

Wow. For us sort of like a point or a line, we know what it means. Rhythm is sort of regularly ordered pattern of durations and strengths of notes and we'll just sort of understand that to be the definition.

So let's go back to this question, what is music with only rhythm?

So Steve Reich was born in New York in 1936. He grew up in California and he studied at Cornell and at Juilliard, and then he traveled to Africa to Ghana in 1970. He wrote Clapping Music in 1972. That really answers this question. He was bringing some of the African rhythms he had learned to Western music and he was using only the human body.

The piece is written for two clappers and they're both clapping the same 12-beat phrase, but one drops a beat behind the other every 12 bars. The entire piece takes about three minutes. It's a fairly long thing and you can see it on YouTube. There are lots of different versions including Evelyn Glennie who does it, both parts by herself which is really impressive.

So here's a short piece that I composed to give you an idea of these ideas. These ideas in this piece are really highly mathematical and I'm pleased to welcome Associate Producer Chris Stoner to help me with this piece. Welcome, Chris. I'm calling this piece, Music without Pitch. Thanks very much. I'm not sure what you're supposed to do at the end of a clapping piece. If you're supposed to applaud again, thanks.

So, is that music? I think that really depends on your own philosophy. For me, that is definitely music. It's sound and it has an aesthetic sensibility. For me, that's enough.

Now, before we dive into Western music, first, I want to take a little bit of a diversion. Rhythm plays a role not only in music but also in something like poetry because words form a rhythm. Indian poetry provides some really interesting connections between rhythm and mathematics and I want to turn to that next.

Indian poetry was traditionally written in Sanskrit and it has two types of words. There are short syllables and there are long syllables, and the long syllables are exactly twice as long as the short ones. So I don't read Sanskrit, but it might be something like long, short, short, long, short.

Now, Pingala was one of these poets and he lived several centuries before the Common Era. He asked an interesting question, "How many different ways are there to put short and long syllables together to get a line of a given length?" If you're thinking musically, you could ask how many different ways can you put one and two-beat notes together to get a rhythm n beats long?

Let's do some quick examples and see if we can figure this out. We can represent this graphically or in fact, musically. You can think about it like squares and rectangles or you can think about rhythm so we could write it out in musical notation.

If you're writing around something one-beat long you have only one choice, just a short syllable. If it's two-beats long, you could do short, short or you could do long. If it's three-beats long, it turns out there are three ways. You could do short, long. You could do long, short or you could do a short, short, short. If you know musical notation, you can write this out in half notes and quarter notes. Four-beats long, there are five ways of doing it. Five-beats long, eight ways. Six-beats long, there are 13 ways of doing this.

Let's look at those numbers. Let's look at those answers that we just got. What's the pattern in there? I think we've seen these numbers before. Those are Fibonacci numbers. Each one is the sum of the previous two. Eight is five plus three. Thirteen is eight plus five. The next number has got to be 21, 13 plus eight.

The poet, Pingala, and later other Indian poets, Virahanka, in around 700 A.D. and Hemachandra around the 12th century, they discovered what we now call Fibonacci numbers. Fibonacci was another name for Leonardo de Pisa. He published his work early in the 13th century, long after the Indian poets. That's a theme we'll run into a lot. We call it something after one person's name, but that wasn't the first person to come up with the idea.

I'll leave this as a question for you. Why is it that the number of ways to write a 12-beat long rhythm is equal to the number of ways of writing a 10-beat long rhythm plus 11? Why is it that we get this pattern that the next one is the sum of the two previous ones? It's an interesting question to think about. Of course, this happens a lot in mathematics.

So some question arises in some field other than mathematics. In this case, it was poetry and we build some mathematics up to answer it. And then mathematicians go off asking many more questions that you didn't actually need in order to solve the original problem, but we just think it's really beautiful and fun.

You could ask what if you included longer words? Say, what if you had words that were one, two or three-beats long? What if you're only allowed to use so many longs? What if you can't put more than two short syllables together?

Here's another question. To get the answer for n beats, do you have to figure out all the ones before it? We think of the answer for n beats as the answer to the previous two questions, $n - 1$ and $n - 2$ but do you actually have to figure out all of those in order to get the nth one?

I'll answer this last question for you even though you might not believe it. The answer is no. You don't have to get all the previous ones. We have what's mathematicians call a closed form solution for this. We can give you a formula which gives you the number of ways of using short and long syllables to form an n-beat phrase. It's called Binet's formula.

And here's Binet's formula. Yes, I know, so the answer has to be a natural number because of the way we phrased the question and this formula doesn't look like it would give you a natural number, but amazingly, it actually does. Of course, like the Fibonacci numbers, Binet was not the first person to discover this either.

So let's go back to Western music and let's talk about a little bit of notation. So a whole note represents four beats and it looks like this. A half note is two beats. Here's one of them. A quarter note is just one beat. An eighth note is half a beat. A 16th note is a quarter of a beat and so on. When they're grouped together, some of these look slightly different. Sometimes, we use bars instead of flags when they're grouped together.

We can make rests for silence of the same length of any of these notes and they look like this. If we want a note that isn't a fraction with a power of two in it, we can use other notation for that. We get things like triplets or quintuplets.

Now, each of these is exactly one beat but it's now no longer divided in half or fourth or eighth. And one more thing if we add a dot after a note, it adds half of the length of the note. The same thing works with rests, but if we had a dotted half note, the half note has two beats, and then the dot adds an additional one beat, which is half of two. So a dotted half note has three beats.

So we have to split these up. We can't have notes, notes, notes, notes, notes. We split them up sort of like we split up English language with sentences, and in order to do that, we need to know how many notes to put in a particular measure. We use the time signature. It actually looks suspiciously like a fraction.

If we're doing something in 3/4 time, each measure has three beats. That's the top number. And each beat is one quarter long. That's the bottom number. Let's see a simple example in 4/4. It's called common time. It's four beats per bar and each beat is a quarter-note long. That's why we get the names of the notes: The whole, the half, the quarter, things like this.

So this is a version of "Twinkle, Twinkle Little Star," the first piece I ever learned. And you can see how the note lengths are used in that phrase.

There are a lot of standard signatures. A very common one is 3/4, three quarter notes per bar. Most waltzes are written in 3/4. Also another common time is 2/4, two quarter notes per bar. Sometimes called cut time is 2/2 or *alla breve*; 2/2 would have two half notes per bar. Another one is 6/8, six eighth notes per bar would also be quite common.

Now, you notice that the top number here can be any natural number where the bottom has to be a power of two. You can do that in any combination and modern composers make more use of the, of stranger options. Here's a measure of 7/16 that I played. It was in a piece I played back in lecture 5, seven sixteenth notes per bar.

Now, some of these time signatures are a little bit more interesting mathematically than others. One of the particularly interesting ones is groups of six. For instance, 6/8 time. Now, the reason six makes things interesting is because six is two times three. It's the product of two different primes. And so you can think of six as two groups of three or you can think of it as three groups of two.

Musically, 6/8 sometimes feels like it's two groups of three, triplets. 1-2-3, 1-2-3. And sometimes it feels like its three twos. 1-2, 1-2, 1-2. Probably the most famous example of this is Bernstein's *West Side Story*. The song is I like to be in America. I like to be in America. 1-2-3, 4-5-6, 1-2-3-4-5-6. Works just like that.

And so, you see how what he's doing is he's gripping those six beats either in groups of three, 1-2-3, 4-5-6, or in groups of two, 1-2, 3-4, 5-6. There's lots of different notations that you can use in order to write something like this in 6/8 and here are a few of those.

Related to this are hemiolas. Now, hemiolas are a particular musical figure that are heard in a piece in which every six beats are usually grouped into two groups of three, and then the hemiola comes when those six beats are grouped into three groups of two. The hemiola comes from the Greek. That's the name. It means one and a half and that's the ratio of the length of the groups, groups of three to groups of two.

A hemiola is used extensively in Western classical music especially by Handel but also Brahms, Dvořák. Many composers use this sort of figure. The effect of using a hemiola is that it interrupts the normal flow. You sort of catch the listener a little bit off guard. If you haven't studied music, it's a little bit subtle, and so I'm going to work hard to try to help you hear this.

So let's hear an example from Handel's Water Music of 1717. Now, the Water Music debuted in front of King George I on the Thames and the orchestra was actually seated—about 50 of them—on a barge in the river. That's part of why it gets the name. And this piece makes liberal use of hemiolas and everyone of these movements, you can hear some sort of hemiola.

And we're going to listen to a little bit from the movement called Hornpipe. It's the second movement from Suite in D Major. The main theme has groups of three, 1-2-3, 1-2-3. And you'll hear eight groups like this and then after that you'll hear the hemiola where instead it's grouped in two, 1-2, 1-2, 1-2.

So let's listen to Handel's hemiolas. We're actually going to listen to this twice. And first, I want you to listen to where the emphasis is and I'll count along. Listen for the hemiola where the emphasis comes every two beats instead of every three. It goes from—if you're counting in six—1-2-3, 4-5-6, 1-2-3, 4-5-6. And then it switches to 1-2, 3-4, 5-6, 1-2, 3-4, 5-6. I'll count this just as 1-2-3 and 1-2 to tell you that it's groups of three or groups of two and even if you can't read music, we'll try to help you follow this with the visuals.

1-2-3, 1-2-3, 1-2-3, 1-2-3, 1-2-3, 1-2-3, 1-2-3, 1-2-3, 1-2, 1-2, 1-2, 1.

Let's listen to that one more time and this time I'm not going to count along. Listen for the effect of the hemiola. By using this hemiola, Handel is signaling that something is changing. The end of the phrase is coming. He's interrupting the previous pattern and he's trying to catch the listener a little bit off-guard. Let's listen to that again.

Now you might ask a very mathematical question. Can we do a hemiola type thing with other numbers other than six? Remember the hemiolas work because six is three times two, but it's also two time three. And that's why we get two groups of three or three groups of two.

You might try to find other interesting combinations like eight is four times two or two times four, but you know the groups of two would fit nicely inside the groups of four so that wouldn't be very interesting. If you did 10, which is five times two or two times five, those are fairly long groups of notes to think about, 1-2-3-4-5, 6-7-8-9-10, 1-2-3-4-5, 6-7-8-9-10. And then you would switch in the hemiola part to 1-2, 3-4, 5-6, 7-8, 9-10, 1-2, 3-4, 5-6, 7-8, 9-10. That's a lot of notes in there.

Now you might think about doing 12 as three groups of four or four groups of three. There are a lot of these numerical games that you can play with rhythms and you can hear a lot of these on Dave Brubeck's wonderful album *Time Out*. He does a lot of interesting mathematical stuff with rhythm.

Next, I want to switch from a single part doing different rhythms to two different parts and these are called polyrhythms if you have two parts in their playing different rhythms. And the opening music—the Chopin that we heard—uses polyrhythms to give it this characteristic sort of agitated unsettled feeling.

Let's dive in and try to understand polyrhythms and I need to tap in order for you to hear these. So let's do a really easy polyrhythm first. We could have four against two, right? So we could write this in common time 4/4 and we could think about it as four quarter notes in one part and two half notes in the other.

So with my right hand I'm going to do the half notes, 1-2, 3-4, 1-2, 3-4. With my left hand I'm going to do the quarter notes, 1-2-3-4, 1-2-3-4. And I can actually emphasize one hand versus the other by letting my wedding ring here hit the wood, 1-2-3-4. That's much louder than this.

So this is what it sounds like when you put them together.

And here's the four.

Let's do something that's just a little bit different. Let's do something in 3/4 time. This is also fairly easy. We're going to have—my right hand's going to do three beats, going to do one beat per bar, 1-2-3, 1-2-3. And my left hand is going to do three beats during that period, 1-2-3, 1-2-3, 1-2-3, 1-2-3. And again, that's fairly easy. You can hear the three clearly, 1-2-3, 1-2-3.

When we musicians first learned to play things like this, we call them triplets. The common mnemonic is to say some sort of berry like straw-ber-ry, straw-ber-ry to get them nice and even.

Let's look at something a little bit more interesting. Let's look at three against two. So now my left hand is going to do three notes again, 1-2-3, 1-2-3. But during that same time, during each one of those groups of three my right hand is going to do two even beats, 1-2, 1-2.

And now, we get something where they don't quite fit together. This is sort of like a hemiola except now instead of playing them sequentially we're actually playing them simultaneously. Here's what it sounds like.

You might hear a little bit of the rhythm from "Carol of the Bells" or sometimes people say "Ham-bur-ger bun, ham-bur-ger bun." There are mnemonics that people use, but let's listen to that and I'll bring out the three using my wedding ring again. And here's the two on my right hand. And you can see how those are going on simultaneously.

Let's look at some musical examples of this. One of the more famous comes in Tchaikovsky's piano concerto. It's Piano Concerto no. 3 and it's in the third movement. This is one of Tchaikovsky's most famous pieces and the time signature is 3/4, three quarter notes per bar. The piano is in three, 1-2-3, 1-2-3, 1-2-3. But the strings end up being in two. They're playing two notes for every three of the piano, 1-2, 1-2.

The rhythm in the piano is actually a little bit more complicated than just three. Instead of going 1-2-3, 1-2-3 like this:

The rhythm is like this, 1-2-3. 1. 1.

I remember the first time I played this we were rehearsing without the piano soloist and the conductor was conducting in three, 1-2-3, 1-2-3. But then the entire orchestra was playing in two and it looked sort of like this, 1-2-3, bambambambambambambambam. It's a weird effect when you're not playing in time with the conductor.

Let's hear it with the correct pitches. Before we hear the real music, I'll play it on my violin and I'll play the piano part as well. Here's the piano part that you're going to hear, 1-2-3.

Hoo, I messed that up a little bit. The orchestra behind them are playing the following: Instead of playing three beats per bar, they're playing just two. So while the piano is going 1-2-3, 1-2-3, the orchestra is doing this. I'll try to keep time with my foot, 1-2-3, 1-2-3. And then it goes on like that.

So let's listen to this piece of Tchaikovsky. And while we listen to this, I'm going to count us through it. So the first time, I'll count with the piano part and that's going to be in three. Let's listen to that, 1-2-3, 1-2-3, 1-2-3, 1-2-3, 1-2-3, 1-2-3, 1-2-3.

And now we're going to hear the same thing again except now I'm going to count with the orchestra. They're playing in two. They're playing two evenly spaced notes in the span of three of the piano's beats. Let's listen to that, 1-2, 1-2, 1-2, 1-2, 1-2, 1-2, 1-2.

And finally, let's hear it without me counting out these beats and see if you can go back and forth in your mind sort of following the piano's three beats, 1-2-3, 1-2-3. And then switching and listening for the orchestra in two. Bambambambam, like that. Let's hear that together.

Now, let's hear it sort of a larger context of the piece. Now, the lead in to the section actually has two hemiolas right before the 3/2 section. So before we listen to the entire thing, let's listen to just the hemiolas and I'll count along to highlight when it goes from groups of three to groups of two. Let's listen to that.

1-2-3, 1-2-3, 1-2-3, 1-2, 1-2, 1-2, 1-2, 1-2, 1-2, 1. And then it goes into the three versus two section.

So now, let's hear the entire passage. I'm not going to count anything, but you'll hear definitely in three. And then you'll hear the hemiolas, and then finally, you'll hear the three against two polyrhythm.

So you might ask a natural question, why is it that composers use polyrhythms? Let's talk about that for a minute. When you use polyrhythms, you get the sort of sense of instability. You get sort of a sense of turning around, unsettling before resolving back into a normal rhythm. The two rhythms sort of form two competing forces and you get this rhythmic tension. And then finally, you release that rhythmic tension when they fall back into line again.

Now, last time we were talking about tension with pitch, right? That was dissonance. And today, we are talking about tension with rhythm. There's also a mathematical question, how do you calculate polyrhythms? You know, if you have three versus two, what you're doing is one part is dividing something into three equal parts. The other is dividing that same time into two equal parts. It's actually a lot like adding fractions. You need sort of a common denominator. You need some sort of equal-spaced piece that you can divide this measure into.

And so, if you have two versus three, you divide that bar into six equal parts. That's the right-sized piece so that you can split that into three and you can split it into groups of two. If you were doing p versus q, it would require dividing the time into the least common multiple of p and q, right? That's exactly what you need to do if you were adding the fractions $1/p$ and $1/q$.

So let's look for a second at three versus four. So I want to demonstrate this for you first. So my right hand is going to do three beats, 1-2-3, 1-2-3. And my left hand is going to do four beats, 1-2-3-4, 1-2-3-4, all in the same span of time.

There's actually a phrase, a mnemonic to help you remember how to do this. It's "Pass the gosh darn butter, pass the gosh darn butter." And now I'll demonstrate so you can more clearly hear the four and the three with my wedding ring again. Or to emphasize the right-hand side.

Now if you want to write this in music, what time signature might you use? Well, the easiest way to do it is in 12/8, but alternatively, you could write the same pattern in 6/8. You could even sort of use this triplet notation that we talked about earlier to write it in 4/4 or 2/4.

So now, I want to hear how Chopin used three against four and to hear that, let's go back to the piece we were talking about earlier, the piece we heard at the opening. You see Frédéric Chopin, he was a French and a Polish 19th-century pianist. He was also a composer, of course, and he was a master of the keyboard. He really revolutionized fingering on pianos.

He wrote *Fantasie Impromptu*, the piece we heard at the top. That was in 1834 and the tempo marking for this piece in Italian, of course, is *allegro agitato*. Now the *allegro* means lively, joyful but the *agitato* means agitated, unsettled. The agitation here is created by this polyrhythm, three against four.

Now, it's written in 4/4 time. There are four quarter-notes in each bar. The right hand in this piece is playing 16th notes, 1-2-3-4, 1-2-3-4, 1-2-3-4 in every beat. The left hand is playing triplets, three per beat, 1-2-3, 1-2-3, 1-2-3, 1-2-3.

So let's listen to each hand separately and slowly. And what I've done here is I've put this on a computer and so you'll hear this, and this is just the right hand and this is the computer playing it. And you can hear the groups of four, 1-2-3-4, 1-2-3-4 like that.

Now the left hand at the same time is playing triplets. So in each beat they're playing 1-2-3, 1-2-3. So let's look at the left hand and then see what that looks like and this left hand you can see the triplets and again, we're going to hear it played by computer so you hear it exactly and very precisely. Let's listen to that.

Finally, let's listen to the left and the right together. Now, remember that this piece is marked *agitato*. It's supposed to be agitated. Listen for the left hand playing the threes and the right hand playing the fours. Listen for the agitation caused by this polyrhythm and listen how they match up every beat. They come back and sort of match up together. Let's listen to that. That felt a little bit cold and sort of mechanical and that's because it was played by a computer.

So let's listen to a real pianist play this with feeling and we're going to also add the first few opening bars of this piece. I want you to listen to how Chopin is using the mathematics of polyrhythms to create this agitated feeling and also how the pianist plays with this rhythm moving a little faster and a little slower to create a sort of emotional sense to this. And I hope we now better understand this piece and what we were listening to at the beginning of this lecture. So here again is Chopin's *Fantasie Impromptu*.

It's such a beautiful piece. I'm sort of sad we can't take more time to listen to the entire thing, but let's move on to more complicated polyrhythms. So you might ask why and how you would play something like three against five or four against seven or five against 11 or for that matter p against q for any numbers p and q. Three against five, you would need 15 divisions. Again, p against q would need the least common multiple just like fractions. If you're trying to do four against seven, you would actually need 28 subdivisions.

There's another mnemonic for that if you want to do four against seven. It's "Walk down the hall with a new tennis ball." And that's four on one side and seven on the other.

Now, some of these crazy polyrhythms are actually used. Let's look at how Chopin used some of these more exotic polyrhythms. In his Nocturne Opus 9 no. 3, in a span of just five bars, there, it's filled with polyrhythms. There are hard ones. Three versus five, three versus seven, three versus eight even but there are also some easier ones: Three versus one, three versus nine, three versus six. Those all fit nicely, but something like three versus eight, that's very complicated. So let's listen to just these five bars and how Chopin is using polyrhythms.

Let's also listen to one more sort of extreme example from the Grieg Piano Concerto. It's in the first movement in the *cadenza* where the orchestra drops out and it's just the solo pianist. In this section, the left hand is making runs seven notes per beat and the right hand is playing a melody plus eight notes per beat. You know if you wanted to do this exactly, you would have to divide each beat into 56 really tiny pieces. Here's what that sounds like. Of course, pianists don't actually think in those 56 little pieces. Pianists actually just sort of learned to have their hands do different things.

We could take polyrhythms to maybe their logical limit and Charles Ives does a really excellent job with that. He was son of a Civil War bandleader. He was really famous for using church and traditional melodies. He wrote in the 1910s a Fourth Symphony, and in addition to some of the polyrhythms we talked about, he actually requires the piano to be tuned a quarter-step sharp. That's much more than the tuning I was doing in the last lecture. Orchestras actually usually use an upright piano. They don't want to hurt the soundboard on their nice 12-foot Steinway.

Now on the second movement of the Fourth Symphony, the polyrhythms are taken probably to their logical extreme. They're so extreme that two different parts of the orchestra are in two completely different rhythms. In fact, two conductors are usually used to do this piece. One conductor sits quietly during the opening part, and then at some point, the second conductor stands up and conducts part of the orchestra while the main conductor is conducting the other part. And at some point, the first part finishes and the second conductor sits back down and they finish the piece.

Just to be clear, here's what polyrhythms are all about. The point is that it's a musical tool used to create a sort of unbalanced feeling with rhythm and you're creating rhythmic tensions. Now, these are used throughout Western music but also, for instance, in something like African drumming.

There's a mathematical aspect to polyrhythms and that's similar to fractions and common denominators. For most performers, the mathematics is really implicit. Nobody's sitting there thinking about the little divisions in order to do that. You just learn to do these two things simultaneously. Polyrhythms are just sort of rhythmic tools.

But what if we combined rhythm with pitch? So far, it was just rhythmic patterns, but if we add pitch, we can do some more interesting things. Now, we're going back to just a single part, a single instrument playing and you could think about playing a rhythmical pattern that's five notes long, something like this.

1-2-3-4-5. It's five notes long. It's four beats long. But you could also think of taking a pattern of pitches that's three long, maybe A, B, C. And now you could put those pitches with those notes and you notice that the five notes and the three pitches don't match up. And so, it sort of turns around and it's a while before you get back to the beginning, but it would sound like this. And how often would it repeat? Well, you take the least common multiple of three and five, you get 15. It repeats every 15 notes. And since there's five notes in each of these bars, it repeats every three measures.

Musically, you get sort of a sense of turning and turning before you return to the beginning. It's almost like you have two gears and they have different sizes, right? And so one of them turns a lot more and it's sort of every once in a while they mesh up perfectly, but then they sort of go out of sync again, and finally, again, they come back and mesh up perfectly.

Let's hear some examples of this phenomenon. George Gershwin was born in Brooklyn in 1898. He was the younger brother to famous lyricist, Ira

Gershwin. He composed pops music, musical scores, classical music. He was all over the place. A lot of it was in the tradition of French composers like Ravel and Debussy, but he also brought in influences of jazz and folk music.

In 1924, he composed what's probably his most famous piece, *Rhapsody in Blue*. It's a work for piano and orchestra. And at least, recently, it's definitely his most heard work because United Airlines adopted it as their theme song. This piece makes use of these repetitious phrases again and again and again. And we're going to hear two examples from this piece and I'm going to play them on the violin first and then we're going to hear them with piano and orchestra. Let's look at these examples.

Let's look at the examples here. The first example that I'm going to play is it's exactly what I was just playing. It's the same rhythm we had last time. It's one of the main motifs or patterns and it gives you this sort of sense of turning and it only repeats every 15 notes. And, it sounds like this.

You hear the sense of sort of turning and instability in that? It finally resolves when the rhythms and the pitches line up again. And after the strings play a lyrical melody, we're going to hear the piano and part of the orchestra enter and they're going to be playing exactly this rhythm, and then it all happens again.

So let's turn to that and let's listen as the piano plays this repeated rhythm that sort of winds around and finally, ends up resolving.

Let's hear one other example of sort of a rhythmic pattern like this and it's also from *Rhapsody in Blue*. Here we have six notes per bar, 1-2-3, 4-5-6, 1-2-3, 4-5-6, but it's an eight-note scale that's being played. The scale sounds like this.

And so, it's that eight-note scale but it's wrapped in six pieces and so it's going to repeat every 24 notes. That's every four bars. Every three times you go up the scale, they're going to match up again. So it's going to sound like this. And you hear that sort of rotation, that sort of instability.

In *Rhapsody in Blue* this happens near the end of the piece, this turning sensation and the composer here is using it to build tension. So let's listen to this piece and let's look at how it looks like. So again, we're going to build tension by having this repeated rhythmic structure that doesn't exactly match up with the eight-note scale. So it's going to turn and turn again until we finally end up at a chord. Let's listen to that.

Notice that first what the composer, what Gershwin was doing is he's building up rhythmic tension with this pattern of rhythms and pitches that aren't matching up. He builds up all of that and then he pauses, and then hits you with this chord which is full of dissonance, pitched dissonance like we've had before. And so, you have this rhythmic tension first and then this tension in terms of the pitches after that.

There are lots of other examples that you can pull of this sort of rhythmic patterns. My favorite is not actually from classical music but from a tune of Bill Withers' "Ain't No Sunshine." You can almost hear him sing that "Ain't no sunshine." In the middle of this tune he sings, "I know" and he sings it 26 times in a row. "I know, I know, I know, I know…" Each one of those "I know" is three 8th notes long and each bar is four. And so, there's a sort of turning and every four "I know" he's sort of back on beat and you get this sense of rhythmic, sort of instability from that.

In the opening of Strauss's *Til Eulenspiegel's Merry Pranks*, there's a seven-beat phrase played by the horn but the piece is in 6/8 time. And so, the seven-beat phrase in 6/8 time is sort of unstable like that and you need 42 notes before it repeats again. It's actually quite a prank to play at the beginning of a tune called somebody's Merry Pranks.

In Messiaen's Quartet for the End of Time, we probably have the most extreme example that I know of. Messiaen writes competing patterns that are 17 and 29 notes long. If you think about those 17 and 29 notes long, it's going to take 493 notes before you get back to the beginning of this pattern again. It's going to take essentially until the end of time.

So I want to be clear about the main point from today. Everywhere songwriters are adding interest to their pieces with rhythmic patterns that give us a sense of turning and finally resolving. Now, musicians tend to think about and understand the tension and resolving, and they're not so much thinking about the mathematics behind it.

And that's the main point for today, but I want to end with a little bit of math and musical sort of coda. We can use basic rhythms, note lengths to do some really interesting mathematics.

Here's a question that we can actually answer, a mathematical question that we can answer with a musical notation. So here's the question. Let's look at the sum one-half plus a quarter plus an eighth plus a 16th plus a 32nd plus a 64th, on and on and on. Just keep going with that.

Now, you might think—and many have, including many of my students—that if you keep adding positive numbers, well, you keep adding positive things. That sum has to go to infinity. After all, you just keep getting bigger and bigger and bigger. You must be going toward infinity.

Somewhat unexpectedly, I think, the series converges. It actually adds to one. If you go all the way to infinity, if you keep adding numbers like this forever, you get one and we can prove it with rhythms. Let's look at this musical proof.

Let's think about writing a measure of music in 4/4 time, that's four quarter notes per measure and let's start out with just a whole note. A whole note takes four beats, and so we have one measure. Mathematically, we have one note that has four beats and that equals one measure. So it's just one equals one.

Now, replace that whole note with two half notes. Those are two beats each. We still have one whole measure, but now, mathematically, we're looking at two half notes, that's half plus a half equals one measure. Now, replace the second half note with two quarter notes—those are one beat each. We still have one whole measure but now, if you think about it mathematically, we have half plus a quarter plus a quarter and that equals one.

Replace the second quarter note with two 8th notes, each one-half of a beat long and we still have one measure but now, mathematically, we have one-half plus a fourth plus an eighth plus and eighth equals one. Replace the second 8th note with two 16th notes, each one of those is a quarter of a beat, we still have a whole measure but now, we have one-half plus a fourth plus an eighth plus a 16th plus a 16th equals one.

Let's just keep going with this pattern and see where it leads us. Each time we keep taking the last note, replacing it with two notes, each of which is half as long as the one we replaced, that leaves the total length of the rhythm exactly the same. It's always just one measure long. But what happens if we keep doing this infinitely, forever?

Now, musically if you wanted to do this, you'd have to play an infinite number of notes, each half the length of the previous one. But if you look at it mathematically, we would be proving that one-half plus a fourth plus an eighth plus a 16th plus a 32nd plus a 64th, on and on to infinity equals one.

Now, mathematically, this is called a geometric series. Each term is equal to the previous one times a fixed constant. In this case it's one-half. These geometric series turn out to be incredibly important and they arise in lots of different applications including, interestingly, your home mortgage and how it's amortized.

So I hope you've enjoyed this little math and musical coda and today's lecture on rhythm. Now that we have pitch, we have scales, we've done chords, and now we've done rhythm, now, we're ready to write some really interesting music.

So next time we're going to talk about musical and mathematical transformations and how they're used in compositions and especially in Bach.

Thanks for joining us.

Transformations and Symmetry
Lecture 8

S o far in this course, we have discussed the mathematics of the musical experience. We started by coming to understand a single note and varying its pitch; then we combined notes into chords and scales; and finally, we added rhythm. Now, we're ready to start composing music. In this lecture, we will discuss parallels between musical and mathematical transformations. A transformation is the process by which one expression is converted into another that is equivalent in important respects but differently expressed or represented. Transformations add beautiful structure to both mathematics and music.

Geometrical, Functional, and Numerical Transformations

- Geometrical transformations are, perhaps, the simplest to begin with. Let's consider any figure in a plane and let $r(x)$ be the reflection of that figure over the x axis. We actually have two transformations here: reflecting the figure over the x axis (the reflection transformation) or doing nothing (the zero, identity, or "do nothing" transformation).

   o The operation in this case will be one transformation followed by the next (composition). If we do nothing and then do nothing again, the net result is doing nothing. If we do nothing and then reflect, the net result is a reflection. If we reflect and do nothing, again, the result is a reflection. But if we do a reflection and another reflection, the net result is the identity transformation.

   o A "group table" is an array listing all the possible outcomes from our operation of one transformation followed by the next. In our case, this will be a 2×2 table.

- Some functional transformations are similar to geometrical transformations. For the function $f(x)$, the identity transformation would be doing nothing, but we could also do a negation—we could look at $-f(x)$. This flips the function over the x axis. Again, we have two transformations here—the identity transformation and the negation transformation—and the operation is composition.

o   Of the possible four pairings with this transformation, the interesting one is taking the negation and the negation again, which gets us back to the identity.

o   Note that the transformations are not the graphs but how the graphs are changing. The transformation isn't the picture but how the picture changes.

- Let's think about addition with regard to the set of even and odd numbers. The set consists of all the even numbers and all the odd numbers. We can construct a group table for transformations of this set that tells us: even + even = even, even + odd = odd, odd + even = odd, and odd + odd = even. The identity here is even because it operates on all the other elements without changing them. Both evens and odds are their own inverses.

- Mathematicians call this group Z_2, and we think of it as addition modulo 2. The question to think about here is: If we divide by 2, what is the remainder? The answer is that the remainder is always either 0 (for evens) or 1 (for odds). We can represent all even numbers with 0 and all odd numbers with 1. The identity in this group is 0, and each of the elements is its own inverse.

Musical Transformations

- With a musical transformation, we could have no change in a melody (the identity), or we could do an inversion. We can think about this as a group because we have two transformations, and we can look at the structure of the group. Remember, we are not looking at the melody itself but how the transformation changes the melody.

- Each of Bach's 14 canons on the Goldberg ground was written using transformations. The canons give us insight into how Bach used transformations to create increasingly complicated music. The canons are based on an aria from the *Goldberg Variations* and are all written on a single sheet, totaling perhaps six or seven minutes of music. The underlying ideas are very similar to group theory.

- Geometrically, an inversion is flipping something over the x axis; functionally, it's multiplying by a negative sign; and musically, it's flipping all the intervals up. In canon 3, Bach puts this together as follows: the original melody (the identity transformation); the inverted melody, four notes after the melody; and a repetition of the sequence.

- In addition to musical inversion—playing a melody upside down—we can also have a retrograde—playing a melody backwards. If we construct a group table, we again have two transformations: the original melody (the identity) and the retrograde. The retrograde followed by the retrograde results in the original.
  ○ The corresponding transformations in geometry are reflecting around the y axis instead of the x axis.

  ○ In terms of functions, instead of looking at $-f(x)$, this transformation looks at $f(-x)$.

  ○ Bach put together retrograde transformations in canon 1. We hear the theme twice, then the retrograde, then both played together.

- Can we do both the retrograde and the inversion? There's a problem when we try to construct a three-element group. We don't have a transformation for a melody that is played retrograde and then inverted. Mathematically, we would say that this operation is not closed. We can fix the problem by adding an element that is exactly a retrograde inversion.

- In canon 2, Bach puts together not the original melody but an inversion of the melody and then adds the retrograde inversion. We hear the inversion played twice, the retrograde inversion played twice, and both played together.

- In canon 5, Bach introduces a new melody and its inversion. If you listen closely, you can hear two baselines in this piece. One is the main theme, and the other is the main theme's inversion.

Group Theory

- A group is defined as a set and an operation. An operation takes two things in the set as input and produces one thing in that set as output. For us, the operation was composition—doing one transformation and another.

- A group must also have four other properties: (1) It must be closed (the output must always be in the set); (2) it must have an identity (one element acts like 0 does in addition; it leaves all the other elements alone when we do the composition); (3) it must have inverses (there must always be a way to get back to the identity); and (4) it must have associativity (the grouping of elements doesn't matter).

- Let's consider addition with the natural numbers: 1, 2, 3, ….
  - We can construct a closed group table for this set, but there's no identity. There's no way to solve the equation $a + x = a$. We can fix this problem by adding 0 to the set, which means we're working with the set of whole numbers.

  - The table associated with the whole numbers is closed, has an identity, and has associativity, but there's a problem with inverses. There's no way to solve the equation $a + x = 0$. We can fix this by adding negative numbers to the set, which means we're working with the set of integers.

  - With addition of integers, we get a group; in fact, we get what's called a "commutative group."

- Let's now return to group Z_2. We've seen many copies of this group: geometrical (reflections), functional (negating functions), evens and odds (addition mod 2), and musical (inversions). All of the tables for these groups have the same structure; we simply change the names of the columns and rows. These are called "isomorphic groups."

- What is Z_2? To answer this, let's look at an easier question: What is 2?

  o The idea of 2 is an abstraction. When you're looking at two apples, what's there? Apples, not 2. In some sense, 2 is what the sets of two eyes, two ears, two fingers, and two apples have in common.

  o The same is true of Z_2. None of the group tables we saw is Z_2; Z_2 is what all of those examples have in common. Both the number 2 and group Z_2 are abstract mathematical concepts— separate from the physical world.

Musical Transformations Revisited

- The four musical transformations we identified earlier (identity, inversion, retrograde, and retrograde inversion) fulfill all the properties of a group. But rather than a 2×2 chart, this is a 4×4 chart; it's clearly not Z_2.

- Considering that this is a four-element chart, we might guess that it would be Z_4. Recall that we're looking here at remainders when we divide by 4. The possible remainders are 0, 1, 2, and 3, but our table has a different structure. In the musical group we're looking at, every element is its own inverse. If we do the inversion and then the inversion, we get the identity. But that's not true in Z_4. If we add the element 1 to itself, we don't get back to the identity, 0. That tells us that these two groups are not isomorphic.

- Let's consider another representation of the same group in geometry. Here, the four elements are: the identity transformation, reflection over the x axis, reflection over the y axis, and reflection over both, or rotation of 180 degrees. That table has the same structure as the one for our musical group.

- In functions, the four elements would be: the identity transformation, $-f(x)$ (reflecting over the x axis), $f(-x)$ (reflecting over the y axis), and $-f(-x)$ (reflecting over both, or rotating 180 degrees). Again, this table has the same structure as the one for our musical group.

- To see the correct numerical example, we have to look at something called $Z_2 \times Z_2$, the "Klein four group." $Z_2 \times Z_2$ is not just numbers; it's actually ordered pairs of numbers, for example, 0 and 1 in one coordinate and 0 and 1 in the other coordinate. The operation here is coordinate-wise addition modulo 2.
  - Let's try $(0, 1) + (1, 1)$. We add the first coordinates, $0 + 1$, to get 1. The second coordinates are both 1, but in modulo 2, $1 + 1 = 0$. When we add these two elements $(0, 1) + (1, 1)$, we get $(1, 0)$. Is this a group?

  - The answer is yes; this is the same group table as the musical one.

- Interestingly, there are only two mathematical groups with four elements: Z_4 and the Klein four group.

Transpositions
- In music, a transposition is moving up or down in pitch. For example, instead of starting on the key A, we could start on D. That would be transposing up a fourth because D is the fourth note in the A-major scale. When we do this in music, it's easily recognizable as the same tune, played a bit higher.

- A corresponding geometrical transformation would be taking a figure and translating it up. For functions, we could think about adding c to $f(x)$. It's just a vertical translation when we're looking at a graph.

- The group structures of these transformations are interesting. We can find the inverse if we transpose up (we just transpose back down), but transposition has infinitely many elements. In theory, we could keep transposing up as many intervals as we want. At any point, if we wanted to go back down, we could transpose infinitely many steps. The table for this group is infinitely large.

- One way to keep the table from being infinitely large is to work by note names, that is, to work what's called "modulo octaves." This approach treats every A on the piano as if it's the same and every C-sharp as the same.

- Think about transposing up one half-step. If you transpose in this way 12 times, in terms of note names, you get back to where you started. You may start on A and go up 12 times, but you end at A. This is similar to adding 1 to itself but then somehow getting back to the beginning.
  o We actually see something every day that does exactly this: a clock, with the 12 acting as 0. This group is called Z_{12} or "clock arithmetic." In Z_{12}, if we add 10 + 3, that's the same as adding three hours to 10 o'clock; we don't get 13 o'clock but 1 o'clock.

  o Transposition by half-steps is exactly the same thing. We go up 12 half-steps and get back to the beginning.

- What if we transpose up a major third, which is four half-steps? What group would we generate if we did this? This group (M_4) has three transformations: do nothing, up four half-steps, and up eight half-steps. The table for this group has the same structure as Z_3; it's addition modulo 3.

- What happens if we combine M_4 with an inversion? This group is not commutative. The M_4 transformation followed by an inversion is not the same thing as the inversion followed by the M_4 transformation.
  o To find a geometrical representation of this requires us to look at symmetries on an equilateral triangle. The group table for these transformations in geometry is isomorphic to the musical group M_4.

  o Mathematicians call this group the "dihedral group of order 6," and it is the smallest noncommutative group we can construct.

- Some mathematical researchers are working to construct musical versions of these mathematical groups.

Symmetry

- Group theory is seen as the language of symmetry in mathematics. Mathematicians categorize objects by their symmetry group.

- The outline of a violin has only one symmetry. It can be reflected over the x axis, but there is no other way to transform that picture and get back to the same picture. In contrast, the outline of a barbell has three symmetries. It can be reflected over the x axis, reflected over the y axis, or rotated 180 degrees. That means the symmetry group for the barbell is a copy of the Klein four group.

- Among the interesting objects that can be categorized by their symmetry groups are frieze patterns. There are just seven different symmetries on frieze patterns and no more. There are exactly 17 different symmetry groups for a wallpaper form.

- In chemistry, group theory is used to classify crystal structures. In physics, it's used to study subatomic particles.

All 17 wallpaper symmetry groups appear in the wall mosaics of the Alhambra in Spain.

Augmentation and Diminution

- Yet another transformation in music that has this group structure is augmentation and diminution, that is, stretching and shrinking by a factor of 2. The augmentation of a melody is twice as slow, and the diminution is twice as fast.

- We can think about the group structure involved in these transformations as follows: Augmentation is taking the inverse of diminution. We can also augment as many times as we want, each time stretching the notes twice as long; thus, this group is infinite.

It actually has the same structure as the integers, where the integers serve as powers of 2: 2^n.

- Augmentation and diminution are among the transformations Bach was working on in his 14th canon.
  - This canon has four parts: The top voice is supposed to play the music as written; the next voice is supposed to play it augmented (twice as slow as the original) but also inverted and transposed; the next voice is supposed to play it augmented again (four times as slow as the original) and transposed again; and the bottom voice is supposed to play it augmented yet again (eight times as slow as the original) and also inverted and transposed.

  - Amazingly, the bottom voice is the original melody from the Goldberg variation.

  - As we listen, notice that all the parts are the same in some sense, but they're transformed from the original melody.

Suggested Reading

Benson, *Music: A Mathematical Offering*, chapter 9.

Harkleroad, *The Math behind the Music*, chapter 4.

Questions to Consider

1. What are groups, and how are they used to study symmetry transformations in mathematics?

2. What are the musical transformations, including inversion, retrograde, retrograde inversion, transposition, and augmentation/diminution?

3. How are musical transformations and group theory connected?

Transformations and Symmetry
Lecture 8—Transcript

That was a Canon by Bach. By the end of today's lecture I hope that you'll hear this piece completely differently by the understanding the underlying mathematical structure to it.

So far we have been talking about the mathematics of the musical experience. We started understanding a single note and varying its pitch and then we combined notes into chords and scales, and finally we added rhythm. That means we're finally ready to start composing music. Today we're going to talk about parallels between transformations that are musical and those that are mathematical, and how they bring structural beauty to actually both of these subjects.

What is a transformation? Well, a transformation is a process by which an expression is converted into another that is equivalent in some important respects but differently expressed or represented. So something stays the same but something is changed. The main point today is an analogy that transformations add beautiful structure to both mathematics and to music. You know, I personally think that this analogy may account for some of the psychological, maybe even the neurological connections between mathematics and music.

Today we're going to back and forth between many different strands. We're going to talk about geometrical transformations. We're going to talk about functional transformations. We'll talk about musical transformations and we'll also talk about Bach's use of these transformation. Along the way, the branch of mathematics we're going to use today is called group theory. There's a wonderful little coda for today, we're going to play for you a table Canon that illustrates many of these ideas incredibly well.

Why are we looking with this analogy instead of doing what mathematics has actually used explicitly? Well, Gottfried Leibniz, he was a philosopher and a mathematician. He was one of the co-inventors of calculus along with Isaac Newton. This is what he said about math and music. He said, "Music is a secret exercise in arithmetic of the soul, unaware of its active counting." Such a great quote, "Music is a secret exercise in arithmetic of the soul, unaware of its active counting." I think what he means is something like this—that music uses many different mathematical structures, but those structures are hidden. They are implicit. They're not explicit. Now last time we were dealing with an explicit use of mathematics in music. Even the words we use to describe rhythm are highly mathematical. Today, instead of looking at explicit uses, we're going to be unpacking the implicit mathematics that Leibniz is talking about that he says is hiding inside the music. We're going to talk about musical transformations and their connection to the mathematics of group theory.

First, let's hear an example of a musical transformation. So the first piece I ever learned was "Twinkle" and it sounds like this. And let's look at a transformation of that. This musical transformation is called an inversion and we're going to flip that melody upside down. Any time I was supposed to go up, I will now go down. And it sounds then like this. And we're going to hear lots more of these musical inversions as we go along.

To understand these musical transformations, let's look at geometrical and functional transformations first. Probably the simplest transformations we could talk about would probably be geometrical. So think about a figure in a plane. It could be any figure. The point is it is not with the figure but how we transform it. Now, let's let r_x be the reflection over the x-axis. That's actually very similar to the musical inversion we just played, which is flipping it this way. So we have two transformations here—we could either reflect it over the x-axis or we could do nothing. We could leave it where it is. And we need a name for that. Let's call that zero or the identity or the do nothing transformation.

We also need to talk about operations. The operation here is going to be one followed by the next. You do one transformation and then you do another transformation, and you see what the net result is. Interestingly, in mathematics they actually call that composition of transformations.

So let's look at this geometrical transformation. We have two transformations. We have the do-nothing transformation and then we have the reflection transformation. And what we're going to do is one after another. If we do nothing and then do nothing again, the net result is doing nothing. If we do nothing and then reflect, then the net result is just a reflection. If we reflect and then do nothing, we just get the reflection. But if we do a reflection and then reflect again, the net result is just the do-nothing transformation. The end result is the same as if we had just done the single transformation, do nothing. We're going to call the zero transformation the identity transformation. This is the do-nothing transformation. The reason we call it the identity is because if we take any transformation and then take the identity transformation, we just get whatever we started with. In this case, if we take a reflection and then the identity, we just get the reflection. It works the other way around. If we do nothing and then take the reflection, that's just the same as the reflection. It acts a little bit like zero does in addition.

Now, we're also going to talk about inverses. And the inverse here, if we reflect over the axis, the inverse of that is going to be what gets us back to the identity. The inverse of the reflection is another reflection and so the reflection here is its own inverse. So now we have two transformations. We have a set of transformations, just two of them, the do-nothing (the identity) and the reflection. The operation is doing one followed by the next. We can actually write out what's called a group table. It's an array listing all of the possible outcomes from this operation. Now for us we have two transformations. We have two inputs and two inputs for the other one, and that gives us outputs that form a 2x2 table.

Now, let's look at some functional transformations that are actually really similar. If you take a function, you might graphic but you might just think of it as a function, like $f(x)$. And the identity transformation would be to do nothing, but we could also do a negation. We could take $f(x)$ and instead of leaving as just $f(x)$, we could look at negative $f(x)$. If you're thinking about this instead of the representation of the graph, it flips the function over the x-axis. And so now we have two transformations. We have the do-nothing transformation, leave it the same, or the negation transformation where we put a minus sign in front of it. Again, the operation is composition, we could do nothing and then we could take the negation, or we could take the negation and then do nothing. Now, of all of the possible four pairings, only one of them is really interesting. If we take the negation and then the negation again, we get back to the identity. We get back to the do-nothing. Graphically, that would be if we flip it over the axis and then flip it again we're back to where we started. Now as before, the do-nothing transformation is the identity. As before, the negation is its own inverse. That's the one where if you negate it and then negate it again, you get back to the identity, the do-nothing transformation.

Again, I want to be clear that the transformations here aren't the graphs but it's how the graph is changing. The transformation isn't the picture, but how the picture changes.

Let's look at a numerical example now. Let's think about addition on odd and even numbers, not the individual numbers, but let's think about the set of the evens and the odds. So we just have two things in our set, all of the evens and all of the odds. The operation we're going to work with here is addition. And we can construct a group table for this. If you take even numbers plus even numbers, you get even numbers. If you take even numbers plus odd numbers, the result of any one of those is going to be an odd number. If you take an odd plus and even, you get odd. Finally, if you take an odd plus an odd, you get even. The identity here is even because it operates on all the other elements without changing it. If you take something and add an even, you get that something back again.

If we think about inverses, both evens and odds are their own inverse because again we figured out that even is the identity and so you're asking the question, "If we have an even, what should we add to it go get an even?" And the answer is an even. If we ask that question with an odd, "If we have an odd, what should we add to that to get an even?" The answer is an odd.

Let's look at another way to write this. Mathematicians call this group Z2 and we think of it as addition modulo 2. What you should really think about is if you divide by 2, what is the remainder? Because the remainder is always either 0 or 1. Zero if it's even and 1 if it's odd. And so, when we write it this way, 0 sort of stands for all of the even numbers, because you always get a remainder 0, and one sort of stands for all of the odd numbers because that's always the remainder when we divide by 2. When we construct a table for that, it looks like this. And the only thing that looks weird in this table that's not sort of the standard addition we know is that 1+1 is now 0, because 1+1 is 2, but the remainder when we divide by 2 is 0. And that's why 1+1 is 0 when you are looking in Z2. Now in this particular group, the identity here is 0—if you take anything and add 0 you're going to get that thing back again. Again, each one of these elements is its own inverse, 0+0 is the identity 0 and 1+1 is also the identity 0.

Let's turn to a musical example now. We can have no change in a melody and that would be the identity transformation, or we can do the inversion, what we heard earlier. So here's a melody and this is a melody we're going to talk about a lot today. So that's a nice melody. If we invert it, here is what we get. And we can think about this as a group because now we have two transformations. We have the do-nothing transformation or this inversion. The operation here is to do one after another and we can look at the structure of this group. We can figure out what its table looks like.

Now we need to remember that we are no looking at the melody itself. We're looking at how that transformation changes this melody. So, let's construct this table. Now some of the outputs are obvious. If you do nothing and you do nothing, you've done nothing. If you do nothing and then an inversion, that's just an inversion. A little bit trickier is if you do an inversion and then do another inversion, you get back to the identity, you get back to the do-nothing transformation. Now, you've probably noticed that all of the group tables we've looked at, they are all very similar. Mathematicians would say they are all copies of Z2. They're all, what we would call, isomorphic.

Before we get to more of that, let's look at how composers use musical transformation when they're composing music. In particular, we're going to talk a lot today about Bach and how he used these transformations. The piece that we're going to talk about today a lot is Johann Sebastian Bach's 14 canons on the Goldberg ground. Fourteen canons, so, these are 14 individual pieces. The 14th Canon is actually what we played at the beginning of today's lecture. The number is BWV1087 in Wolfgang Schmieder's system. These were not found until 1974. A copy of these 14 canons was found in an original copy of the *Goldberg Variations* that Bach owned at one point. We know they are actually Bach because a couple of these canons appeared elsewhere before that.

Now these are some of the really brilliant fugues and canons that Bach wrote that have incredible mathematical structure to them. So, there are 14 canons and each one is compactly written using transformations. These are simple, yet beautiful. I think the proper way to view these is that some of the early ones, especially, are sort of studies, where Bach is studying this simple melody and figuring out how to use it, how it fits with itself in different transformations. And those are stepping stones to more complicated canons and throughout the 14 canons, every once in a while, there's a much more complicated canon, which is more like what we think of as beautiful, complicated music. But I think because of this, we actually get a lot of insight into how Bach put puzzle pieces together and how he used transformations to do that. And I think you'll agree once we learn about these, that this process that he uses has a highly mathematical flavor to it.

So, the 14 canons are all on a single sheet of music. It's six, maybe seven minutes of music, all on a single sheet. It's written with brilliant cleverness and the ideas underlying it are very similar to group theory.

Today we're going to talk about the first five canons and we're also going to skip and talk about the 14th Canon, the one you heard at the very beginning. Now these canons are based on a line from an aria, an aria from the *Goldberg Variations* and that's where this piece gets its name. You heard it a minute ago. I'll play it for you again.

And so we've talked about many of the transformations. The one we're going to talk about now is this inversion. So, geometrically, it's flipping something over the axis. Functionally, it's multiplying by a negative sign and musically, it's flipping it up for all the intervals before when they went down and now they're going up. And it sounds like this. And now Bach puts this together, the do-nothing transformation, the original melody, and the inverted melody, and he delays one by four beats and then he repeats it. Let's listen to Canon 3 and see exactly how he does this. You see, Bach used this inversion, he was sending a message to the musicians to play this inverted. The way he did that was that he wrote both parts on a single staff but he put a second clef and the clue to the second clef is actually where the sharp is placed. It's placed in an odd place and that sharp only makes sense if it's read upside down, if it's read inverted.

Let's listen and what we'll hear is the melody first and on the second time of the melody the inversion starts, four notes after the melody starts. Let's listen to that. Let's listen to a different transformation. Instead of inversion playing something upside down, there's another transformation that plays a melody backwards. This is called retrograde. So let's go back to "Twinkle, Twinkle," and listen to that. So again the melody of "Twinkle, Twinkle" is this.

The inversion that we've already heard—the transformation we've already heard—is the inversion. But now let's take the original "Twinkle, Twinkle" melody and play it retrograde, back to front, starting at the end of the melody and working back forwards. And it sounds like this. If you remember back, when we talked about the definition of transformation, something was the same but something was changed, some aspect is the same, some aspect has changed, and I think you hear that in these transformations of melodies. There's some element of the original melody there, but something else has changed.

Let's see if we can write this out in the group table. We have two transformations here. We have the original and then we have retrograde. So the trivial transformation is the do-nothing transformation and then the other transformation we're working with is the retrograde, to play something backwards. When we fill out the group table, most of the entries are fairly straightforward but one of them is interesting, the retrograde followed by the retrograde. If you play something backwards and then play that backwards, you get back to the original, so composed with the retrograde is back to the original—the trivial identity transformation. The corresponding transformations in geometry are reflecting around the y-axis instead of the x-axis. In terms of functions, instead of looking at $-f(x)$, this transformation is looking at $f(-x)$. If you think about the graph, that is also flipping it over the y-axis.

The structure of the tables related to these transformations is exactly the same as we've seen before, but these are just more representations of the Z2. So, how did Bach use the retrograde transformation? In order to understand that, let's go back to the *Goldberg* theme. So the theme again is this. If we play that retrograde back to front it sounds like this. Bach puts these together in Canon 1. So, let's listen to that. We're going to hear the theme twice and then the retrograde and then he's going to play them together. Again, Bach is using these transformations as sort of a trick because he is writing all of the music on a single staff but he gives a clue to the musicians. You see, there's a second clef at the end and it's backwards and that's the indication that the second player is supposed to play retrograde. Both parts are on the same staff, but you hear it as a duet. So let's listen to that.

Now there's another question we could ask, "Can we do both the retrograde and the inversion?" What would that table look like? Is that a group? Well, let's see. We would have the trivial transformation, the do-nothing transformation, that's just the original melody. We have the inversion reflecting it over the x-axis and we have the retrograde playing it backwards. Maybe there's a three-element group in there. Maybe we could write out the table for that. But when we try to there's a problem here. See, if we play something retrograde and then invert it, that's not a transformation that we have. We can't complete the table because we don't have a name for that. Mathematically what we would say is that this operation is not closed. We don't have a transformation that does that. Now we could fix that. We could add an element which is exactly this thing, and that, musically, is called the retrograde inversion, backwards and upside down.

Let's go back to "Twinkle, Twinkle." Here's "Twinkle, Twinkle" again. If we now do the retrograde inversion to that, we are playing it backwards and upside down. It sounds like this. Let's look at how Bach used this new transformation, this retrograde inversion in his music.

In Canon 2, Bach puts together not the original melody but an inversion of the melody and then he adds the retrograde inversion. So if we listen to this, we are going to hear the inversion played twice and then we're going to hear the retrograde inversion played twice and then we're going to hear them together. After these first four canons give Bach enough information about this melody, he then uses them in Canon 5. So let's turn to that one.

You see these first four canons are maybe study pieces before he finally gets to writing more complicated, more interesting music. So in Canon 5, he is using these same ideas and he also introduces a new melody and its inversion to write some really beautiful music. If you listen closely, there are two baselines to this piece. One is the main theme and the other is the main theme's inversion. So let's listen to Canon no. 5. Now that's starting to be really, really beautiful music.

Let's dig into some of the mathematics behind it, which is group theory. Now, we've already seen a few groups. But what's the definition of a group? Well, we need a set, for us that was transformations or we saw some with numbers. But we need a set and we also need an operation. An operation takes two things in that set and it spits out as an output one thing in that set. For us the operation was composition doing one transformation and another.

There are four properties we have to have in order for something to be a group. It has to be closed. That means the output is always in the set. It has to have an identity. That means that one element acts like zero does in addition. It leaves all the other elements alone when you do the composition. We have to have inverses. There's always a way to get back to the identity. And finally, we have to have associativity. That means the grouping doesn't matter. To understand these, let's look at some examples when one or more of these properties fail.

So let's think about the natural numbers, that's probably the easiest set of numbers, 1, 2, 3, 4, 5, 6, on and on up like that. Let's look at addition. Now when we write out a table, notice that it's closed. All the outputs are natural numbers. They're all things in our set. But notice that there's no identity. There's no zero. There's no way to solve the equation A+something equals A. Now we could try to fix this. We could just add zero to our set and when we do that we get something that are called the whole numbers.

When we look at the table associated to the whole numbers, we've done better. This is definitely closed, all the outputs are whole numbers. It has an identity now, for any A, A+0 is equal to A. And it works the other way as well, 0+A equals to A. But there's a problem with inverses. A+something equals 0, there's no way to solve that right now, and 3+something equals 0. You need a negative 3 and a negative 3 isn't in our set of whole numbers. So why don't we fix this by adding all the negatives in. When we add the negatives in, we get a set called the integers. Now we are looking at addition on the integers and now we have a group. Notice that it's closed, all the outputs are integers. It has an identity, 0 is the identity. It has the inverses. The inverse of -5 is 5. The inverse of 7 is -7. You can always find something to add to a number to get back to zero. It also has associativity and that's this grouping idea, A+B+C is the same thing as A+B+C . The parenthesis, where we put the parenthesis, does not matter. This is a group. In fact, it's a particular kind of group.

If you notice, you know from grade school that A+B is the same thing as B+A. The property there is called commutative. You can see this on the table, there's symmetry over the diagonal. If you take A+B it's the same thing as B+A. That means that there's symmetry across this diagonal. Mathematicians call these kinds of groups commutative.

Let's go back now to another group that we've seen repeatedly. Let's go back to Z2. We've seen lots of different copies of Z2. We've seen geometrical ones, reflections. We've seen functions, negating functions. We saw evens and odds; that was addition mod 2. We saw musical inversions, that was one table. We saw retrograde. All of these tables really have the same structure. We're just like changing the names of the columns and the rows in these tables. We call these isomorphic groups. That's what mathematicians call it. They have the same sort of structures. These are all versions of the same group Z2. We're just changing the names. So what is Z2 itself? I think that is sort of a philosophical question. Here's what I mean by that.

Let's go back to an easier question, what is 2? What is the number 2? You know, babies answer this from sort of experience. You know, these are two eyes, two ears, two fingers. None of those is two. When you're looking at two apples, what's there? They're apples. They're not two. In some sense, two is what all of those sets have in common. It's a very abstract idea, and the same is true of Z2. All of those tables that we saw, all of those groups, none of them is Z2. Z2 is what all of those examples have in common. Both the number 2 and group Z2 are very abstract mathematical concepts. They're separate from the physical world. This is a trade of mathematics which is really interesting that you could do a lot of mathematics without actually referring to anything in the physical world. And we're going to talk more about that in lecture 12.

Let's go back to some complicated math and some complicated music than just Z2. Let's go to musical transformations. Now we have inversions and we have retrograde and when we tried to put them together we found it was not closed, and we needed another transformation in order to make that closed so we can add the retrograde inversion to fix this. So now we have four transformations: the identity, the do nothing transformation; inversions; retrograde; and retrograde inversions. Let's write out the group table for that. And when we write out the group table for that, we can check, it's closed, it has an identity, the do-nothing transformation. It has inverses, in fact, each one of the transformations is its own inverse and, in fact, it's associative. Now what group is that? Because it's clearly not Z2 after all. You know this is a 4 x 4 chart; it's not a 2 x 2 chart. Let's see if we can find the same group somewhere else. Where else might we see this group, the same group? Well, it's a four-element group, so we might guess that it would be Z4.

So we're looking at numbers and the remainders when we divide by 4 instead of Z2 with remainders when you divide it by 2. If we're looking at Z4, the possible remainders when you divide by 4 are 0, 1, 2, and 3. But when we look at that table, it has a different structure. You see, in the group we're looking at, the musical group, every element is its own inverse. If you do the inversion and then the inversion, you get the identity.

It's a little harder to see but if you do a retrograde inversion and then you do a retrograde inversion, you also get back to the identity. That's not true in Z4. If you look at the element 1, if you add 1 to itself, you don't get back to the identity zero, 1+1 is 2. If you look at 3, that's a little bit tricky, because 3+3, we normally think of that as 6, but we're looking at remainders mod 4 and so the remainder when you divide 6 by 4 is 2. So 3+3 is 2. That's also not the identity so neither one nor 3 is its own inverse. That tells that these two groups are not isomorphic. So you might ask what group is this then?

Let's go back to geometry and see another representation of the same group. In geometry, we might have to do-nothing transformation, we might have to reflect about the x-axis transformation, we might have the reflection about the y-axis transformation, and then in order to make a closed group we would need to do both. We would need to reflect about the x-axis and then the y-axis. If you think through that, that's actually the same thing as doing a

180-degree rotation. So now we have four elements. We have the trivial, the do-nothing transformation, reflect over x, reflect over y and reflect over both, or rotate 180 degrees. When we write out that table, it has the same structure as our own group. Each one of those elements is its own inverse, and I think you can think through why, because there's a symmetry that's really the same properties; we're just flipping things in two dimensions. We're flipping things over the x-axis or over the y-axis. Let's see if we can find a functional example of the same group.

In functions, we could do nothing and that's the trivial transformation. We could take $-f(x)$, that's reflecting over the x-axis. We could take $f(-x)$, that's reflection over the y-axis, or we could do both. We could look at $-f(-x)$. And when you think through that, that's actually a 180-degree rotation as well. This is another representation of the same group. Every element in this group is its own inverse. Let's see if we can find a numerical example, because when we looked for a Z4, that was not the right numerical example.

To see the correct numerical example, we have to look at something called Z2 cross Z2. The name of this group is actually the Klein 4-group. Klein was a 19th-century German mathematician. It's the same Klein as the Klein bottle if you've heard of that. Z2 cross Z2 is not just numbers, it's actually ordered pairs of numbers. So you have two coordinates, a 0 and 1 in one coordinate and a 0 and 1 in the other coordinate. The operation now is a little bit complicated. It's coordinate-wise addition modulo 2.

So let's do an example to see this. If we had the ordered pair 0, 1 and we were adding 1, 1 to it, we would look at the first coordinates first. So the first coordinate is 0 and 1, we add those, and we get 0+1, that's 1. Now the second coordinates are both 1, 1+1 is not 2, we're working modulo 2, 1+1 is 0. When we add these two elements, 0,1 + 1, 1, we get 1, 0. Is it a group? Well, we have some properties to check. It has an identity, 0, 0 is the identity. Every element is its own inverse, you can think through that. You can actually understand this in relation to the other groups we've talked about. You can think about the first coordinate is telling you whether or not you're flipping over x of the x-axis. If it's a 1 you flip; if it's a 0 you don't. You could think about the second coordinate as flipping over the y-axis. If it's a 1 you flip and if it's a 0 you don't. And so it is indeed exactly the same chart that we've seen before; the same group table.

Now it's an interesting mathematical fact that there are only two groups with four elements and we've seen both of them now. One is Z4, that was remainders when you divide by 4, and now this other one is this group of transformations that we've seen several times that we now have a name for, the Klein 4-group, or Z2 cross Z2.

So let's go back to musical transformations. Here's a new transformation for us to do. A transposition. A transposition is moving up or down in pitch. You could think of it as modulation; it's a version of that. Let's hear an example of this transposition and I'll play it for you on my violin. Let's go back to "Twinkle, Twinkle." The idea of a transposition is normally we start on the key A. Instead of that we could start on D. That would be transposing up a fourth because D is the fourth note in the A major scale. It would sound like this. When you do that, it's easily recognizable as the same tune, it's just a little bit higher. Now there are corresponding mathematical transformations. If we're thinking about geometry, you could think about just taking a figure and translating it up. For functions, you could think about taking $f(x)$ and adding C to it. It's just a vertical translation when you're looking at the graph.

When you look at these transformations and you look at their group structures, it gets really interesting. You see if you have, you can find the inverse if you transpose up, you just transpose back down, but it has infinitely many elements. In theory, you could just keep transposing up as many intervals as you want. At any point, if you wanted to get back down, there's an inverse transformation to do, so you could transpose infinitely many steps. The table for this group is infinitely large and that's a little bit strange. Now one way to keep it from being infinitely large is to work by note names, to work what's called modulo octaves. That is to treat every A on the piano as if it's the same thing and ever C-sharp is the same, whether it's a C-sharp down here or a C-sharp way up there.

Let's think about this. Let's think about transposing not up a fourth, but up one-half step, go one key at a time. If you transpose up a half-step and then up a half-step and you keep doing that. If you transpose 12 times, in terms of note names, you get back to where you started. You may start on A and go up 12 times, you would end at A. It's actually just like adding 1 to itself, but then somehow getting back to the beginning again.

We actually see something mostly every day that does exactly this, and it's a clock—1, 2, 3, 4, 5, 6, 7, 8, 9. You could think of 12 as the 0. You could think of it as a zero and so you go back to the beginning again and you start over. That group is called Z12 and sometimes Z12 is simply called clock arithmetic because of that. If you think about it in Z12, if you take 10+3, that would be like taking 10 o'clock and then going three more hours and you don't get 13 o'clock, you get 1 o'clock, right? And so, it's just like Z12.

Transposition by half steps is exactly the same thing. You go up 12 half-steps and you back to the beginning. You could think about it as a circle, up 1, 2, 3, 4, 5, 6, 7, 8, 9 and then when you've finally done 12, you're back to the start.

Let's see another transpositional group. Let's look at transposing not up a half step, but up a major third. Now a major third is four half steps. So maybe we'll call it M4, for modulating up four half steps. Let's think about the group that you would generate if you did this. Well, you have the trivial transformation, do nothing, and then you could go up four half steps. If you did up four half steps followed by up four half steps, that would take you eight half steps, that's a minor 6th. And if you did up eight half steps followed by up four half steps, you'd be going up 12 half steps. But if you go up 12 half steps and you're working modulo octaves, 12 half steps gets you back to the same note name you had before. And so that is the identity, going up 12 half steps is really the same thing as leaving it where it is. It's the trivial transformation.

Now we can write out the chart. We have three transformations here–do nothing, up four half steps, up eight half steps, and that's it. When we write out the table, we see that it actually has the same structure as Z3. It's addition modulo 3. We're looking at remainders when dividing by 3 and, of course, those remainders are always either 0, 1, or 2. So this transpositional group that we've come up with, starting with transposing up four half steps is really another copy of Z3. What happens if we combine that with inversion, then we get something that's really interesting because this group is not commutative. So, again, we're going to do two transformations here. We're going to do inversions and we're going to look at up a major third, four half steps.

So let's take those in turn. Suppose we take a melody and we invert and then we go up a major third. That's different from going up a major third and then inverting over where we originally started. This transformation puts the melody much too low. That's telling us that this group is not commutative. The M4 transformation followed by the inversion is not the same thing as the inversion followed by the M4 transformation. That's a little bit weird. I wonder if we can find sort of a geometrical representation of that. What would that look like?

It turns out that you can find a geometrical representation, but it's not quite as simple as the other things we have done. You need to look at symmetries on an equilateral triangle. So there are rotational symmetries. You could think of rotating 120 degrees. We'll call that ro. Rotation of 120 degrees. If you do that twice you get a rotation of 240 degrees. If you do that three times, you get back to the identity. On the other hand, an equilateral triangle also has a reflectional symmetry. Let's look at the vertical one. You can reflect over that vertical line and there's two diagonal reflections that also work. Let's call those r2 and r3, reflection over one diagonal and the other diagonal.

You can take these transformations and write out a group table and if you do, it's actually isomorphic to the musical group that's generated by going up four half steps, M4, and the inversion. Let's see why that's true. You see, going up four half steps plays the same role as rotating 120 degrees. The reason is if you go up four half steps, do it again and do it again, you get back to the same note name you started at. You get an octave higher but we're working modulo octaves. With the rotations, you rotate 120 degrees and then another 120 degrees and then again, you're back to where you started with because a full rotation is 360 degrees. In both cases you do it three times and you get back to the identity.

The reflection works the same. If you reflect and then do it again, you get back to the identity. The inversion, the musical transformation, the inversion does exactly the same thing. If you invert and do it again, you get back to the identity. If you look at the tables for both of these groups, you have exactly the same structure. Mathematicians have a name for this group. This is called the dihedral group of order 6, and it is the smallest non-commutative group that you can construct. You can generalize on these dihedral groups, instead of using an equilateral triangle you can use an n-gon like a regular square or regular pentagon or higher order things like that.

We can also ask some interesting questions about these. If we can generate these groups we can ask, Are there musical versions of these? What do the musical versions sound like? Which of these mathematical groups that we construct can be realized as a musical group? This is actually the subject of current really interesting research that some of my friends are doing.

Let's go and look at symmetry. Let's look at an example of symmetry. Because after all group theory is probably seen as the language of symmetry within mathematics. Mathematicians categorize objects by their symmetry group. If you take the outline of a violin, there's only one symmetry it has. You see you can reflect it over the x-axis and you get the same thing, but there's no other way to transform that picture and get back to the same picture. On the other hand, if you had like the outline of a barbell, it actually has three symmetries. You could reflect it over the x-axis, you could reflect it over the y-axis or you could do 180-degree rotation. That means the symmetry group for that barbell is a copy of Z2 cross Z2, that's the Klein 4-group.

Mathematicians categorize objects by their symmetry group and one of the interesting objects you can categorize is called Frieze patterns, strips of patterns that repeat. If you do the mathematics, there are seven different symmetries on Frieze patterns and no more. We could extend this. Instead of looking at Frieze patterns, we could look at entire wallpaper symbols. If you look at wallpaper symbols, you can actually find out that there are exactly 17 different symmetry groups on wallpaper. If you look closely at the Alhambra in Spain, all 17 of those groups appear in the Alhambra. There are no more than 17. Seventeen is the right number. That's how many symmetry groups there are for a wallpaper pattern.

Group theory is the language of symmetry and it is actually useful in a lot of different places. In chemistry, they use group theory to classify crystal structures. In physics, it's used to study subatomic particles. There are lots of really interesting uses for group theory. But let's go back to music and let's hear one last type of transformation that has that sort of group structure.

The transformation we need to talk about is called augmentation and diminution, stretching and shrinking by a factor of 2. Let's go back to "Twinkle." Here's the original melody. Its augmentation is twice as slow, whereas if we go back to the original melody and take its diminution, it's twice as fast—like that. So that's augmentation and diminution. You can think about the group structure involved in these transformations. If we augment, it's inverse is taking the diminution. We could also augment and then augment again and then augment again. We could stretch these notes as long as we want, each time taking them twice as long. So this group is definitely going to be infinite. If you think about it, it actually has the same structure as the integers. You can add 1 to itself as many times as you want, that's why that group is infinite. What does this group sound like?

Let's go back to Bach, because the opening music we heard was Canon 14. The name of Canon 14, it says four parts with augmentation and diminution, it's a canon in four parts. So we need to hear exactly what those sound like. So let's go back. Remember all of these canons are based on a single line of music. So let's hear that line of music and let's hear it with diminution and with augmentation. So let's hear, the original theme that Bach is working on—all these canons is the theme from the Aria from the *Goldberg Variations*. If we do the augmentation of that, it's twice as slow. On the other hand, if we do the diminution of that, it's twice as fast. And those are the transformations Bach is working with on his 14th Canon.

Bach wrote this 14th Canon in a single line and the only instructions are the title, that it's a four-part canon with augmentation and diminution. Let's hear just the single line without the four parts, but just the one part. Let's listen to that. That's the one line of music. By itself it's beautiful. It's a little tricky in places, but it hides the puzzle that people quickly figured out. The solution to Bach's Canon is that it's actually in four parts. So let's look at the solution.

If we look at the solution there are four parts to that. There are four parts. The top voice is supposed to play the music as written, like I just played it. The next voice is supposed to play it augmented, twice as slow, but also inverted and transposed, some of these transformations we've been talking about. The next voice is supposed to play it augmented again, now four times the length of the original and transposed again. The bottom voice is supposed to play it augmented yet again. It is now eight times as slow as the original and also inverted and transposed. Amazingly, the bottom voice is just the original melody from the *Goldberg Variations*.

While you listen to this, I want you to listen for all of the parts. All of the parts are the same in some sense but they're different in some other sense. They're transformed from the original melody. Let's listen to this. Let's actually listen to that one more time. It's such a great piece. Let's listen to it and let's see, I want to make sure we understand what's going on. Each part is read from the same music, but each part is using a different transformation. Each part is derived in some sense from the *Goldberg* ground, just those eight notes, and when I say derived, I mean using these transformations. These transformations have a very mathematical structure. These transformations that decades later would be called group theory. Group theory wasn't around in Bach's time. Later it would be called group theory. So let's listen one more time to the 14th Canon.

Finally, today we have a musical coda and I think it's going to be a whole lot of fun. We're going to play a table canon for you. Now, this is a duet. It's written for two violins and the idea is you take this duet and you take the music and you place it on a table between the two players. You see one person is supposed to play this music right side up, starting here. The other person is supposed to play it upside down, starting here.

Mathematically speaking in terms of these transformations, one person is playing the original music, the identity, and the other person is playing it upside down and backwards, the retrograde inversion. Now this piece is attributed to Mozart and probably unlikely that it's actually Mozart, but as you listen I want you to think about how the composer had to write a part that fit well with its own retrograde inversion. Think about the mathematics going on in this. This is one of the many transformations that link music to mathematics and, in particular, the mathematics of group theory.

To help me play this, I want to welcome my good friend, Dr. David Kung, from St. Mary's College of Maryland, probably the ideal person to play this with. Welcome. Thanks, Dave, it's my pleasure to be here and I think we should play the *Table* canon.

Thanks for watching. Thanks for joining us.

Next lecture, we're going to talk about, appropriately, self-reference.

Self-Reference from Bach to Gödel
Lecture 9

W e can point to many different versions of self-reference: talking about yourself, looking in a mirror, and using references to a work of art in the work itself. Self-reference creates beauty and a bit of strangeness in both mathematics and music, and the self-reference in these two subjects seems somehow similar. In this lecture, we'll discuss different levels of self-reference, from basic, to intermediate, to advanced, looking at both musical and mathematical examples. As we progress on this continuum, we'll see that infinite loops begin to appear, and these loops take on stranger meanings.

Basic Self-Reference

- Basic self-reference in classical music is fairly common. Western composers like to take snippets of earlier parts of a piece and play them later to sort of refer listeners back and keep the parts of the piece connected.

  o One of the most popular pieces of all time does this: Beethoven's Ninth Symphony, just before the "Ode to Joy." After an opening raucous blast, Beethoven intersperses a vigorous cello line with references to earlier movements. The piece quotes earlier parts of itself.

  o Many similar examples of basic self-reference can be found in the Western concert music repertoire.

- Mathematicians use basic self-references all the time in the form of functions—sequences that refer to themselves. Think, for example, about the Fibonacci numbers, a sequence that recurs everywhere—in pinecones, sunflowers, Indian poetry, and much more. Each term in the sequence refers back to earlier terms. In mathematical notation, the sequence is $f_n + 1 = f_n + fn - 1$. The name for this sort of self-reference is a "recursively defined function."

- If we have a function defined on a small interval, say 0, 1, and we want to repeat it—we want it to go on and on and do exactly the same thing—we write $f(x) + 1 = f(x)$. What is $f(2)$? It refers back to $f(1)$; $f(2)$ is $f(1) + 1$, and that should be $f(1)$ according to our equation. What is $f(1.5)$? That refers back to $f(0.5)$; $f(1.5)$ is $f(0.5) + 1$, which is the same thing as $f(0.5)$.

Intermediate Self-Reference

- Basic self-reference in music is a piece referencing itself. Intermediate self-reference in music might be a composer referencing himself or herself. One of the most famous examples of intermediate self-reference in music is Sir Edward Elgar's *Enigma Variations*.

- To understand intermediate self-reference in the work of Bach, we need to know a little bit about music in Germany, in particular, the system for naming notes. In Germany, our B-flat is indicated with a B, and our B is indicated with an H. Thus, in the German system, Bach was able to encode his name in his music. We hear examples in *The Art of the Fugue* and the *Brandenburg Concerto* No. 2.

- Other composers have honored Bach in the same way, by writing BACH into their music. Still others, including Robert Schumann, Franz Schubert, Johannes Brahms, and even Dmitri Shostakovich, have also written their names into their music. In some cases, if the letters don't match up with the notes, they use tricks of musical nomenclatures or puns to accomplish the self-reference. Shostakovich shortened the German form of his name to DSCH, used the fact that S in German notation is E-flat, and arrived at D, E-flat, C, B.

- Here's a fun math version of intermediate self-reference: If you pick an answer at random from the following choices, what is the probability that you will be correct? (A) 25 percent, (B) 50 percent, (C) 0 percent, or (D) 25 percent. We can see the self-reference here: The answer is the probability of picking the correct answer.

- o Each answer is equally likely, so that is a 25 percent chance of picking each one. But the 25 percent appears twice; if we pick at random, there is a 50 percent chance of picking 25 percent. Perhaps the answer should be 50 percent. But 50 percent appears only once, and the chance of picking 50 percent is 25 percent.

- o Neither 25 percent nor 50 percent could be correct, so the correct answer should be 0 percent. But 0 percent appears only once, and there is a 25 percent chance of picking it. No answer is the correct percent chance of picking that answer.

- o A sneaky way to answer this question would be to write in a fifth option: (E) 20 percent.

- • In some sense, all differential equations are a form of self-reference. Consider, for example, the differential equation $y' = 0.5y$. This is among the simplest differential equations we could write. The equation asks: How quickly does y change? The answer to that question is: The change is half the size of y.
  - o This equation models something like exponential population growth. Think about starting with 100 rabbits, and at every time step, half of them reproduce, so at the next time step, we have an additional 50 rabbits. Then, with 150 rabbits, at the next time step, we get an additional 75 rabbits.

  - o The key self-reference here is that the function appears on both sides of the equation; it is a function referring to itself.

- • In an earlier lecture, we looked at the wave equation, which is another example of a differential equation (a partial differential equation). Recall that $u(x,t)$ represented how far above the median line the vibrating string went at position x and time t. Notice that $u(x,t)$ occurs on both sides of the equation. It is a form of self-reference; u is related to itself in this particular way.

- • Recall that the golden ratio (phi) we discussed in Lecture 5 is like pi, a number with special properties, and it is also rational; it cannot be written as a fraction. We usually think of the golden ratio not in terms of its continued fraction but as $1 + \sqrt{5}/2$, the ratio of the sides of pi.

o   If we have a rectangle with sides that are exactly on that ratio and we remove the largest possible square, the remaining rectangle has the same proportions as the original. From that, if we remove the largest possible square, the remaining rectangle has the same proportions as the original, and so on.

o   If we inscribe a curve inside each one of these squares—roughly a quarter circle in each square—we get a logarithmic curve.

• We have seen that the golden ratio is $1 + \sqrt{5}/2$, but we have also seen it as a continued fraction with all 1s. How do we know those two are the same?

o   Let x be the continued fraction with all 1s. The denominator is just another copy of x. It is just 1 plus a fraction with an infinite sequence of further fractions all involving 1s; that is what x is. That means that the whole expression x is actually equal to $1 + 1/x$, the entire expression again. The value x appears on both sides of the equation.

o   To solve, we multiply both sides by x, and we get $x^2 = x + 1$. We then subtract $x + 1$ from both sides, which leaves us with a quadratic equation: $x^2 - (x - 1) = 0$.

o   We then apply the quadratic formula: $\dfrac{-b \pm \sqrt{b^2 - 4ac}}{2a}$, which gives us phi: $1 + \sqrt{5}/2$.

• A geometrical version of self-reference is the Möbius strip. To construct one, we take a long strip of paper, which appears to have two sides—a front and a back—and we twist it once and fasten the ends together. Now, the front side continues on what was the back side, which continues back to the front side. The strip has just one face and one edge.

o If we cut the Möbius strip down the middle and keep cutting all the way around, we end up with a single piece of paper that has two faces and two edges.

o If we cut it in thirds, we get two separate loops that are interlocked.

© Ryan McVay/Photodisc/Thinkstock.

Self-reference creates beauty and a bit of strangeness in the everyday world and in mathematics and music.

Advanced Self-Reference

• Musical examples of advanced self-reference are rare. One of the few is a "crab canon." This is a duet formed by playing a piece of music forward and backward simultaneously. Bach wrote one in response to a musical challenge posed by Frederick the Great of Prussia in 1746.

o Written out, a crab canon has two parts, but the second part is the same as the first played in reverse. In the language of transformations, the second part is simply the retrograde of the first part. In Bach's crab canon, the second part reads the music retrograde, or from the end to the beginning.

o In a "table canon," the second part plays retrograde inversion from the end to the beginning but inverted—upside down. If we were to write out the table canon on one long musical staff, we could then represent an infinitely long musical score by forming a Möbius strip.

o Canons such as these and those we heard in earlier lectures represent the pinnacle of self-reference in music.

• For advanced self-reference in mathematics, we turn to Kurt Gödel.

o In 1910, Alfred North Whitehead and Bertrand Russell published *Principia Mathematica*. Their goal was to provide axioms that would give a stable base for mathematics, in much the same way that Euclid had done for geometry, except they were trying to do this for arithmetic and all of the theorems that come with arithmetic.

o Whitehead and Russell, along with David Hilbert, sought axioms that were consistent (so that both a statement and its opposite could not be proved) and complete (axioms that proved all the true statements). If a statement was true in their system, they wanted to make sure it could be proved using just the axioms they provided.

o This is a particular view of mathematics that with the right axioms, there might be only two kinds of statements in the world: true statements, all of which would be provable, and false statements, none of which would be provable. Gödel's work ruined the dreams of these mathematicians.

o The liar's paradox is a tricky version of self-reference. Consider the statement s = This statement is false. It can't be true because the statement says that it is false, and that's not possible. But if s is a false statement, then "This statement is false" is false, so the statement must be true. Thus, s can be neither true nor false. Gödel used this kind of self-reference to burst Whitehead and Russell's dream.

o Given a set of axioms strong enough to prove basic arithmetic truths about the natural numbers, Gödel gave a way of producing within that system the statement g = This statement is not provable.

o Is g itself provable? It cannot be provable because then the statement would be both provable and not provable. That would introduce inconsistencies; thus, g is true, exactly because it is not provable.

○ Kurt Gödel put this in his 1931 masterpiece, *On Formally Undecidable Propositions in Principia Mathematica and Related Systems*, and with this, he destroyed the dreams of Whitehead, Russell, Hilbert, and many other mathematicians. His first theorem states that no theory strong enough to do arithmetic is complete. There are true but unprovable statements. His second theorem states that no theory strong enough to do arithmetic can prove its own consistency. A system might be consistent, but we cannot prove within the system that it is consistent.

Suggested Reading

Hofstadter, *Gödel, Escher, Bach.*

Nagel, Newman, and Hofstadter, *Gödel's Proof.*

Questions to Consider

1. In what ways is self-reference used by classical composers in their music?

2. How did Gödel use self-reference in his work that revolutionized mathematics?

Self-Reference from Bach to Gödel
Lecture 9—Transcript

Math and music and this lecture is on self-reference. I hope it is good. That is a little bit strange. What is self-reference? Well we actually closed last lecture with an example. I welcomed myself on screen to play the Mozart *Table* canon. Now, there are many different kinds of self-reference. There are sort of everyday common types of self-reference. You can talk about yourself; you can talk about yourself maybe in the first or maybe in the third person. When you look in a mirror that is a version of self-reference.

If I were to write a research paper I could say in the research paper see theorem 2 which happened earlier in the paper. Or I could reference earlier work that I myself had done. That is a form of self-reference. Now, it would be weird if in a paper I would cite that paper. Maybe, in a 2006 paper that I wrote I could cite Kung 2006; that is a hint of weirdnesses to come. There is self-reference in popular culture in everyday life. We think of something like the chicken-and-the-egg problem; that's which came first. That is a version of self-reference.

If you ever see two mirrors that are parallel to each other and you look at them and you can see the light bouncing back and back, you can see reflections and reflections. That is a form of self-reference. Magritte, the famous Belgian painter, painted a picture, *Treachery of Images*, in which it says "This is not a pipe," of course, it is a picture of a pipe. The opening of this lecture where we saw infinitely many copies of me watching myself; that is a form of self-reference.

You see it in Sci-Fi movies, *Back to the Future*, Marty McFly, that is Michael J. Fox's character, he helps bring his own parents so that they can produce himself. *Matrix, Inception*, people dreaming about themselves; remember in *Matrix* the oracle says to Neo, "Don't worry about that vase," and then Neo turns and knocks over the vase. Would he still have broken it if the oracle had not said anything?

Even in literature there are versions of self-reference. In *Don Quixote*, Cervantes' protagonist, he understands that he is being written about. The character in the book talks about the book itself. Italian writer Italo Calvino wrote a book called *If On a Winter's Night a Traveler* in which a character sits down to read a book titled *If On a Winter's Night a Traveler*. Gabrielle Garcia Marquez wrote *A Hundred Years of Solitude*, a wonderful book, and in the final scene Aureliano II reads a book that prophecies his family's history, including his reading that very book all before the apocalypse erases the town of Macondo.

Now self-reference in math and music are both important in their own ways, but my main point today is this, self-reference creates beauty and a bit of strangeness in both mathematics and in music. The self-reference in these two subjects seems similar. Now like last lecture on transformations, this is really an analogy, this is not math directly applying to music or explaining music in some way, but I think that these two things, self-reference and mathematics in music, are very similar.

I personally think that in your brain there are neurological connections, that somehow it's the same schema needed to understand both mathematical and musical self-reference. Note that I just got your neurons to process thoughts about themselves, another form of self-reference. A lot of this was brought to the fore by Douglas Hofstadter in his book *Gödel, Escher, Bach: An Eternal Golden Braid*. I remember back in high school I joined the paperback book club to get a copy of this book. Now, it is a 1980 masterpiece of fantastical nonfiction. It won the Pulitzer Prize that year in general nonfiction.

This book elucidates the common connections among Bach's music, Escher's art, and Gödel's mathematics and I know that Gödel's work is probably the least well-known of these three. It includes ingenious dialog sort of like Plato would have written with hints of the mathematician Charles Dodgson, who you probably know better as the author Lewis Carroll. I had actually forgotten how brilliant these dialogs are. You know in one dialog there is a story about creating a record player. Each record player created has a resonant frequency and if you make a record with exactly that frequency, it will resonate and the record player will resonate and destroy itself. Now, you could make a new record player to play that record, but that new record player would have its own resonant frequency and there would be a record that would destroy it; really brilliant ways of explaining difficult material in wonderful ways.

On the surface, this book is about math, music, and art, underneath Hofstadter is really talking about deep concepts. He is talking about self-awareness. He is talking about cognition.

Today, we are going to talk about different levels of self-reference. There is basic self-reference; things like I am Dave. There is no strangeness, there are no loops, and there are lots of musical and mathematical examples. We could also have intermediate levels of self-reference. That is something like this sentence is true and now you can start to see infinite loops appearing. That sentence refers exactly to itself, which refers to itself, and again and again.

The mathematical examples of intermediate self-reference become more interesting and the musical examples are a little bit harder to come by. And finally, we are going to get to advanced self-reference; things like this sentence is false, and now the loops take on stranger meanings. You get contradictions. Musically, Bach was able to make music with these sorts of loops. Mathematically, these sorts of loops produce really unexpected consequences and we are going to look at very, very difficult mathematics from as recently as the 1930s.

But, let's start by looking at self-reference in music. That opening was a little bit strange; let's skip forward a little bit and see what music has to say about basic self-reference. My friends, composers have manipulated this quirky at times, headache-inducing technique of self-reference in myriad ways. Just to make myself perfectly clear, my main point today is this, self-reference creates beauty and a bit of strangeness in classical music, which is of course more properly called concert music. Let's look at basic self-reference in classical music, which is pieces that reference themselves.

Now, basic self-reference in classical music is fairly common. Western composers like to take snippets of earlier parts and play them later to sort of refer you back to keep those things connected in a piece. One of the most popular pieces of all time does this. In fact, Beethoven's Ninth Symphony does this right before it gets to the famous "Ode to Joy" so let's examine exactly how he does this. Beethoven's Ninth Symphony was finished in 1824. It was first performed in Vienna with Beethoven sitting right next to the conductor unable to hear a thing.

The last movement, the fourth movement is the one that contains Schiller's poem "An die Freude" or "To Joy," hence the name "Ode to Joy." After an opening raucous blast, Beethoven intersperses a vigorous cello line with references to earlier movements. The piece is quoting earlier parts of itself, this basic form of self-reference, the symphony is referencing itself. Let's hear these themes from the earlier movement separately and then as self-reference at the beginning of the last movement. The theme from the opening movement, the opening movement is marked *Allegro ma non troppo*, fast, but not too fast, and it sounds like this.

That is sort of the opening motif from that. In the second movement, we have a theme that is much faster. The second movement is marked *scherzo*, a joke, and it is in a fast three and it sounds like this.

And then we get to the third movement, *Adagio molto e cantabile*, very slow, smooth in a singing way. And here is the opening line for the violins, the theme from the third movement.

So, beautiful! Now let's see how Beethoven references these when we get finally to the fourth movement. What you are going to hear, the fourth movement is market *Presto*, fast, and what you are going to hear is this splashy brass theme, and then you are going to hear alternating the cello theme with quotes from the earlier movements. Do not worry; we are going to show you on screen which parts are which. Let's listen to the first few minutes of the last movement of the Ninth Symphony of Beethoven.

My friends this is hardly the only example of self-reference in the concert music repertoire, examples leap from the pages of the scores of western music, Mahler's First Symphony quickly comes to mind, *Der Titan*, they are as numerous as over-zealous rabbits reproducing their way into over-populated oblivion. If we only did not have to share the stage with math we could hear more of them, but for now let's see how mathematicians use self-reference.

Mathematicians use basic self-reference all the time, functions, sequences that refer to themselves. Think about the Fibonacci numbers, sequence that comes up everywhere, pinecones, sunflowers, Indian poetry; remember it is 1, 1, 2, 3, 5, 8, 13, to get to the next you add the two previous terms. This is a form of self-reference. You see, each term refers back to earlier terms in math notation $f_{n+}1$ is equal to $f_n + fn - 1$. There is a name for this sort of self-reference in math and computer science. These are called recursively defined functions. Recursion here is the function f recurring on both sides of this equation.

We can look at other examples of mathematical self-reference. If we have a function defined on a small interval, say 0, 1, and we want to repeat it again, we want it to go on and on and do exactly the same thing, we write $f(x) + 1$ is equal to $f(x)$. What is $f(2)$? It refers back to $f(1)$, $f(2)$ is $f(1) + 1$ and that should be $f(1)$ according to our equation. What is $f(1-1/2)$? That refers back to $f(1/2)$, $f(1.5)$ is $f(0.5) + 1$ and so that is the same thing as $f(0.5)$.

You actually get these long chains. You get $f(5)$ is equal to $f(4)$ is equal to $f(3)$ is equal to $f(2)$ is equal to $f(1)$. We can look at it graphically. Anytime you have a function defined on 0, 1, we can replicate that between 1 and 2 and we replicate that between 2 and 3. All because of the self-reference contained in this equation $f(x) + 1$ is equal to $f(x)$.

We can also create loops of this and you probably have seen this if you have taken a computer science class. When I was programming I was using outmoded languages like Pascal and Fortran, but we used to create loops and we used to use counters to do things. We would start a loop and then we would set the counter to be equal to 0 and then we would do some sort of work and then at the end of the loop we would say counter equals counter + 1. There is the self-reference. And now unless we are done we go back to the start of the loop. The self-reference here is that the counter is equal to the counter + 1. It refers back to itself. It actually refers back to an earlier state within the chain.

I know that self-reference in mathematics gets much more complicated than this and I am sure the same is true of self-reference in music. Let's see what self-reference in an intermediate level of complexity looks like in music. For composers, basic self-reference was a piece referencing itself. Intermediate self-reference in music might be a composer referencing him or herself. Now there are two famous examples of this that we are going to hear about today; one is Johann Sebastian Bach and the other is Sir Edward Elgar. Let's take the Elgar first.

Edward Elgar was a British composer, born in 1857. He was one of the first composers to really embrace recorded music. He recorded orchestral works with a label HMV as early as 1914. One of Elgar's most famous works was probably *Pomp and Circumstance*. You probably hear this when you go to graduations, you might hear it again and again and again, but he did write many other tunes including a very famous piece called *Enigma Variations*. The *Enigma Variations* were composed in 1899.

Back in 1898, in that fall, Elgar was finished teaching violin lessons in his house. He lit a cigar and he started just improvising on the piano. In another room, his wife Alice said, "I like that tune play it again," and Edward played it again and again and again. He started playing it how his friends and family would play it and that is how we get the name of this piece. You see Elgar took the original tune to his grave. We do not know what the original tune is, we only now know how Elgar thinks his friends would have played it. That is how we get *Enigma Variations*; the original tune is still an enigma.

One of the more famous is actually *Variation No. 9* called *Nimrod* after a friend of his, Augustus Jaeger. We get *Nimrod* because Jaeger in German means hunter and nimrod was Babylonian, the hunter before the Lord. Let's look at Elgar's self-reference that he uses in this piece. You see the first variation in this piece is labeled in the score CAE and that stands for Caroline Alice Elgar. It is the second one where the self-reference comes in. The last segment of this piece is labeled in the score EDU and that is for Edu or Edward and that is Edward Elgar himself. This is the self-reference.

You see Sir Edward Elgar composed this little bit of music that we do not know and this is Sir Edward Elgar himself telling us how Sir Edward Elgar would play this theme that Sir Edward Elgar took to his grave. This is self-reference in music. Let's listen to this last movement of the *Enigma Variations*.

240

That was Elgar's self-reference. To understand Bach's self-reference we need to know a little bit about music in Germany and in particular how they notate the names of the notes. We have talked about how we notate names in our system. We have A and C-sharp and E-flat and things like that. In northern Europe, including Germany, there B was our B-flat and then to indicate our B they use the name H. Why was this so important to Bach? Because now in the German system BACH, all four of those are now notes and so it would sound like this if you played BACH in the German system.

And so Bach because of this German system could encode his name in his music. Now he could do this up an octave; he could do it down an octave like that.

He could encode his name in these pieces as much as he wanted and he actually wrote BACH, this little phrase, this motif, into many different pieces. Let's look at some of those examples. The most famous might be *The Art of the Fugue, Die Kunst der Fuge*. In *Contrapunctus No. 14* this is unfinished. His son C.P.E. Bach, Carl Philipp Emanuel Bach, wrote in the score [German phrase]. In this Fugue the name Bach has written in the countersubject, where it is actually written into the music, the composer died. C.P.E. Bach is telling us that this is the last thing that Bach was writing.

It turns out there is some disagreement whether or not that is actually true, whether or not Bach wrote this and then passed away. There are some indications that C.P.E. Bach might have written that in much later, but it remains that the motif BACH is written into this particular fugue. Let's listen and we are going to start exactly where he starts quoting BACH, BACH, this is where Bach is using self-reference in his own music. Let's listen to that.

Let's listen to one more example of Bach self-referencing himself and this comes from the *Brandenburg Concerto No. 2*. Interestingly, the *Brandenburg Concerto No. 2* is sometimes used as intro music for Great Courses. Near the end of the first movement the bass line plays BACH and it sounds like this.

Let's listen to a short clip first where it is just this particular phrase and here is what it sounds like in the flow of the piece. This is toward the end of the first movement in Bach's *Brandenburg Concerto No. 2* of 1721. Listen for Bach referencing himself in the bass line.

Other composers actually honored Bach in the same way. Other composers would write BACH into their music as sort of an homage to Bach. There is actually an entire website devoted to exactly this. Some other composers did more of self-reference spelling their own names. There are a lot of problems, of course. There are problems that the letters do not always match up with the notes and so they used tricks of musical nomenclatures, sharps, flats, linguistic tricks, puns, in order to do the self-reference. This includes Robert Schumann, Franz Schubert, Johannes Brahms, even Demetrius Shostakovich. Imagine if you are Shostakovich and you are trying to write your own name into your piece and your name is Demetrius Shostakovich. He actually did this by shortening the German form of his name. In German, Shostakovich is written Sch at the beginning and so what he would do is he would write in DSCH as a short for Demetrius Shostakovich. Now where does the S come from you might ask? S in German notation is E-flat and so his name would sound like this.

Again, he is using German notation and a bunch of short hands in order to write himself into his music. He is doing self-reference. I find these musical forms to be fun and intriguing and I wonder what mathematics looks like as intermediate self-reference. Let's see.

Here is a fun math version of self-reference that I would probably put at the intermediate level and it has made the rounds in math circles lately. Multiple choice, if you pick an answer at random from the choices below the probability that you will be correct is and your choices are A: 25 percent, B: 50 percent, C: 0 percent, or D: 25 percent. You see the self-reference here? The answer is the probability of picking the correct answer. If you are sort of a puzzle person you might want to take a break for a second and think about this. We are going to analyze the possibilities.

There are four answers, each of which is equally likely, so that is 25 percent chance of picking each one. But, the 25 percent appears twice and so if we pick at random there is a 50 percent chance of picking the 25 percent. Maybe the answer should be 50 percent. Ahh, but 50 percent appears only once and the chance of picking 50 percent is 25 percent. Neither 25 percent nor 50 percent could be correct so the right answer should be 0 percent, but 0 percent appears once and there is a 25 percent of picking it. No answer is the correct percent chance of picking that answer. There is a cheeky way around this. You could write in as option E 20 percent and then that becomes the right answer.

Let's look at more mathy examples of self-reference at the intermediate level. In some sense all differential equations are a form of self-reference. Let me tell you what I mean by that. Let's think of the easy differential equation y prime = $1/2y$. This is among the simplest differential equations you could write. The meaning of this one is how quickly does y change; that is y prime, the change in y, and the answer to that question is the change is half the size of y. You could use this and you could use other constants besides $1/2$, but this would model something like exponential population growth. Think about starting with 100 rabbits and maybe at every time step half of them reproduced and so you have half of them at the next time step, so you get an additional 50 rabbits.

But now, you have 150 rabbits so now when half of them reproduce you get an additional 75 rabbits; that is the exponential growth part. As things keep going faster and faster you spiral upward. The key self-reference here is that the function appears on both sides of the equation. It is a function referring back to itself.

Back in lecture 1, we were studying a vibrating string. We looked at the wave equation, which is another example of a differential equation, actually it is a partial differential equation. The wave equation looked like this; remember that $u(x)$ and t represented how far above the median line our string went at position x and time t. Notice that it occurs on both sides of the equation. It is a form of self-reference, u is related to itself in this particular way. Every differential equation, and in fact every partial differential equation, is some form of mathematical self-reference.

We can also look at geometrical examples. Let's look back to the Golden Ratio, which we talked about in lecture 5. Remember we looked at its continued fractions with all 1s. Remember that the Golden Ratio here is like *pi*, a number with special properties, and it is also rational. You cannot write it as a fraction. The Golden Ratio, we normally think of the Golden Ratio not in terms of the continued fraction, but in terms of it being 1 plus root 5 over 2 , the ratio of the sides of *pi*.

The main property geometrically of the Golden Ratio is that if you take a rectangle whose sides are exactly on that ratio and remove a square, the largest square you can, the remaining rectangle has the same proportions as the original. From that, you can remove the largest square and the remaining rectangle has the same sides as the proportional and you can do that again, and again, and again. In fact, if you inscribe a curve inside each one of these squares, roughly a quarter circle in each square, you get this beautiful curve and it is actually called a logarithmic curve. When we look at that it is this spiral, and it is just one example of a logarithmic spiral and there are others depending on the size, but this is the one that related to the Golden Ratio.

We have seen that it is 1 plus root 5 over 2 , but we have also seen that it is this continued fraction with all 1s. An interesting mathematical question, if you are being skeptical you should be asking how do we know those two are the same. In order to see that, it takes some algebra and a little bit of self-reference. Let's look at the continued fraction with all 1s and let's call that value x. The denominator, when we look at the denominator in that expression, it is just another copy of x right? It is just 1 plus a fraction with an infinite sequence of further fractions all involving 1s; that is what x is. That means that the whole expression x is actually equal to $1 + 1 / x$, the entire expression again.

We write out this equation in algebra and it is just that x is equal to $1 + 1 / x$ and here is the self-reference because x appears on both sides of this equation. When we solve this we just multiply both sides by x. We get x^2 is equal to $x + 1$. We can subtract $x + 1$ from both sides giving us this quadratic equation. Remember, to solve a quadratic equation there is a formula, coincidentally enough called the quadratic formula. When we apply that formula we might remember this from high school $-b$ plus or minus the square root of $b^2 - 4ac$ all over $2a$. We apply that in this particular case and we get *phi*, we get 1 plus root 5 over 2 . We actually get 1 plus or minus root 5 over 2 , we know it cannot be the minus sign because that value would be less than 1/2 and our number is clearly bigger than 1.

Let's look at a geometrical version of self-reference, the Möbius strip. It is probably the easiest geometrical version of self-reference we can come up. We take this long strip of paper and it appears to have two sides or faces, a front and a back, and we can fix that with a little bit of self-reference. We twist once and tape the ends together and now the front side continues on to what was the back side, which continues all the way around back to the front side. It is the Möbius strip. If you think about it, it has just one face and one edge.

How weird is this Möbius strip? To show you the strangeness of self-reference I will do two demonstrations with this strip. First I am going to cut it down the middle and I am going to cut it exactly in half down the middle the long way and if you are intrigued about this you should guess what is going to happen when I do this. When I cut it down the middle I keep cutting all the way around and amazingly I end up with a single piece of paper and now it actually has two faces and two edges.

Another thing I can do with this Möbius strip, instead of cutting it in half I can cut it in thirds and when I cut it in thirds, now again you might want to think about this and pause for a second, but when I cut it in thirds one of the surprising things you will notice is that I do not have to start my cut over, it is actually one very long cut and when I do this the result is fairly surprising. I get two separate loops, but they are interlocked. There is a shorter one, which is a thinner version of the Möbius strip, and then there is the longer one, which is a version of what we had when we cut it exactly in half except now that is thinner. The properties of the Möbius strip are very strange indeed. There are other topological beasts that have similarly strange properties and like most of the self-reference you see it is a little bit above the basic level I would say.

Well that, I think, is intermediate self-reference in mathematics. Let's see what our musical friend can show us about intermediate self-reference in music. My friends I fear that musical examples of advanced self-reference are nearly as rare as pigs actually taking flight. There are only a few, precious few examples of self-reference ingenious enough to earn the label of advanced; one is definitely a crab canon.

Now this is a masterpiece of musical form and contrapuntal complexity. It is a duet formed by playing a piece of music forwards and backwards simultaneously. Let's look at a crab canon of Bach. In 1746, Bach was challenged by Frederick the Great of Prussia: compose a canon based on a theme of his choosing and he chose a very odd little theme. I will play it for you on violin. Here is the theme that the King of Prussia gave to Bach to compose a fugue on.

That is a very little odd theme indeed. On the spot, Bach was able to improvise a three-part fugue based on that theme, but he apologized that he could not do better and when he returned to Leipzig from Potsdam, he wrote a six-part fugue based on the same theme. This is known as a musical offering. One of the parts of the musical offering is a crab canon so let's look at that.

The crab canon when you write it out has two parts, but if you notice the second part is the same as the first played in reverse. In the language of transformations the second part is simply the retrograde of the first part. This hauntingly beautiful melody based on a theme not of his own choosing magically fits with its own retrograde to form a duet. Let's listen to this crab canon.

In Bach's crab canon, the second part reads the music retrograde or from the end to the beginning. In a table canon, the second part plays retrograde inversion from the end to the beginning, but inverted, upside down. My friends, you may have seen this type of canon demonstrated in an earlier lecture in this math and music course that you're currently watching. I certainly do not want to replay that piece, it simply cannot be correctly attributed to Mozart, but let's look at this again. Let's look at the table canon.

Now a table is such a boring piece of furniture to use, let's find a more interesting way to represent this piece. Suppose we were to write out the table canon on one long staff, it would be much too small for you to read, but you can imagine it written out here and it would start here at the beginning and you would be able to go through, you would play through the middle and then you would get here to the end. Then player two would be playing from the end, but upside down through the middle and finally to the beginning.

It's a little hard to read music upside down so let's see if we can give these guys a little bit of help. I am going to rip this exactly in the middle, you notice the middle here is split and I am going to flip them over and tape them together with a twist. When I do that let's see what it looks like. Here I am taping together and then you see here is the end of the word "middle" and here is the beginning of the word "middle" and they need to be flipped in order to tape together. Let's do exactly that. Now I am going to tape just to make sure it stays together.

Let's think about what the players are supposed to do. See player one is supposed to play starting here at the beginning, keep going, there's the middle, play through the middle right here and finally get to the end. Player two on the other hand is supposed to play starting at the end and upside down and here we go. They are supposed to keep playing, keep playing. Notice that they get to the middle, upside down, and they keep playing and they keep playing and finally they get to the beginning upside down.

Amazingly, if both players wanted to keep going, if they wanted to repeat this they could just keep going. The second player would just start again at the end upside down on this confounded strip that sort of works out nicely. I am sure mathematicians have some name for it. The piece would just keep repeating musically. A mathematician might say that this is infinitely long in some way.

Canons such as these and those you heard about in earlier lectures, they represent the pinnacle of self-reference in music. There simply is nothing better. Let's see what the ultimate in self-reference looks like in the mathematics world. Finally, we have come to the Gödel and Gödel Escher Bach for advance self-reference in mathematics.

First, we have to understand the context in which Gödel was doing his work. In 1910, Alfred North Whitehead and Bertrand Russell published *Principia Mathematica*. Their goal was to provide axioms that would give a stable base for mathematics, sort of the same way Euclid did for geometry except they were trying to do this for arithmetic and all of the theorems that come with arithmetic. Whitehead and Russel along with David Hilbert sought axioms that were first consistent so that you could not prove both a statement and its opposite; that would be a problem, and second complete axioms that proved all the true statements. If a statement was true in their system they wanted to make sure that they could prove it just using the axioms that they provided.

This is a particular view of mathematics that with the right axioms there might be two kinds of statements in the world. There would only be true statements, all of which would be provable, and then there would be false statements, none of which would be provable. Gödel's work ruined their dreams. Before we can talk about Gödel's work, let's back up a little bit to the liar's paradox. This is again a tricky version of self-reference. Consider the statement s: this statement is false.

Let's think, is s a true statement? Well, no because if it is true than the statement says that it is false and that is not possible. Is s a false statement? Well, if s is a false statement this statement is false is false so the statement has to be true. So, s can be neither true nor false. Gödel used this kind of self-reference to burst the bubble of Whitehead and Russell's goal, their dream. You see if you had a set of axioms strong enough to prove basic arithmetic truths about the natural numbers then Gödel gave sort of a recipe, a way of proving, a way of producing within your system the statement g: this statement is not provable.

Let's think about why that works. G, this statement is not provable. Is g itself provable? Well, it cannot be provable because then the statement would be both provable and not provable and we would have inconsistencies and so g is true, exactly because it is not provable. The world is not quite as black and white, sort of true and provable versus false and provable. We have managed to find, Gödel managed to find within the true statement something that was necessarily not provable.

Kurt Gödel put this in his 1931 masterpiece *On Formally Undecidable Propositions in Principia Mathematica and Related Systems – Part 1* and in this he destroyed the dreams of Whitehead, Russel, Hilbert, and many other mathematicians. This first theorem says that no theory is strong enough to do arithmetic is complete . There are true, but unprovable statements. His second theorem actually says something different. It says that no theory strong enough to do arithmetic can prove its own consistency. Remember consistency is that you cannot prove both *s* and not *s*. A system might be consistent, but you cannot prove within the system that it is consistent.

I would really love to walk you through the details of Gödel's work. This work is incredibly difficult and when I was an undergraduate I did an entire semester's independent study with Professor Bird just on the completeness theorem, an entire semester to prove the incompleteness theorem. The core ideas here involve coding statements about mathematics with numbers so that you can talk about those statements within the mathematical language. The key to all of this is actually unique prime factorization that every natural number can be written as the product of primes in exactly one way. Really I think this is the height of mathematical self-reference. This is a self-referential statement that shows the futility of axiomatic systems for arithmetic.

Mathematicians since Gödel have had to deal with this fact and it has spurred surprising new areas of research. Anyway, what Gödel does is create a sentence that talks all about itself. It is sort of like this entire lecture. I hope you have enjoyed our tour through the strange worlds of self-reference in both mathematics and in music. Next time, we are going to move away from these implicit connections between the two subjects of math and music and we are going to see how composers explicitly use mathematics in composing their works. Thanks for joining us.

Composing with Math—Classical to Avant-Garde
Lecture 10

In the last few lectures, we've been talking about composing music. Scales, rhythms, transformations—these are all important aspects of composition, but in each case, the mathematics is sort of embedded; it's implicit. The composers aren't necessarily thinking about the math, although now you know that they really are doing some math. What if the mathematics were explicitly used in composition? What would a math-based composition sound like? In this lecture, we'll explore ways to explicitly use mathematics and the tools of mathematics to write and analyze music. We'll take a chronological tour through explicit uses of mathematics in composition, going from 1600 up to modern times.

Musical Dice

- The waltz by Mozart we heard at the beginning of the lecture is an example of algorithmic music, produced by a set of rules. It actually stems from an 18th-century European tradition called Musikalisches Würfelspiel, "musical dice games."

- The idea was to compose a large number of measures, all in the same key, and then to make the measures harmonically interchangeable, sort of like puzzle pieces. The players would then write out a chart with instructions on exactly how to pick from these measures, and musicians would play the music based on the roll of a pair of dice. Today, there are online sites that allow you to play a similar game.

- To count the number of waltzes Mozart could compose with this game, we need to use something called the "multiplication principle."
    - A simple version of this is as follows: If you have 3 shirts to choose from and 4 pairs of pants, that gives you 12 possible outfits ($3 \times 4 = 12$). If you have 3 shirts, 4 pairs of pants, and 2 belts, you have 24 different outfits.

o   With Mozart's algorithmic waltzes, there are 11 choices for each of the measures (because the dice can roll anything from 2 to 11), and there are 16 different measures to choose. That's like having 16 different parts of an outfit; thus, we have 11^{16}, which is roughly 4.5×10^{16}, or 45 quadrillion.

o   But Mozart did not actually have all those possibilities. Look closely at the eighth measure. If you roll a 2, you get measure 30. If you roll a 3, you get measure 81. If you roll a 4, you get measure 24. But when you look at those measures, they are all exactly the same. The roll doesn't matter.

o   You'll always get the same thing for measure 8. In other words, there aren't 11 ways of choosing measure 8; there is really only 1 way to choose measure 8. Similarly, with the 16th measure, there are really only 2 choices.

o   To incorporate that information into our analysis, we need to revise the original number of choices, 11^{16}. Two of those 11s become a 1 and a 2, which leaves us with fourteen 11s. The number we get is 2×11^{14}, or about 759 trillion.

•   Is each one of those 759 trillion options equally likely? The answer is no because the odds of rolling different combinations of dice are different. For example, you have about a 3 percent chance of rolling double 1s but an 11 percent chance of rolling a 9 because there are more ways to roll a 9 (4 and 5, 5 and 4, 3 and 6, 6 and 3). Thus, you're much more likely to get some measures than others.

•   Mozart wasn't the first to compose algorithmic music; the first composer to do so was probably Giovanni Andrea Bontempi.
    o   In 1660, he wrote something called "A New Method for Composing for Four Voices, by means of which one thoroughly ignorant of the art of music can begin to compose." The idea was to give people with no composition skills tools to compose music. Other composers who used this method included Joseph Haydn and C. P. E. Bach, Johann's son.

    o   These Baroque and classical examples of math-based composition are much more tame than what we'll hear later on.

The Progression toward Atonality

- The 19th century continued the progression toward atonality. As you'll recall, this means having no tonal center, no main key on which to begin and end and to return to throughout a composition. Composers moved away from reliance on a single scale or multiple related scales. By 1900, composers were challenging the notions of what music is.

- In 1885, Franz Liszt wrote *Bagatelle sans tonalité*, "Bagatelle with no tonality." In 1894, Claude Debussy wrote *Prelude to the Afternoon of a Faun*, which again, pushed the boundaries of avoiding tonality.
  - o   This music was not always well-received. In 1913, the premiere of Igor Stravinsky's *Rite of Spring* sparked a riot in Paris.

  - o   That composition represents almost the height of this increase in dissonance, that is, using intervals that are not prevalent in the overtone series.

- The use of dissonance was taken to its logical extreme by Arnold Schoenberg with 12-tone music and atonality.
  - o   Schoenberg was born in Vienna in 1874. He played the violin and cello, and by 1909, he had arrived at his ideas for what he called "pantonal" music.

  - o   Schoenberg was working around the same time that cubism was emerging in the art world, with the work of Picasso and Georges Braque. He was equally revolutionary in terms of his composition and performance.

  - o   In 1920, he teamed with two of his students, Alban Berg and Anton Webern, forming the Second Viennese School.

- All music theory up to that point had assumed tonality—a foundational note or scale—and by design, some of those notes were more prominent than others. Schoenberg had to search to find a replacement for the structure that tonality provided, and he found it in math. His work used the mathematics that we saw in Lecture 8, especially the Z_{12} group, as well as transformations, inversions, retrograde, and retrograde inversions.

- Schoenberg's goal was to avoid any sense of tonality, and his solution was to force himself to use all the notes with equal frequency.
  - He started with a tone row using each piano note once. We're thinking about modulo octaves, so he's using each of the 12 notes once, but he hasn't decided which octave A might come from; C could be from any other octave. And he does this in a serial way. The tone row is sort of the foundation of a series of tones.

  - In 12-tone music, no tone dominates. That's why it's called "atonal music." Schoenberg did this by structure intentionally. He actually preferred the word "pantonal," not atonal, meaning a synthesis of all of the keys, not avoiding any one key.

- Let's see if we can crudely demonstrate Schoenberg's methods with a simple piece. Instead of working with 12 notes, we'll work with 5 notes. Mathematically, we're going to think about working modulo 5, that is, looking at the remainders when we divide by 5, and those would be 0, 1, 2, 3, and 4.
  - We start by randomly ordering those 5 notes—2, 3, 1, 0, 4—then, we transpose. We start at 0 and add 3 to each one. Working modulo 5, we get $3 + 2 = 0$, $3 + 3 = 1$, $3 + 1 = 4$, $3 + 0 = 3$, and $3 + 4 = 2$. That's our tone row: 0, 1, 4, 3, 2. We then write down the inversion of this, the retrograde, and the retrograde inversion, and then we have to translate the numbers into notes. To do that, we think of A being represented by 0, B by 1, and so on up through E, 4.

  - Next, we have to choose such elements as note lengths, the octave from which we will pick the notes, and the rests.

That gives us a piece of music composed using some of Schoenberg's ideas, although he used all 12 notes and we've used only 5.

- We hear the opening of the fifth piano piece from Schoenberg's Opus 23, *Five Pieces for Piano*. Remember, his goal was to explicitly avoid tonality—the predominance of any single key or scale. He did this using a mathematically based tone row system to ensure that in every group of 12 notes, each half note appears exactly once. Such music places heavy demands on both the performer and the audience.

- Schoenberg's system always referred to a starting point, 0. An alternative method is to pick a starting note, go up four half-steps, use that as the reference point, go up two half-steps, use that as a reference point, and go down three half-steps, similar to bootstrapping. With this system, it's difficult to tell whether notes have been duplicated.
  - A Russian math student and music lover named Vladimir Viro encoded the musical parts in this alternative to the Schoenberg system. He then used a music database to digitize a great number of classical compositions and make them searchable.

  - Viro's database searches only changes and pitch, and it can find melodies no matter the key. His mathematical encoding, which is very similar to what Schoenberg did, makes the search possible.

Aleatory, Spectral, and Computer-Programmed Music
- In the 1950s, music took a turn back toward mathematics, reintroducing randomness into concert music. This is called "aleatory music" or "chance music." The most famous composer of chance music, and possibly the most influential composer of the 20th century, was John Cage.

- Cage was known for his radical experiments. He wrote pieces for "prepared piano," where he placed bolts and screws on top of the strings to alter the sounds as he played. He composed for dance accompaniment with Merce Cunningham's group. He composed based on James Joyce's *Finnegan's Wake*. He composed for melting ice sculptures. He composed a piece called *Organ/ASLSP* ("as slow as possible"); one performance of this piece began in 2001 and is scheduled to end in 2640.

Wind chimes play a version of aleatory music, in which pitches are chosen at random by the wind.

- Perhaps Cage's most famous piece is *4'33"* ("4 minutes and 33 seconds"). This is a piece with no notes. It's written for piano in three movements, and it's timed. The pianist is supposed to sit at the piano for three movements that add up to 4 minutes and 33 seconds. This work seems to be a musical version of the mathematical concept of 0.

- Cage began composing chance music around 1950, making a transition from creation to acceptance—accepting the results of chance. He also gave the performer a degree of uncertainty and randomness. Some compositions require the performer to do random things and play based on the results.
  - This kind of composition introduces mathematical questions. What kind of randomness is Cage using? What is the sample space? When we were talking about Mozart's dice game, there was a sample space where 7 and 9 were more likely than 2 or 12. One of the sample spaces Cage used was a Chinese text called the *Yijing*, the "*Book of Changes.*"

o   Cage would compose based on the charts of the *Yijing*, choosing pitches, rhythms, tempo, and so on. One of the results was a 1951 piece called *Music of Changes*.

o   In 1961 and 1962, he used the randomness of star charts to compose *Atlas Eclipticalis*. In 1983, he used the particular rock formation in the Zen temple in Kyoto, Japan, the Ryoanji Temple.

o   Other composers stretched the idea of randomness even further. Charles Dodge, for example, composed a piece called *Earth's Magnetic Field*, in which the pitch changes were taken from the changes in the earth's magnetic field resulting from solar winds.

- Spectral music comes from a European tradition of trying to create the spectrum. Recall from Lecture 2 that the spectrum showed us how much of each overtone we would hear. Mathematically, it was the Fourier transform of the wave form that gave us the spectrum. In Gérard Grisey's *Périodes*, seven instruments were used to re-create the spectrum of a trombone.

- Many programmers are using computers these days to compose program music. One of the most prolific is David Cope, who has done extensive work in this field, including work to emulate Mozart. The algorithms he uses range from fairly simple to highly complicated, bordering on the field of artificial intelligence.

Using Math to Analyze Music
- Music theorists have used mathematics in many different fields to analyze music. Some of the most interesting results here come from the recent work of Princeton's Dmitri Tymoczko, who is working on the geometry of music, in particular the geometry of two-note chords.

- The geometry of a one-note chord is fairly simple. Remember that the notes run from A all the way through G-sharp, and then the next A is really the same thing as the original A if we're thinking modulo octave. Thus, the geometry of a one-note chord is a circle.

- If we had two notes, we would get two coordinates, so we would have A, A-sharp, B laid out on the x coordinate and A, A-sharp, B on the y coordinate. Each two-note chord would be a spot on a 12 × 12 grid.
    - If we had a chord with G and C, physically, we would have many options for playing that because we could pick the G and C from any octave we wanted, but those would all be examples of a G, C two-note chord.

    - What happens if we wrap this into a circle, as we did for the one-note chords? At first, we might think that the two-note chords form a torus, but when we eliminate redundancy in the chords, we find that we get a Möbius strip.

- Tymoczko's work shows us that the space of two-note chords has the geometry of a Möbius strip, and any sequence of two-note chords is really just a path along the Möbius strip. This is a new way to visualize and study music.

Suggested Reading

Forte, *The Structure of Atonal Music*.

Harkleroad, *The Math behind the Music*, chapters 5–6.

Lewin, *Generalized Musical Intervals and Transformations*.

Loy, *Musimathics*, vol. 1, chapter 9.

Perle, *Serial Composition and Atonality*.

Wright, *Mathematics and Music*, chapter 6.

Questions to Consider

1. How have the ideas of probability been used by composers, both in the classical era and in modern times?

2. How did the atonal and 12-tone composers ensure that their compositions didn't accidentally become tonal?

Composing with Math—Classical to Avant-Garde
Lecture 10—Transcript

Let's start by helping Mozart compose a piece of music. Okay, one more. All right, now, just watch and listen. I'll explain what we've just done in a second. That was actually a Mozart waltz. Now you probably don't recognize that work of Mozart. It was one of over 759 trillion pieces that he wrote. Confused? Maybe you know your Kochel listings, that's the complete catalog of all of Mozart. You know that the last work listed in that catalog is the Requiem at #626. Now some numbers are missing and some of them are doubled, but 759 trillion. You know he died at age 35, that's just not possible. What's the catch here? Mozart and I just used mathematics probability, to compose that tune. The composition was mathematically generated. More about that in a second.

So far we've been talking about composing music for a while. Scales, rhythms, transformations—these are all important aspects of composition, but in each case the mathematics is sort of imbedded. It's implicit. The composers aren't necessary thinking about the math, although now you know that they really are doing some math. What if the mathematics were explicitly used in composition? What would a math-based composition sound like? Well, you heard one already today and we're going to hear a lot more throughout today's lecture.

Today we're going to talk about ways to explicitly use mathematics and tools of mathematics to write and to analyze music. Remember when we were talking about transformations and self- reference, those things were analogies. Bach did not use group theory to compose his canons. In fact, group theory hadn't really been discovered and hadn't written down his group theory yet. The canons exhibited similar structures to what would later be called groups. These were powerful analogies. They helped us understand the music better. Today we're looking at explicit uses of mathematics in musical composition and in musical analysis. These ways help us gain an even deeper understanding of how math relates to musical composition. Today we're going to take a chronological tour through these explicits— these literal uses of mathematics in composition, going from 1600 up to modern time.

So let's go to the opening music, Mozart's waltz. It's an example of algorithmic music, produced by a set of rules. Sometimes with chance and as you saw with the dice, today's is with chance. Part of an 18th-century European tradition called Musikalisches Würfelspiel, musical dice games. To quote from the instructions of the Mozart waltz, the goal of this was to compose without the least knowledge of music so many German waltzes as one pleases by throwing a certain number with two dice. It's almost like a musical paint by number sort of thing. You get a different result every time or nearly every time.

So how do they make the music sound good? Well the idea was compose a large number of measures, all in the same key and then to make the measures harmonically interchangeable. They were sort of like puzzle pieces but many different pieces could fit in a particular place in this puzzle. Then they would write out a chart with instructions on exactly how to pick from these measures. Then they would sit back and watch the musicians roll the dice and place a new piece every time. It's sort of like an 18th-century parlor game.

Let's look back at this opening waltz. The instructions say, well, to choose measure one, I was supposed to roll two dice, I got a four and a five, add those together and that gives us a nine, and then find the ninth entry in that column. That particular one was 119. And then I'm supposed to go to the table of measures and look for measure #119 and that's going to be my first measure in my new waltz. Now that's just one of 11 possible openings for the first measure. To get the second measure, I looked at column two. Again, I roll the dice and again I get something between 2 and 12; 2 for snake eyes and 12 for double 6s and then I choose the measure appropriate for that. Now there are 11 choices for column two, measure two. So that makes 11 x 11 possibilities just for the first two measures.

In the opening waltz, well, I happened to roll the following sequence of numbers, a 9, 9, 3, 6, 9, 9, 9, 6, those are the first eight bars and then the last eight bars was a 9, 9, 11, 9, 5, 9, 4, and 6. I was really lucky with the 9s; I don't know why, and that gave us the following measure numbers and those were the measure numbers that I was supposed to pick from the list of measures that Mozart wrote. Let's hear it again now that we know exactly how it was constructed.

It's actually even a little bit more complicated than that because Mozart did not write this for violin. He actually wrote it for piano and there's a baseline. There's a line for the left hand on the piano.

But what if we want to hear more possibilities? If you want to hear more possibilities, instead of taking the time to roll out dice, write out the score and then play it, there are online sites that will generate them and play them, and show you the music very quickly. So, let's actually count the number of waltzes that Mozart was composing in this. And to do that we need something called the multiplication principle.

Now you might know a simple version of this. If you have three shirts to choose from and four pairs of pants, that gives you 12 possible outfits because 3 x 4 is 12. If you had three shirts, four pants, and two belts, now you have 24 different outfits. You multiply those numbers. Let's apply that to Mozart's algorithmic waltzes. Now there's 11 choices for each of the bars because the dice can roll anything from a 2 to an 11, and there are 16 different bars, different measures to choose. So that's like having 16 different parts of your outfit, so you have 11 x 11 sixteen times. When you do that multiplication, 11^{16} is 4.5×10^{16} roughly, and that's 45 quadrillion.

Not so fast, you see, Mozart did not actually have those possibilities. If we look closely at the eighth column, the eighth measure. If you roll a 2, you get measure 30. If you roll a 3, you get measure 81. If you roll a 4, you get measure 24. But when you look at those measures, all those measures are exactly the same. The roll doesn't matter at all. You'll always get the same thing for your measure 8. In other words, there aren't 11 ways of choosing measure 8; there's really only one way to choose measure 8.

Similarly, the last measure of the piece, the 16th measure, there are really only two choices. So now we have to incorporate that into our analysis and so now instead of 11^{16}, two of those 11s become a 1 and a 2, and then we have fourteen 11s. So the number we get is 2×11^{14} and that is 759 trillion and a few more. It's actually a number that's larger than the U.S. National debt. It's hard to find a number that's larger than the U.S. National debt, but we've done it.

Now, is each one of those 759 trillion from compositions? Is each one of those equally likely? No. You see when you roll two dice, what happens, the odds of getting snake eyes, double 1s, and the odds of that happening are 1 in 36, just about a 3 percent chance. The odds of rolling a 9 on the other hand— well, you could roll a 4 and a 5, a 5 and a 4, a 3 and a 6, a 6 and a 3, it's 4 out of 36, it's one-ninth. It's about 11 percent chance of rolling a 9. You're much more likely to get some measures than others. Actually, 7 is the most likely sum. Seven happens about 1/6 of the time, about 17 percent. The measures listed in the middle of the table are most likely. The measures listed at the top and the bottom are least likely. Now I happened to roll a lot of 9s, that means the piece you heard was actually very unlikely to come from this process.

Mozart wasn't the first to compose algorithmic music. The first attempt that I know of is Giovanni Andrea Bontempi in 1660. He wrote something called "A New Method of Composing for Four Voices" by means of which one thoroughly ignorant of the art of music can begin to compose. You can see how this is like a paint-by-number. People with no composition skills can use these tools to compose music. It was a fun game. The idea was to make composing easy and fun. Now, are these compositions real music? That's a good question.

In 1757, Johann Philipp Kirnberger wrote the "Eveready Polonaise and Minuet Composer." Now this was not just for a couple of lines, but for two violins and piano. Now, like Mozart's later work, Mozart's work of 1787, he used rolls of dice to determine which measures and all those measures were prewritten. Other composers jumped on the musical dice game band wagon. Joseph Haydn did so and C.P.E. Bach, that's Johann Sebastian's son. He was one of 20 or more kids that Bach had and he was the one who wrote the note about Bach's death. There were other composers as well. Now, in our modern age we can use computers to produce such music and we can generate these results very quickly and play them. You wouldn't have to sit in the parlor and keep rolling the dice.

These Baroque and classical examples of math-based composition are much more tame than what we're going to see later on, the later uses of mathematics in music. Remember back in lecture 5, we talked about the co-evolution of composition in tuning. The 19th century continued the progression towards atonality. Remember this is having no tonal center, no main key, no note that you kept coming back to again and again that you probably started the piece and ended the piece on. Throughout that century they were moving away from this reliance on, you know, single scale or multiple related scales. By the time we get to 1900, composers were really challenging the notions of what is music. In 1885, Franz Liszt wrote Bagatelle sans tonalité; a Bagatelle with no tonality. So intentionally avoiding this sort of tonality.

In 1894, Claude Debussy wrote "Prelude to the Afternoon of a Faun," which again pushed the boundaries of avoiding tonality. Now, this music was not always well-received. In 1913, Igor Stravinsky premiered his "Rite of Spring." It's a ballet with orchestra. The premier was at a new theater, Théâtre des Champs-Élysées, in Paris. During the performance, audience members argued out loud about the ruckus music with strong accents off the beat, bom, bom, bom, bom, bom, just like that, and sort of seemingly random accents, and the radical choreography by Nijinsky. Now perhaps they were spurred by hot weather and the fact that many of the people in the audience were tourists. Whatever the cause is, they actually came to blows over this and it evolved into a full-blown riot. Police were actually called in all over an artistic performance, "The Rite of Spring." This represents sort of nearing the end of the increase in dissonance, using intervals that are not prevalent in the overtone series. There were less reliance on standard scale and keys. This was finally taken to its logical extreme by Arnold Schoenberg with 12-tone music and atonality.

So let's look at that. Schoenberg was born in Vienna in 1874. He played the violin and cello and by 1909 he had arrived at these ideas of atonality. He did so with a couple of pieces, one was three pieces for piano, which is Opus 11, and the other is a song cycle written around the same time. If you think about the art world, this is right around the same time as the rise of Cubism with Picasso and Braque. Schoenberg was revolutionary in terms of his composition and in terms of performance. He founded the society for private musical performances. At the society, there were no critics allowed, there was no advanced program announced beforehand, and there was no applause after the pieces.

Now by 1920, he had teamed with two of his students, Alban Berg and Anton Webern. And they formed what they like to call the Second Viennese School. Their implication in calling the Second Viennese School was that they were the natural heirs to Haydn, Mozart, and Beethoven, who would be considered sort of the first Viennese School.

Now all music theory up to that point had really assumed tonality. It assumed that there was a primary key, a foundational note or scale. And by design some of those notes were more prominent than others. Schoenberg had to search to find a replacement for the structure that tonality provided and he found it in math. His work used the mathematics from lecture 8, things about group theory, especially things like $Z12$, the group with 12 elements in it, and transformations, eversions, retrograde, retrograde inversions.

Those ideas are all very key in Schoenberg's work. His goal was to avoid any sense of tonality. To avoid scales, avoid relying on a specific set of notes, avoid the tonal center, to not return to a particular note. His solution was to force himself to use all the notes with equal frequency. He started with a tone row using each piano note once. We're thinking modulo octaves, so he's using each of the 12 notes once but he hasn't decided which octave A might come from. He's looking at C and now for C it could be any other octave. And he's doing this in a serial way. The tone row is sort of the foundation of a series of tone.

In 12-tone music, no tone dominates. That's why we call it atonal music. He did this by structure intentionally. Schoenberg actually preferred the word "pantonal" not atonal. Pantonal meaning sort of a synthesis of all of the keys, not avoiding any one key. So let's see if we can crudely demonstrate Schoenberg's methods with a simple piece. Instead of working with 12 notes, let's work with five notes. Now, mathematically, we're going to think about working modulo 5, looking at the remainders when you divide by 5 and so those numbers would be just 0, 1, 2, 3, and 4.

Now, let's randomly order these five notes. Let's choose 2, 3, 1, 0, 4. Now we're going to transpose. We're going to make sure we start at 0. Let's add 3 to each one, so we add 3 to 2 and we get 0. Remember, we're working modulo 5. And 3+3 is 6, which gives us a 1; 3+1 is 4; 3+0 is 3; and 3+4 is

7, which gives us a 2 in working mod 5. So that's our tone row, that's row1, 0, 1, 4, 3, 2. Now let's write down the inversion of this, the retrograde, the retrograde inversion, and then finally we have to translate these into notes. We're translating the numbers into notes.

When we do that, let's think of A being represented by 0, B is 1, all the way through E is 4. And now we have to choose things like the note lengths, which octave we're going to pick these notes from, the rests. So, we're going to do that and I've written out a piece of music and by design once we have this chart, each note appears exactly once in each row and when we write our music based on this, we get to choose the note values and how long and put rests in when we want. Now, there's an important note about this, because I chose just five of the notes on our scale, it's violating a key principle of Schoenberg. You see, he used all 12 notes equally likely and I've completely ignored seven of them. But let's hear what we have here. When we take this and we play it, it sounds like this. That should give you some idea of the methods that Schoenberg was using.

But now let's turn to the actual 12 tones that he was working with. So, Schoenberg and his colleagues used a more complex version. It's the same idea, but with 12 note names, A, A-sharp, all the way through G-sharp. And what we're going to hear is something from Opus 23. It's five piano pieces. We're going to listen to the fifth one. The tone row that Schoenberg was using in this composition is the following. He got these numbers and then those corresponded to these notes.

These are the notes you'll hear at the very beginning, but before we get to the music, we have to add the transformations. So, he took the tone row, he took the inversion, the retrograde, the retrograde inversion, and all of these. All of these weren't enough and so what he did is he took that tone row and he used the transposition of that tone row to get the first column and then he wrote out the transposition of the original tone row along each of the rows.

For instance, one of the notes on that first column was a 3 and so that's transposing up three half steps from the original tone row. If you look, the row with 3 starting it is exactly three numbers above the original row. Now he adds one more layer of complexity before he gets to the actual composition.

He now has 12 rows to work with, and now he takes each one of those rows and writes out the inversion, the retrograde, and the retrograde inversion. And now he has 48 different rows to work with and by design, because of the mathematics, each note appears exactly once in each of those rows. Tonality is intentionally avoided. No note is more important than the others.

So we're going to listen to the opening of the fifth piece of Schoenberg's Opus 23, five pieces for piano. Remember, his goal here is to explicitly avoid tonality. The predominance of any single key or scale and he did this using a mathematically-based tone row system to ensure that in every group of 12 notes, each note appears exactly once. Remember the tone row here, starting with C-sharp, A, B, G, all of those notes. If you look carefully at the right hand of this piece, it's those 12 notes exactly in a row. Tonality was successfully avoided by Schoenberg.

So let's quickly listen to these the first four opening bars, where you can hear the tone row explicitly in the right hand. Let's listen to them. Now, let's listen to that in context of the larger piece. Schoenberg continues using various lines created from these transformations, from these 48 rows that he has based on the tone row and he is forcing himself to use all of those of notes equally, always avoiding tonality. So here's the fifth of the five pieces for piano by Schoenberg.

Let's look at the attitudes towards Schoenberg, because there really is nothing easy about Schoenberg or really any of the serial 12-tone compositions. They place heavy demands on both the performer and the audience. They are really cerebral. They're pushing music to its furthest limits. If you look up in the *Oxford Dictionary of Music*, it says in the entry on Schoenberg and I quote, "His greatness lies not only in his own music but in his artistic courage and in his powerful and continuing influence on 20th century music. He is likely to remain always a controversial, revered and revolutionary musician."

If we look at other composers, they were all listing these 12 notes out and they were listing these 12 notes out starting with the first one and then going through these 12 notes. They were all doing about the same thing, composing their serial 12-tone music. I want to look at an alternative, but similar system because it has something that's going on in modern times that's very interesting related to it.

You see for Schoenberg, he would write out all the 12 notes and when we think of these in numbers, it's 0 through 11. He would write those out and it's always in reference to sort of the starting point, 0, then 4, 6, 3, 1, always in reference to the starting point. An alternative way of doing this is to pick a starting note and then to go up four half steps. And then to use that as your reference point and go up two half steps. To use that as your reference point, go down three half steps. It's sort of like bootstrapping that we did when we were tuning things.

Now there's a reason that the 12-tone folks wouldn't have liked the system at all because it's hard to tell if you've duplicated notes, so it's not very effective at avoiding tonality. But there is an upside to this that came out in the last few years. It has to do with numerical encoding of a melody and making that melody searchable.

Most classical music, most concert music, is now in the public domain. Around 2006, a teenager named Edward Guo, who is a violinist and a pianist, decided to create an online database of classical sheet music so that everybody could have access to this free and online. He made it into a Wiki so everybody could add music as they saw fit. This is now named the International Music Score Library Project. You can find it at IMSLP.org.

Another teenager used this to create a classical music melody search. It was the Russian math student and music lover named Vladimir Viro who encoded all these musical parts in this alternative to Schoenberg system, where instead of referencing the first note, he is telling you how far to go from that note to get to the next. He used the IMSLP, the music database, to digitize lots of music. Let's see exactly how this works.

So suppose a melody pops into my head. I'm not sure from where, somehow your brain stores music. We're going to talk about that in lecture 12. Suppose the following melody pops into my head. And I just can't seem to remember where this melody is from. What I can do is I can go to Viro's search engine, it's at peachnote.com. I can type in the notes, not how long they are but just the notes. What I would type in is this. You can actually see on the search engine and you can see that it's encoding that as 66. Sixty-six is the piano key, I started on the 66th piano key. Then it encodes it as -2, -2, -1, -2 and what that's telling you is how many half steps to go up or down to get to the next note.

He's completely ignoring rhythm in the same way that Schoenberg and the 12-tone composers ignored rhythm completely. When you hit return, this is what you get. It tells you that this particular note pattern appeared in several places and then it shows you a timeline of when those place happen and, in particular, it shows you that it was Tchaikovsky Fifth Symphony. It even provides you a link to the score.

So let's look at the score. In fact, we found the melody. It was Tchaikovsky's Fifth Symphony that I was thinking about. Let's play it and in its original. Now, it didn't search, in fact, it found it even though the key was wrong. It didn't search 66 and then up and down from there the changes and pitch. It just searched the changes and the pitch. The brilliance of that is that it can find it no matter what key you're working in. So, I was able to find this particular piece. It was able to find it as Tchaikovsky's Fifth Symphony, even though I had the key wrong. I don't have perfect pitch so I wasn't sure where it started. The mathematical encoding of this melody, which was very similar to what Schoenberg used, makes this all possible.

Let's go back to our timeline, looking at other composers and how they explicitly use mathematics in their composition. In the 1950s, music took a turn back toward mathematics, reintroducing randomness into concert music. This is called aleatory music. This is from the Latin alea, meaning dice, and sometimes also called chance music. There's actually a version of aleatory music that you probably hear fairly frequently. Wind chimes are a version of aleatory music, which pitches you hear is sort of chosen at random, not by any person but by the wind.

Now the most famous composer of chance music, possibly the most influential composer of the 20th century was John Cage. John Cage was born in Los Angeles in 1912. He died in New York in 1992. He studied at Pomona College with Schoenberg in the '30s and purportedly Schoenberg said of this his only interesting American student, "Of course, he's not a composer, but he's an inventor of genius." Now it's telling that we get that quote from Cage's version of the events.

Cage was known for his radical experiments. He wrote pieces for prepared piano, so he took the piano and he added bolts and screws on top of the strings and they would bounce around and make sounds. He composed for dance accompaniment with Merce Cunningham's group. He composed for pre-recorded tape with TVs. He composed based on Joyce's *Finnegan's Wake*. He composed for ice sculptures which contained pebbles and the pebbles would fall onto wires when the ice melted and make sounds. He composed a piece called "Organ ASLSP", where the letters A-S-L-S-P were taken sort of an idiosyncratic acronym of "As Slow As Possible." One performance of Organ ASLSP began in 2001 and it's scheduled to end in 2640. John Cage's most famous piece was probably "4 minutes and 33 seconds." This is a piece with no notes. It's written for piano in three movements and it's timed. The pianist is supposed to sit there for three movements that add up to 4 minutes and 33 seconds.

I go to perform this a year ago. An older gentleman in the front row misheard the title and about 2 minutes in I heard him whisper to his friend, this is a lot longer than 33 seconds. For me, Cage's "4 minutes and 33 seconds" is actually a musical version of a mathematical concept. That concept is zero. Both zero and a piece without notes, these are sort of symbols for nothing. I think it requires a certain inspiration to realize that you can do something with nothing. Now, zero was essentially only invented twice by the Mayans and the Indians. The other numbers were invented by lots of different cultures. In Indian it was Pingala, the poet we heard about when we were talking about the Fibonacci sequence. He started to use zero back when he was writing poetry.

Cage was the first to see the complete absence of notes as music. Cage had a lot of different influences and many of these were from the East, India, Japan, Japanese philosophy, especially Zen writings, and other parts of Japanese culture. Now Cage's use of mathematics came in an interesting way. He started composing chance music around 1950. He sort of moved from being a composer, from creating, to sort of, what you would call, accepting; accepting the results of chance. He also gave the performer some sort of uncertainty and some randomness. Some compositions require the performer to do random things and then play based on that.

There are mathematical questions in here. What kind of randomness is he using? Technically, the question is, "What's the sample space?" When we were talking about Mozart's dice game to open this lecture, there was a sample space where 7 and 9 were more likely than 2 or 12. So you could ask questions about Cage's sample space. Now one of the sample spaces Cage used was actually a Chinese text called the *Yi Jing*, the *Chinese Book of Changes*. If you don't know it, it was described to me by one of my older Chinese relatives as like an ancient Chinese magic 8-ball.

Now, Cage would ask the *Yi Jing* to compose and he would compose based on the responses he got from this chart. Choosing from the chart the pitches, the rhythms, the tempo, the dynamics, all based on what he got from this chart. One of the results was a 1951 piece called "Music of Changes." The rest of Cage's life he used chance elements. He used randomness drawn from many different places in his music. In '61 and '62, he used the randomness of star charts to compose "Atlas Eclipticalis". In '83, he used the particular rock formations in the Zen Temple in Kyoto, Japan, the Ryoanji Temple.

He used those rock formations to compose a piece. He was really stretching the idea of randomness and other composers stretched it even further. Charles Dodge composed a piece called "Earth's Magnetic Field," where the pitch changes were taken from the changes in the earth's magnetic field and those changes were due to solar winds. I think you'll agree the effect of this sort of celestial source of randomness sounds, well, it sounds very random. Let's listen to a bit from Dodge's piece.

We are going to take one last stop in this mathematical composition after hearing that Dodge piece, and that last stop is spectral music. Now, spectral music comes from a European tradition. The European tradition was looking at trying to create the spectrum. Remember the spectrum from lecture 2. The spectrum showed you how much of each overtone you're going to hear. And this European tradition was based on that. You could actually see this graph. You could see in the spectrum you have these different peaks at different frequencies and that was the timbre, how high each one of those peaks were. Mathematically, it was the Fourier Transform of the waveform that gave us the spectrum. Remember the jump rope and the drum heads were showing the different modes that something could vibrate in. Now spectral music was trying to use different ways of using that spectrum to create music. One particular piece, Grisey's *Périodes*—seven instruments were used to re-create the spectrum of a trombone, so the entire piece led up to the final chord where these seven instruments were combined to try to re-create the timbre of a trombone.

Now there's some inversions of using mathematics to compose music that we have not covered. In particular, there are a lot of computer programmers who use computers to compose or maybe we should say compute or maybe program music. One of the most prolific is David Cope who has done extensive work, including work to emulate Mozart. The algorithms he uses range from fairly simple to highly complicated algorithms and they are really bordering on a field of artificial intelligence. We're going to save this for lecture 12 when we talk about math and music in the mind.

I do have a little bonus today for the mathematically inclined. So far we've talked about using math to write music and this last bit is going to be about using math to analyze music. Now there are a lot of different ways to do this and different music theorists have used many different methods including statistics. But maybe the most surprising comes from the recent work of Princeton's Dmitri Tymoczko. He is working on the geometry of music, and a lot of his work is very complicated, both mathematically and musically, but one of his early results is probably the easiest to understand.

He looked at the geometry of two-note chords. So let's take a look at that. Now the geometry of one-note chords is fairly simple. Remember you have notes A, A-sharp, all the way through G-sharp, and then A is really the same thing as the original A if we're thinking modulo octave. And so the ends of this wrap around and give you a circle. So the geometry of one-note chords, which are just single notes. The geometry of that is just a circle. When we think about the mathematics of that, that's just Z12, just like addition modulo 12 where you are looking at remainders when you divide by 12.

Another way of thinking about this is that you could take the G-sharp that you ended up at and you could glue it to the A. Or if you got to the A you can glue the two As together and paste them together, and that's how you might get the circle. Now all of this is synching modulo octave, right? So we're treating all of these notes as all of the different octaves of C-sharp as being the same.

What if you had two notes? Then you would get two coordinates. So you would have A, A-sharp, B laid out on the x-coordinate and then you would have A, A-sharp and B on the y-coordinate. And each two-note chord would be a spot on this 12 x 12 grid. If you had a chord with the G and a C, you would find that on the G, C spot in our chart. Physically, you would have many options for playing that because you could pick the G and the C from any octave you wanted but those would all be examples of a G, C two-note chords. Now we have to remember that both the x- and the y-axis, these notes aren't aligned, but we just figured out that that should really be wrapped into a circle. So, what happens when we do that?

Well, look at everything in the x-axis, everything in the first column has As and everything in the last column has G-sharps and those are supposed to be right next to each other. So when we tape those so that they are right next to each other, we geometrically get a cylinder. But now look along the cylinder and now everything in the bottom ring of that cylinder is an A and that should all connect to everything on the top ring of that cylinder, which is G-sharp. When we connect those, the result is what mathematicians call a torus, the surface of a doughnut. So, we might think that we're done.

We might think that two-note chords form a torus, but when we look back at the chart we see that we've done something wrong. The G, C chord we were talking about earlier does not appear just in the G, C part of the chart, it also appears in the C, G spot. So we really double counted our construction of the torus, double counts the chord, so we don't have the geometry quite right yet. These two-note chords don't form a torus. It's actually better than that. Let's see if we can fix this.

In order to fix this, we're going to have to get into a little bit of gluing. Before we were gluing the first column to the last column, we saw that those were supposed to wrap around. But now what we've seen is if we look at it like A, B is the same chord as B, A, and A-sharp, C is the same chord as C, A-sharp. If we look along the first row, all of those are really the same thing as the first column, so really we also have to glue the first row to the last column. That's hard, especially if when we look at the direction of the glued edges. You see, the first and the last column are glued together in the same direction.

If you look at the arrows, the arrows are telling you what direction to glue these. But now the first row is also supposed to be glued to both of those. We're supposed to glue that starting at one corner and ending at the other. So the first row is supposed to be glued to the last column with the bottom left corner glued to the bottom right corner. You just can't do it; you can't do it physically. If you try this with a piece of paper, you'll have to crumble it up and you won't be able to do it. But notice that once we've sort of abstracted it to just this rectangle, we really just have abstracted the core mathematical ideas from this musical thing and now we just have a math problem to do.

So now let's see if we can fix this gluing problem. To fix this remember that there was redundancy and if you looked closely the double counting happen at the bottom and the top of these triangles. The bottom triangle contained all of the chords and the top triangle contained all of those chords again. So, that's where the double counting was. If we want to figure out the geometry of two-note chords, let's just remove the top triangle and if we get rid of the top triangle, then we have every chord represented just once.

Now we only have two edges we're supposed to glue to each other. We're supposed to glue the bottom edge to the right edge, but again the direction of that gluing makes that very difficult. To fix this, we're going to do something that mathematicians actually call surgery. We're going to do topological surgery on this piece. We're going to cut the diagonal and we have to remember which way we're cutting the diagonals because later we're going to want to paste that back together. When you do surgery, you'll want to stitch the patient back up at the end. Let's cut along that diagonal and then let's flip the right triangle over.

Finally, we have to move that flipped triangle and then we have to move it into position where we can glue these two solid lines together. Once we've glued those two edges together, once we've finished repairing that, now look what we have. What we have is just a strip and if you look at the ends, the ends tell us how to glue those together and the ends are telling us we're supposed to glue it together not like we did originally, not like we would get a cylinder but in opposite directions we're supposed to glue the ends together with a twist.

We've seen a strip where we're supposed to glue ends together with a twist before. It was exactly the Mobius strip. We saw in a lecture on self-reference. We saw it in how we constructed a table canon and in a way that both players could play it continuously. We just took that strip and twisted it and pasted it together and that's what we're getting from this geometry of two-note chords. We get a Mobius strip.

So what does this mean? It means that, well, Tymoczko's work shows us that the space of two-note chords has the geometry of a Mobius strip and any sequence of a two-note chords is really just a path along the Mobius strip. This is a new way of visualizing music. If you take anything that has two notes at a time, each one of those pairs of two notes is a particular point on this Mobius strip and then you can follow the composition by just following a path on the Mobius strip. It's a new way to visualize music. It's a new way to study music, the music of chords that have two notes at a time.

Let's look at an example of this. I'm going to play a little bit from Pachelbel's Canon. I think this piece is played at nearly every other wedding that I go to. The piece actually has three identical violin parts and each one is delayed two measures from the previous and so each note has to function in three different ways. It functions first at the melody and then it functions as harmony two more times.

The baseline is probably the most boring part ever written for cello. It is the same eight notes repeated over and over and over again. I've had cellists tell me at the beginning of this piece, "You know, just nod to me when we're done cause then I'll finish. I don't want to have to read the music the whole time." In order to visualize exactly how Pachelbel's Canon sounds and how it looked on Tymoczko's Mobius strip, I'm going to play one of the violin parts and we're going to electronically add a baseline. That gives us two-note chords and we're going to show you where on the Mobius strip each two-note chord is.

You have to remember that this is a Mobius strip. We're going to show it to you as just sort of a rectangle from the screen, but when you go out the top of the right side, you come back in the bottom of the left side. If you go out the top of the left side, you come back in the bottom of the right side. That's the twist and that's what makes it a Mobius strip. So, here's the opening 16 measures of the Pachelbel Canon. It goes on and on like that.

If you want to see more of the geometry of chords, I encourage you to look at Tymoczko's website, which has really lots of interesting information on that. Today we went from Mozart's dice games to Cage's chance music to Tymochko's geometry. In all these cases, we saw that mathematics helps us compose and analyze music. Math also helps deliver it to us in a modern age where we have everything digitized in 0s and 1s, and that's what we'll talk about next time.

Thanks for joining us.

The Digital Delivery of Music
Lecture 11

In the course of these lectures, we've talked about vibrating objects and their overtones, and we've seen how to construct scales and cords. We then used that knowledge to find some compositional techniques that use mathematics. But how does music get to our ears? In this lecture, we will talk about an important but underappreciated subject: the digital delivery of music and the mathematics of that process. Specifically, we'll look at three ways that mathematics has changed the delivery of music in our digital world: the notes we hear, the number of songs we can fit into a smaller space, and how much cleaner music sounds now than it did in the early days of recording.

Delivery of Music

- The original delivery of music was only in person. Before about the time of the U.S. Civil War, no music had ever been recorded to be played back later. People traveled to hear concerts and had only two or three chances in their lifetimes to hear such works as Beethoven's Ninth Symphony.

- The first known musical recording was not from Edison but from Édouard-Léon Scott de Martinville singing "Clair de la Lune" in 1860. It was written to paper by something called a "phonautograph." This recording was not heard in sound until 2008, when it was reconstructed from lines drawn on this paper. The first music recorded onto a replayable cylinder was Handel's *Israel in Egypt*, recorded in 1888 for Edison.

- The move from cylinders to flat discs around 1890 made it possible to produce multiple copies of a recording. With this development came the rise of gramophone companies. Radio broadcasts of live music started around 1906 to 1910, and recording and playback quality quickly improved.

- Earlier technologies for recording sound resulted in degradation of the recorded media. Modern CDs don't degrade over time, but the manufacturing process for CDs introduces more than 10 errors per second on a disk—50,000 errors! Even so, most CDs sound fine when we play them.

The Mathematics of Pitch Correction

- Auto-Tune was invented by Antares Audio Technologies in 1997. It was first heard widely on Cher's album *Believe*. The idea behind Auto-Tune was to provide a digital fix for out-of-tune singing. The process involves two steps: pitch detection and pitch correction.

- For pitch detection, there are several options. Looking at the Fourier transform, we can see where the first peak is; that should be the fundamental frequency.

Victrolas and other gramophones were entirely mechanical, requiring no electricity to play.

The distance between the peaks also gives us the fundamental frequency, because they represent the fundamental frequency added to itself. If we wanted to stay on the wave form side, we could look at the distance between the wave repeating; that period should give us 1/frequency.

- Once we have done the pitch detection and we know a singer is singing at, say, 430 Hz, we can ask whether the frequency should be something else. In other words, is the singer out of tune? If we know that an A natural should be about 440, we can correct that note upward a bit.

- But we can't just shift the graph over 10 Hz because if the singer is singing at 430 Hz, we are also hearing the overtones at 860, 1290, 1720, and so on, when we should be hearing 880, 1320, and so on.
  - The key to remember here is that intervals are multiplicative, not additive, and that tells us how to get our solution.

  - To do the pitch correction, we should multiply, not add. To get from 430 to 440, we need to multiply by 44/43.

- Here's the process for auto-tuning we have so far: We start with a wave form. We compute the spectrum, we detect the frequency, we compare that with a table of correct frequencies, we multiply by a constant, and then we invert. We have to take the inverse Fourier transform to get back to the wave form. Now, we can simply play that corrected sound. In theory, we could adjust the tune of anything with this process, although in practice, it's a bit more complicated.

The Mathematics of Audio Compression
- If we recorded sound at its highest fidelity on a CD, the CD would hold less than two minutes of music. The problem here is that recorded audio and video simply contain too much information. The goal of audio compression is to reduce this amount of stored information while still minimizing the effect on the listening experience.

- The Victrola used a groove that was modeled on the wave form, so that when the needle went through the groove, it vibrated exactly as the wave form did. Digital audio uses 0s and 1s, but it's necessary to convert from a continuous wave form to discrete points that can be represented in this way. That process is called "sampling."

- Sampling a wave form involves identifying a number of points and deciding how tightly to space the points on the wave. More points gives a better sound, but fewer points reduces the size of the file for more storage.

- The mathematics needed for this sampling is called the Nyquist theorem, proved by Harry Nyquist in 1928. What Nyquist proved is that if we sample at frequency f, so that we are putting points every $1/f$ seconds, we will save information on all waves that have a frequency of less than $f/2$. If we think about this in terms of the Fourier transform, we will retain all the information on frequencies that are less than half of the frequency we are sampling.

- The limit of human hearing is about 20,000 Hz. The Nyquist theorem tells us that if we sample at more than 40,000 Hz, we will accurately reproduce all sounds that are less than 20,000 Hz. The common sampling rate for audio CDs is actually 44,100 times per second.

- We still need to decide what vertical levels we will sample. How many levels can we actually distinguish? The rate that has been determined for CDs is 16 bits, which doesn't sound like much. But if we have sixteen 0s and 1s, that gives us 2^{16} different levels, or 65,000 levels at which we can sample.

- Once we know how many samplings per second we need to do and what the possible output levels are, that information gives rise to the bit rate—how much data per second of music. If we want CD-quality sound, we need 1400 kilobits per second, that is, 1.4 million 0s and 1s in each second of music.

- To make the file size even smaller, MP3 compression is used. MP3 uses perceptual coding, retaining the parts of the data that people are likely to notice and dropping the parts that people are unlikely to notice. This is an area called psychoacoustics, which looks at such issues as the threshold of hearing. Perceptual audio compression is a very complicated subject. It's also a great example of the intersection of different fields, in this case, math, music, psychology, and computer science.

The Mathematics of CD Encoding

- As mentioned at the beginning of the lecture, even a new CD can have about 50,000 errors, yet it still sounds fine when we play it.

What's used to address the error issue in manufacturing CDs is the Cross-Interleaved Reed-Solomon Code (CIRC).

- A sales representative taking an order on the phone from a customer knows immediately whether or not the customer has read his or her credit card number correctly. How?
  - The representative's computer performs a series of calculations that must result in a multiple of 10 to verify that the correct credit card number has been entered. Using 10 as a credit card check digit catches 70–80 percent of all errors made in entering credit card numbers.

  - Similar check digits are used on airplane tickets, UPCs, bank routing numbers, ISBNs on books, and vehicle identification numbers. Internet communication includes check digits in the packets of information sent back and forth.

- Once errors are detected in this way on a CD, they need to be corrected. To understand the error correction process, we need to go back to 1947 and the work of Richard Hamming at Bell Labs.
  - Hamming developed a system to detect and correct errors on a very early computer. In his system, only four out of every seven pieces of data were true data; the other three were check digits.

  - Imagine that we are sending a digital message of 1, 0, 1, 1, and we are going to append three digits to the end. We put the original four digits into four regions on a chart, and then we add digits in regions 5–7 in such a way that each circle has an even number of 1s. That gives us our check digits, 0, 1, and 0, and we can now put all seven digits in order; the message block reads: 1011010.

  - The person on the receiving end of the message can put those numbers into the same chart to determine whether or not there was an error in transmission and, if so, how to correct it.

o Not every sequence of seven 0s and 1s is a valid block, but how different are two valid blocks? What is the distance between two valid blocks as measured by the number of digits by which they differ? The answer is always three or more. In our example, the distance between what was sent and what was received was only one, and because of that, we knew the message had to be wrong.

o The 7-4 Hamming code has a message length of four set inside a block length of seven. That gives an information rate of 4/7; about 57 percent of the digits that are sent are actual data, and the others are check digits. This particular system can check one error and correct one error. An extended Hamming code enables checking for two errors and correcting for one.

• The next step in encoding a CD is called interleaving. A scratch on a CD may corrupt a number of 0s and 1s in a row, and the solution to avoid losing that bit of music is to intersperse the data from any one moment in the music in a number of different places on the CD. We see an example of interleaving with the message "Math is my favorite." A further example shows how the Hamming code and interleaving can be used to correct a message with a transmission error rate of 20 percent.

• Instead of using a Hamming code, manufacturers of CDs actually use what's called a Reed-Solomon code. This code replaces the single digits that we were just talking about with groups of eight digits. Because of that, a Reed-Solomon code is really working in a particular group, a field called Z_{256}. The resulting Reed-Solomon code can detect up to three errors and correct up to two errors.

• How good is this system? As we said, it results in about 50,000 errors on a disk—but that's out of about 20 billion bits!

• Mathematics is encoded somewhere in all of the ways that we deliver music digitally now. And these ideas are not just used for

CDs but for communicating in deep space missions, receiving satellite TV, and storing data on your hard drive.

Suggested Reading

Benson, *A Mathematical Offering*, chapter 7.

Loy, *Musimathics*, vol. 2, chapter 1.

Pohlmann, *Principles of Digital Audio*.

Questions to Consider

1. How are mathematical tools, such as the Fourier transform, used to correct singers' pitch and compress digital music?

2. What are error-correcting codes, and how do they ensure that scratched CDs still play without problems?

The Digital Delivery of Music
Lecture 11—Transcript

Welcome back. We are nearing the end of our long journey that started with vibrating objects and their overtones, and then we figured out how to construct scales and cords. We used those to find some compositional techniques that all use mathematics. But now, how does the music get to our ears, how is the music delivered? Today, we are going to talk about a little known subject. It is very important, but underappreciated, the digital delivery of music and the mathematics of that process.

First, let's take a quick tour of how music was delivered through the years. The original delivery of music was only in person. I think it is really hard to imagine a world without any recorded music. Prior to about the U.S. Civil War no music had ever been recorded to be played back later, all of those performances of Bach, Beethoven, Mozart, all gone. You wanted to hear Beethoven's 9th, you got to hear it maybe two or three chances in your entire life because it had to be live. People traveled around to hear a concert. Hector Berlioz was famous for traveling Europe extensively both to conduct, but also to hear concerts. He was a particular fan of concerts conducted by Franz Liszt.

Early recordings were really scratchy. The first known musical recording is actually not Edison, but it comes from 1860. Édouard-Léon Scott de Martinville was singing *Clair de la Lune* and it was written to paper by something called a phonautograph. This recording was not re-read; it was not heard in sound until 2008 from lines drawn on this paper. It was reconstructed and played for us to hear.

Now, the first music recorded onto replayable cylinder was 1888. It was Handel's *Israel in Egypt* and it was done for Thomas Edison. It took 4,000 voices and the sound from 4,000 voices; it sounds incredibly faint. It is really scratchy. You can find this online and you can listen to it. It is oddly at the National Park Service website.

They moved on to better sounds and there were important milestones that were achieved. They moved from cylinders to flat discs around 1890 or so and that made multiple copies of a recording possible, much easier to produce, and you saw the rise of the gramophone company. Radio broadcasts of live music started around 1906–1910 and the recording and playback quality quickly improved. Through all of this, no mathematics was needed. The waveform was transferred directly to the medium that held the recording. They were really limited only by the quality of the recording instruments and the playback instruments.

Let's listen. Here we have a Victrola machine. This is from right around 1905–1906 and we have here an album that I rescued from the scrapheap at a library and most of the tracks on this album are in very poor condition, but we can actually listen to the first one alright. The amazing thing about this is it requires no amplification. There is no electricity here. It's just mechanical so let me get it going and let's listen to what it sounds like.

It is really amazing to me that this recording requires no electricity at all to play. There is nothing plugged in. We have done some video trickery in this course, but we are not using any trickery at all here. In fact, I can show you what the volume control on this is. Here, I will start it over.

That is how you control the volume on these old Victrolas. Now, it is a wonderful thing to be able to record music and play it back, but it actually degrades over time. Every time you play this it gets a little bit worse. In fact, it is particularly bad. This album is vinyl. It is from after the 1950s when albums were made out of vinyl, but we are using the original technology, the original needles and they are fairly heavy and it actually degrades the vinyl. It rips the vinyl off. If you look closely on the end of that needle you can see a little bit of vinyl on it. What happens is the recording degrades over time.

Let's compare this with some more modern technology. Let's play a CD so here we have a CD. It is the Bach Brandenberg Concertos. It is brand new. I am going to unwrap it for us and this is how we play CDs. We pop it into a machine and we assume that it starts just fine.

There we hear the Bach Brandenberg Concertos. Now, this is brand new right. This came right out of the package. You saw me open it. It is digitally encoded. It is all 0s and 1s encoded on here and while it is true that these 0s and 1s never degrade like the album over there would, it is also true that in the manufacturing process there are over 50,000 errors, more than 10 errors per second on this disk. If you take a used disk, this one is nice and shiny and new, but if you take a used disk there are probably half a million errors, half a million errors on this disk. Did you hear any errors? I mean I did not think I heard any errors. Let's see if we can hear any of the errors; there are probably 50,000 errors that are on this CD.

Now, I didn't hear any errors on that at all, but let me do something and then I want you to think about it. I brought a knife with me today. We all know if I took a knife to this album and I scratched it we all know what that would sound like, you would get this annoying click every time it went around. Let's take this CD. Here, I'll slice it. There, you can see I put a nice slice across this with a knife. Maybe now that we've added more errors we're going to hear it just like we would on the album. So, let's hear it. Now, this album has a lot more than 50,000 errors. I scratched across every single line of data on this.

I don't know about you, but I think that sounds the same. I didn't hear any errors on there. Maybe that wasn't enough errors. Maybe I didn't put enough errors on there, so let me add some more errors. Here's a permanent marker, and you can see the scratch there. I'm just going to sign my name across here, so there, there is my name scratched across this so now I am going to play it again. Now this has many more than 50,000 errors. I put tons of errors, some all in a row. Let's see what happens when I play this on this machine here.

That sounded perfect still. I did not hear any errors there at all. In the days of the Victrola, you did not need any math or any electricity to produce music. In today's modern times, music is delivered digitally and digitally delivered music is full of mathematics. That is what we are going to talk about today. The three main topics we are going to talk about today are these: We are going to talk about three different ways that mathematics has changed the delivery of music in our digital world. We are going to talk about how it has changed the notes that we hear; how mathematics makes bad singers sound good. That is something called Auto-Tune.

We are going to look at how much music we can carry and how we can fit more songs into smaller space, how we can stream more things wirelessly over the Internet and that is the mathematics of audio compression and finally we are going to look at how much cleaner music sounds because of math; the example that we just saw on a CD. Compared with records, cassettes, 8-tracks, music sounds much better when it is delivered digitally and part of that is error correcting codes. So, those are the three topics. We are going to talk about the notes we hear, how much we can carry, and how much cleaner the music sounds because of math.

Let's look at the first of those. Now, this is a bit of a departure from our usual focus on classical music. Auto-Tune was first heard widely on Cher's album *Believe*. It was an effect that was greatly exaggerated so we could hear it, but the technology comes from 1997. It is from Antares Audio Technologies and it was recently called one of the 50 worst inventions by *Time* magazine. The idea is that even when a singer sings out of tune you can fix it digitally. Now, originally this was done just in the studio. It took a long time to process this computationally. At this point, they can do it live in performance. When the singer sings out of tune, the correct notes come out of the speakers because they are fixing it so quickly.

There are other versions other than Auto-Tune, but Auto-Tune has become what is called a proprietary eponym. Think about things like Frisbee or Xerox. Now, it is not just used to fix pitch, it is actually also used for effects. The rapper T-Pain uses Auto-Tune a lot to give his music a particular quality.

There are two steps that we are going to talk about in Auto-Tune. The first is pitch detection and the second is pitch correction. Let's talk through an example of this. I am not a particularly good singer. I can't control my voice, I haven't had any training, but I can use this demonstrate, so here's the finale of Beethoven's Ninth in German. *Freude, schooner Götterfunken tochter aus Elysium* and now I am going to ask Gordy, our sound engineer to play that back to us with Auto-Tune and the computer is going to correct the pitches and you will hear it sounds much better.

Exactly how does this work? Well to do it live it requires fast computers, but it also involves some interesting mathematics and the two parts that we are going to talk about are the pitch detection and then the pitch correction. Think back to lecture 2 on timbre. We figured out that the waveform of a sound might look like this and these are the pressure changes of the sound wave. We can also take the Fourier Transform to get the spectrum and then we are looking at the frequencies. Now, if you want to do pitch detection, if we want to know exactly what pitch I was singing at we can do that. We have several options. If we want to look at Fourier Transform we could look where that first peak is; that should be the fundamental frequency, but also the distance between those peaks because all of these sounds have this very arithmetic sequence of notes. It is just the fundamental frequency added to itself each time. The distance between the peaks should also give us the fundamental frequency.

Finally, if we did not want to go to Fourier Transform, if we wanted to stay on the waveform side we could look at the distance between the wave repeating, what that period is that should give us one over the frequency. Any one of these methods will give you a singer's frequency. Let's say somebody sings at 430 Hz, once we have done the pitch detection and we know that she is singing at 430 Hz now we could ask should it be at 430 Hz or should it be something else. Is she singing out of tune? If we know the frequencies of the notes, if we know what the frequencies of an A-flat are for an equal timbre scale at about 415.3 Hz and an A-natural should be about 440. Well, the 430 that we are hearing is probably close to the 440 so I think that should be a 440; that should be upwards a little bit. It should be a little bit sharp. We should correct that note.

How do we do the pitch correction? Well, to do the pitch correction you might think that we should go from 430 Hz to 440 Hz and so we should just add 10 Hz. In other words, we should just shift the graph over 10 Hz. That does not work. Remember the overtone series is multiples and so if the singer is singing at 430 we are also hearing the overtones at 860, 1290, 1720, all the multiples of 430. What it should be is multiples of 440, which are 440, 880, 1320, 1760. If we were just to add 10 Hz to her voice we would not get the right sequence. We would get 440; that would be correct, but then 870, 1300, all of the rest would not be correct.

The key thing here is to remember that intervals are multiplicative, not additive, and that tells us how to get our solution. To solve this we should really be multiplying, not adding, and to get from 430 to 440 we are going to multiply by 44 over 43. To think about this, we would take the spectrum and we need to stretch it by a factor of 44 over 43. Remember when you do algebra $g(x)$ over 2 is the same graph as g except it is stretched by a factor of 2 and so we can find the new spectrum in this way. We can just stretch it by a factor of 44 over 43.

Now, we sort of in theory have a process that we will work. At least, this is one process that could work. We start with a waveform; we get the waveform from the recording. We compute the spectrum, we detect the frequency, we compare that with a table of correct frequencies, probably equal tempered frequencies. We multiply by a constant to correct it and then we have to invert. We have to take the inverse Fourier Transform to get back to the waveform and now we can simply play that corrected sound. In theory, this is how we can fix the tune of anything like that.

In practice, it is a little bit more complicated. There is some analog to digital switching that has to go on that is called sampling. We will talk more about that later. We also have to split the voice up into individual notes. When a singer moves from one note to another we have to redo all the computations and we have to figure out when exactly she might be moving from one note to another. We also have to make sure we don't change the initial attack. Remember earlier, we took the attack off of a note. You could not hear it as a banjo, but when we put the attack back on it was a banjo, that's telling us that the attack is very important and so we have to make sure we do not change that initial attack.

Finally, one of these computational issues is that the Fourier Transform and the inverse Fourier Transform are computationally very difficult. There is actually something called a Fast Fourier Transform, which is a little bit better. It works a little bit faster, but all of these are much slower than you would need in order to do things live and so Auto-Tune does everything on the wave sound. It does what is called time domain pitch correction and they manage to do that fast because there is no Fourier Transforms involved.

I hope this does give you an idea of the issues that are involved and some of the mathematics involved in fixing pitches. That takes care of fixing the notes that we hear with Auto-Tune. Let's move on to the second topic; how math changes how much music we can carry or we can stream.

The problem is you simply never have enough space and my iPod seems to always be full even when I get a new one that's larger. This is even more of an issue for streamed audio. We don't want streaming audio, internet radio or the audio that comes with a streaming video. We don't want to take up all of the bandwidth of this pipe coming into our house of digital information. The problem here is that recorded audio and video just take up too much information. If we recorded sound at its highest fidelity and put that on a CD, a CD would actually hold less than two minutes of music. Imagine having to do that. If you want to hear Beethoven's Ninth Symphony at 70 minutes long, you would need 35 CDs. Every two minutes you would be switching CDs to hear the next part. That would just be a complete mess.

The goal of audio compression is to reduce this, to reduce the amount of stored information while still minimizing the effect on the listening experience. Now, this is a really interesting area. It is sort of on the border among mathematics and psychology, electrical engineering, computer science, and there are a lot of incredibly complicated details when you study this topic. We are just going for the main ideas today.

First, we have to talk about analog versus digital signals. The Victrola here uses a groove that is modeled on the waveform so that when the needle goes through that groove it vibrates exactly like the waveform does. Digital audio uses 0s and 1s and we have to find a way to convert from this continuous waveform to discrete individual points that can be represented by 0s and 1s and that is called sampling. Now, this is a really key decision because we are going to sample this waveform at a bunch of points this way and also at a bunch of heights and we have to decide how tightly we should space the points on the wave. If we have more points we are going to get a better sound. If we have fewer points, on the other hand, the sound might be worse, but the size of the file will be smaller.

The mathematics needed for this is actually something called the Nyquist theorem. Harry Nyquist proved this in 1928, and as far as I know, Nyquist was actually the first person to prove this and so the name Nyquist theorem is appropriate in this case. What he proved is that if you sample at frequency f so that you are putting points every $1/f$ seconds, you are putting exactly f points per second, what you are going to do is you are going to save information on all waves that have frequency less than $f/2$. If we think about this in terms of the Fourier Transform, if we think about decomposing this complicated wave into its individual component frequencies, you are going to retain all of the information on frequencies that are less than half of the frequency you are sampling.

The limit of human hearing is about 20,000 Hz. The Nyquist theorem is telling us that if we sample at more than 40,000 Hz, 40,000 times per second, that will accurately reproduce all sounds that are less than 20,000 Hz. Just to be safe we sample at a little bit higher rate. The common sampling rate for audio CDs is actually 44,100 times per second. It is a little higher for video equipment and that has to do with getting it exactly right with the frames of video, about 48,000 for video.

If we sample at higher rates, the audio is just not that different. We cannot audibly tell the difference between those and the file sizes become much bigger. So, we have our answer. We are going to sample at about 40,000 points per second and now we have to decide if want to discretize this, if we want to make this into 0s and 1s. We have to decide what are the vertical levels that we are going to sample are nice continuous waves because again, the analog on the Victrola was a continuous amount. You could put any amount on that wave as you want, but digitally we can only have certain levels because it is 0s and 1s. So, how many output levels do we want?

We turn to psychology to figure this out. The question we could ask is how many levels can we actually distinguish? When we do that we come up with the rate for CDs as 16 bits. Now, 16 bits does not sound like a lot, but if you have 16 0s or 1s that is giving you 2^{16} different levels. That is 65,000 different levels that you can sample at. Once you have how many samplings per second you have and what the possible output levels you have, that gives rise to what is called the bit rate, how much data per second of music. If you want CD quality sound, you have to have 1400 kilobits per second, 1.4 million 0s and 1s in each second of music. If you want to fix the scratches and the bad data, you have to stay tuned to later when we get back to correction of these errors.

If you want further compression, if you want to make the file size even smaller it gets a little bit more complicated and that is called MP3 compression. MP3 compression is one of the many different ways we can compress music and make the file sizes even smaller. MP3 uses perceptual coding. You keep the parts of the data that you think people will notice and you drop the parts that you do not think they will notice. This is an area called psychoacoustics, what can and can you not hear. It is really partly the ear and it is partly the brain. Some of the issues that come up are the threshold of hearing. What is the softest sound you can hear? It turns out that the answer is different at different frequencies and this curve gives you the threshold of hearing.

If a sound does not rise above this line then there is no use keeping it in a recording; people will not hear the difference because it is below our threshold of hearing. If you want to drop it you need to do a little mathematics; you need to create what are called bandpass filters in order to get rid of those. There's another very cool thing they do with this, which is called masking. Say you have a loud sound at about 300 Hz; that actually keeps you from hearing a soft sound at 320 Hz. The louder sound masks the sound that is close in frequency. This is much more pronounced for nearby frequencies than when frequencies are far apart.

This actually has a biological effect. It's the resolution of the auditory systems within the cochlea that are giving rise to this phenomenon. Let's listen to this. The first recording we're going to hear is going to have pitches and they are going to have one pitch and then two pitches and then one pitch and then two pitches and the frequencies of these pitches are going to be quite far apart. As we go through this, the second pitch is going to get softer and softer and softer and what you'll notice is you can continue to hear these and the reason you can is because they are far apart. The second pitch gets progressively softer, but you can always hear it. Let's listen to that.

Now what if those two notes were much closer in pitch? That's when we get masking. What we are going to hear now is that the higher note starts to disappear. It's masked by the lower note and after awhile you're not going to be able to hear the higher note even though they're at the same levels, the same loudness, as the example we just played. Let's listen to that. The MP3s that you might download use this phenomenon. They calculate when will a sound be masked. If it will be masked by a louder sound which is close to it in frequency we can drop it from the waveform. Every time we drop a sound the file gets a little bit smaller.

Now perceptual audio compression is a very complicated subject. It uses many different levels for these different uses. You can have low values of compression. You can have high values of compression and it's a great example of the intersection how different fields can work together, math, music, psychology, computer science. But let's hear the different levels of compression.

When you import a CD sometimes it asks you what level of compression you want, how big is the file that you want to save. If you have less compression you're going to have better sound, but bigger files. If you use more compression you are going to get worse sound and smaller files. Here's a demo; here is a passage of Bach. This is from the Gavotte in Partita no. 3. Let's hear it first with no compression; so this is essentially CD quality sound coming through.

And now, let's hear that with a lot of compression; so we're going to compress this a lot and you should hear that the sound is much worse.

And now I want to let you hear the progression as we go from no compression down to this last level, a lot of compression. I'm going to play this piece five times in a row and every time we are going to get a little bit more compression and you should hear the sound getting a little bit worse, the quality of the sound is getting a little bit worse. The tradeoff is that the size of the file is getting smaller each time.

That's a quick tour of some of the issues involved in the compression of music. Again, the whole point of this is that you want to be able to fit more tunes on an iPod or stream music without eating too much of your bandwidth up. CDs have no compression other than the fact that they have been converted from analog to digital at 44,000 Hz. The amplitudes are set at 65,000 different levels. Interestingly on a CD, since there is no perceptual compression Cage's "4.33" would use the exact same number of 0s and 1s as any other 4:33 excerpt of music.

But, there's another issue with CDs especially and that is errors. CDs use a very smart, really ingenious bit of mathematics in order to fix the problem of errors and here I am talking about scratches, manufacturing defects, people signing these, things like that. Now, remember from the beginning that even a very well produced CD can have about 50,000 errors. If it's scratched it would have more. If it is signed it has even more, but somehow the disk plays perfectly, we heard that at the beginning. And, that is the last topic of today; the mathematics of CD encoding.

This has a technical name. What's used on CDs is called the Cross-Interleaved Reed-Solomon Code (CIRC). The main ideas in here are error detecting codes, error correction codes, and finally interleaving, and we're going to walk through all three of these. Interestingly some of this mathematics you use every day and not just on CDs. Error detecting codes, error correcting codes, things like this come up when you are using the Internet, when you are using credit cards, when you are at the grocery store, all sorts of places so let's first look at error detecting codes.

Here's a conversation that happens all the time. A representative answers the phone and says something like thank you for placing your order at The Teaching Company, may I have your credit card number please? The customer reads off a credit card, maybe this one here, 313242 on and on, and the representative as soon as the customer is done reading that number might say I am sorry could you read that again. How does the representative know that they got something wrong? Well, certainly if they just could not hear a number then they would ask that, but sometimes if they've heard all the numbers perfectly, if the customer made an error, the representative knows that the customer made an error and the reason is the representative's computer is using what is called an error detecting code. The credit card number is wrong and the representative knows it.

Let's look at how exactly she knows it. Here's how this works. You take a credit card number and you double every other digit starting with the first digit. If this were our credit card number we would double the 3 and then the 3 again; we would double the 4, the 3, all of these things. We would double all of these numbers. And now if some of the doubled numbers might have two digits; for instance over here we doubled an 8 and we got 16 and we have two digits we have to subtract 9 from that so instead of 16 we are going to replace that 16 with a 7 and we need to do that any time we get a two-digit number when we double it.

Now we take our long string of digits and we simply add them and in this case we get 75. Now if the answer to that had been a multiple of 10 then we knew that the credit card number would check, it would be possibly correct. It might be exactly what the customer wanted. If it doesn't add to a multiple of 10 we know the credit card number is wrong, at least one of the digits is incorrect. Ours in this case, we got 75; that is not a multiple of 10 and so we know that ours is wrong. The salesperson's computer does all this computation immediately and simply tells the salesperson you need to get that number again.

This is called a credit card check digit and it catches all single-digit errors and that is about 60 percent of all errors that are made on a credit card. In fact, it catches almost all neighboring transpositions. If you take two numbers and switch the order that accounts for another 10–20 percent of all errors. Together this check digit is catching 70–80 percent of all errors made when you read a credit card number to somebody else. The information rate on the other hand, the first 15 digits are actually encoding important information. It is last the digit, which is called a check digit, and so our information rate is 15 out of the 16 digits we use contain actual information. The last digit is only the one that is extra.

Check digits like this save companies and customers valuable time and money. There are lots of other uses of error checking codes. Airplane tickets, the UPCs, when you are reading the items at a shopping center sometimes you will hear a beep, beep, beep, it gives you a different beep because it read it incorrectly and how does it know it read it incorrectly? Because it is doing an error checking algorithm and finding out that it did not check and so it asks you to rescan.

Bank routing numbers include check digits, ISBN numbers on books. The VIN numbers on cars include them now, but they've only included check digits since 1981. Internet communication includes check digits in the packets that you are sending back and forth. Now, that is not good enough for music. Error checking isn't good enough to fix things on a CD. If you check and find that there is an error what are you supposed to do about it? Detecting errors is not good enough. Error correcting would be much better.

To understand error correcting we have to go back to 1947. Richard Hamming was working at Bell Labs in 1947 and he had access to a very early computer on weekends. Now, there was a long line of scientists who were really eager to try out their programs on this new machine, this new computer. What they would do is they would put their programs on queue over the weekends and they would have these programs just run. If there were an error in your program the computer would detect the error and it would just stop. You would be kicked out of the line and it would start the next scientist's program.

You would have to go back, fix it, and go back to the end of the line and run your computer program again. Hamming thought if the computer could detect the error and fix it, then the program could just continue running. There would be no stopping. The advantages of this are that it would find and fix the errors. The downside was the information rate. In his original system only four out of every seven pieces of data were true data, the other three were check digits. Let's look at how his system worked and let's look at it in the example of sending a short message. Digital messages are all 0s and 1s, letters, sounds, video, audio, they are all encoded as just 0s and 1s so imagine sending a very simple message, just a four-digit message, 1, 0, 1, 1 and imagine that you transmit this message to somebody else in some way and they read it. It's sort of like the kids game "Telephone" where you keep telling a message to one kid after another and it goes down the line and you know that sometimes the message gets badly garbled by the end.

Error correcting codes help get around these problems that you have in telephone games like this. Let's try to send our message. Our message has four digits, 1, 0, 1, 1 and we are going to append three digits to the end. Those are the check digits and we have to tell you exactly how we are going to append these digits. We take this diagram and we put the original message, those four digits, into regions 1, 2, 3, and 4 in order. Now, we are going to add digits into regions 5–7 in such a way that each one of these three circles has an even number of 1s. Let's look at region 5. In that circle, there are two 1s already so it must be a 0 so that there is an even number. Region 6, there are three 1s in that circle and so it must be a 1 in region 6. In region 7, there are two 1s and so it must be a 0. Now, we have figured out our check digits. Our check digits are 0, 1, and 0 and now we can put all seven digits back in order and we get what is called a block. This message is encoded in a block and the block reads 1011010.

Now, let's think what happens if there is an error in transmission? You send this block to a friend, 1011010, and through this telephone game your friend reads 1001010 so we know there is an error, but your friend does not. What can your friend do? Your friend puts those numbers into this same chart and then checks the circles. Do the circles all have an even number of 1s in them? No. In this particular case, the top circle and the left circle both have an odd number of 1s and if there's only 1 error then that error has to be in region 3. That is the region that is in exactly the circles with an odd sum and it is not in any of the circles that has an even sum.

Because of this, we know that region 3, the 0 that's there should really be a 1. We fix that. We write out the block, 1011010, or rather your friend does this writing and your friend has detected the error and corrected the error. That is an amazing bit of mathematics.

There is another way to think about this and that has to do with distance in some space. Remember the received block was 1001010 and that was not a valid block. It was not correctly encoded. The correct block was 1011010. Now, not every sequence of seven 0s and 1s is a valid block. How different are two valid blocks. If we think about the distance as measured by the number of digits in which they are different then the distance between two valid blocks is always three or more. The distance between what we sent them and what our friend received was just 1. Those messages were different only in one of the digits.

Because of that, we knew that it had to be wrong. The message that was received was a distance one away from a correct message. What correct message was it? Well, the one that we sent and that is how the error correcting went. If you wander too far away from a valid block, more than one digit, then things might be a problem. But, if you only wander one digit away then you can not only detect the error, you can correct it.

Let's look at what happens if it's more than just one error. Suppose we send the original message we did before, but now our friend incorrectly reads it with two errors, 1001011. When our friend puts the numbers into this figure the bottom left circle has three 1s in it. Now, the easiest fix if we assume it is just one error than it must be an error in region 6. We must change that 1 to a 0 and when your friend fixes that they get 1001011 and our method just screwed up the message a little bit more. What we're seeing here is that this method cannot detect or fix two or more errors, but it does detect and fix one error.

Hamming codes, more precisely the 7-4 Hamming code that we have seen, have a message length of 4 set inside of a block length of 7. That gives an information rate of 4/7, about 57 percent of the digits that are sent are actual data and the others are check digits. This particular system can check one error and it can also correct one error. The distance between valid blocks is 3. You can extend this and do more complicated mathematics and you can get what is called an extended Hamming code, which checks for two errors and corrects for one.

The next step in encoding a CD is called interweaving so let's look at that. You see CDs have a particular way that they have errors. Sometimes errors are randomly placed and that might be the manufacturing process, but sometimes when you scratch a CD it corrupts a lot of the 0s and 1s all in a row and the solution to get around this, to not lose that bit of music, is to intersperse the data, to spread out the data from any one particular moment in music in a lot of different places. Let's look at an example of this with letters.

Suppose that my message is math is my favorite; that is a great message, and suppose during the sending of this message we lose four letters in a row. Boy our message is not clear, we cannot really figure out what that message is going to say. The solution is to interweave the message and let's look at how we do that. We put these letters in a 4 x 4 grid horizontally, but then we send the message vertically. Let's interleave math is my favorite and see what it looks like.

Here we put the message in horizontally and then we read down instead of across m-i-f-r-a-s-a-i. It does not look like much of a message, but when we send the message if we were to lose say four letters in a row, this is called a burst error, think about a scratch on a CD. We put the remaining letters in a grid down and now we read across. What we have done is we have spread out those errors into different parts and so we can easily read this as math is my favorite. There is no problem because we spread out the errors.

Let's put error detection, error correction and this interleaving together to see how a CD works. Let's think about encoding these 16 digits on a CD. The first thing we are going to do is we are going to split it up into groups of four and so now we have four groups of four and now our first try might be to add check digits to each group of four. Each group of four we can run through the Hamming code, get three additional digits and it would look like this. Now, we can write that in a 4x7 grid and interleave and that would be a good way to do things, but we can do better and that is called cross interleaving.

Again, the goal is to encode these 16 digits and so we did what we did before. We split them into groups of four. We add three digits and now we write them in a 4x7 grid, but before interleaving we're going to add three additional rows at the bottom and then we are going to read the columns and we're going to add three check digits using our Hamming code in order to figure out what those digits should be.

Now, we have a 7x7 grid and now we interleave that and so now we read those vertically instead of horizontally. This would be a cross interleave Hamming code. Let's see how it deals with errors.

Let's introduce two kinds of errors. Let's suppose we send this 49-digit message and we have some errors that are single-digit errors. These are sort of random, think about manufacturing errors where a 1 should be a 0 or the other way around, but we also have this big scratch here in the middle and it is completely unreadable. We do not know if those are 0s or 1s. What I have demonstrated here is a huge error rate. It's about 20-percent error rate. Is it fixable? Let's try to decode it.

We write the data in the grid and now we check the columns and we check them with our Hamming code. Column 5 checks out perfectly when we put those numbers into our circle figure. But, columns 1, 2, 6, and 7, there is one error in each one of those, which we can detect and correct using our Hamming code. Columns 3 and 4, there are too many errors in there. Our Hamming code does not help us and that's where we use the interleaving. Now, instead of reading the columns we read the rows and now in each row there is at most one error, which is detectable and correctable. We correct those errors, we reverse the interleaving. We keep only the top block, the 4x4, which were the 16 digits, removing all of the rest, which were check digits and now compare it with the original. That was amazing. We get the exact original message back precisely without a single error.

Let's review what exactly we just did. We took our 16-digit message, we added check digits in one direction. We interleaved that and added more check digits and then we managed to correct a sent message with a transmission error rate of 20 percent. That is really phenomenal work that we did. I want you to notice how both the Hamming code and the interleaving played a really important role in doing this.

It turns out that CDs are a little bit more complicated than that. Instead of using a Hamming code they use what is called a Reed-Solomon code. I want to just give you a quick idea of the ideas in that. A Reed-Solomon code replaces the single digits that we were just talking about with groups of eight digits. Because of that a Reed-Solomon code is really working in a particular group, it is actually a field called Z_{256}. The resulting Reed-Solomon code can detect up to three errors and it can correct up to two errors, and that's what we need in CDs.

Now, we have the basic ideas in place. We use a Reed-Solomon code, we use cross-interleaving and then there are a couple of extra things we have to deal with. There are two channels. We listen to things in stereo now so there is a left and right channel and those have to be interleaved. There is extra data like track information, timing, there are some technical issues, but all of these are taken into account in encoding a CD. How good is this system? Well, remember a reasonable error rate was 50,000 to a half million errors on a disk. That's out of about 20 billion bits. All of these are corrected. On a CD-ROM if you think about it, all of them have to be corrected because otherwise programs would crash.

If we have a scratch, if we have a burst error, not like an individual manufacturing error, if we have a burst error, a burst error 2.4-mm-wide, that is 3,500 bits in a row, can be completely corrected with this amazing algorithm that we have, this cross-interleaved Reed-Solomon code. I was lucky, if I had signed with a thick Sharpie instead of a thin one then it would have probably skipped instead of playing perfectly.

What I hope is that you get the ideas that mathematics is packaged into all of the music that we have. Mathematics is encoded somewhere in all of the ways that we deliver music digitally now. Every CD is encoded the same way. The brilliant mathematics that people have invented, Hamming, Reed, Solomon, is used so that this disk still plays perfectly when I put it in. It is not just CDs, these ideas are used for communicating in deep space missions, satellite TV, even storing data on your hard drive, all of these involve error correction, error detection codes.

In all of today's topics, there was mathematics helping improve the musical experience. We learned how mathematics is used to fix the notes we hear, how we use mathematics to increase how much music we can put on a device, and how we use mathematics to not just detect, but correct errors in CDs and other communication. Next time is the culmination of our journey, the culmination in performance when music reaches our minds. We're going to talk about math, music, and the mind next time.

Thanks for joining us. Let's hear a little bit of error corrected Bach to take us out.

Math, Music, and the Mind
Lecture 12

Throughout these lectures, we have looked at a central question: How can mathematics help us understand music? And we've seen a great deal of evidence for connections between math and music: vibrations, scales, compositional techniques, and so on. In this final lecture, we're going to look at deeper connections; we'll refer back to everything we've learned—all the details—but to make a larger point: The connections we make between mathematics and music are in our minds.

Differences between Math and Music

- Mathematics and music are clearly not the same thing. What aspects of music are completely nonmathematical?

- Although computers can generate melodies using mathematical algorithms, real musical composition is not mathematical. The results of computer composition have no themes or coherence.

- The Fourier transform can explain how the overtones of an oboe are different from those of a clarinet, but orchestrating a melody—deciding which instruments should play which parts—is a nonmathematical art.

- Mathematics can guide us in tuning a piano and predict the sounds that will come out when we hit the keys, but math cannot tell a pianist how hard to strike each note or how the tempo of a piece should ebb and flow.

- Of course, there are also some things that math does that music simply can't. Virtually all scientific advances rely on some form of mathematics, and music cannot make that claim at all. Music can and should be seen as the pinnacle of civilization's creative works, along with other arts, but it isn't useful in the same way that mathematics frequently is.

- Music also seems much more accessible than mathematics. Everybody likes some form of music, even if they don't understand it or can't play it themselves. Of course, the same can't be said for mathematics.

Infant and Child Development
- Almost from birth, infants start to think both mathematically and musically. For example, when babies are just three or four days old, they can distinguish three dots from two dots. This is evidence of "subitizing," that is, instantly counting without counting individual items.

- By about five months, infants can do basic addition, recognizing that $1 + 1 = 2$. In experiments at the Infant Cognition Center at Yale University, babies have been shown to look longer at a screen that shows only one doll when two were expected. Older infants differentiate both between the items shown (a doll versus a block) and the number of items shown.

- Some mathematical capabilities seem to be innate or nearly innate, but what about music? Conditioned head-turning experiments in the United Kingdom have shown that infants seem to have early preferences for fast, loud, and familiar music. Additional research has shown that even after a year, babies preferred music they had heard in the womb over similarly styled and tempoed music.

- Infant brains are structured in ways that allow them to process these fundamentally important aspects of both math and music—even before they can use language or walk. The brain somehow comes wired to process, to remember, and maybe even to understand both math and music.

Patterns and Prodigies
- Our brains are marvelous at pattern matching and pattern predicting, and these abilities are at the core of both mathematics and music. One area in which we see the importance of pattern matching is with prodigies, children who perform at an adult level in a given

field. Note that we often associate prodigies with three fields: music, math, and chess.

o   In music, we have such prodigies as Mozart and, more recently, the cellist Yo-Yo Ma and the violinists Hillary Hahn and Sarah Chang.

o   In math, we have Srinivasa Ramanujan, who grew up in poor conditions in India and eventually moved to England to work with the most renowned mathematicians in the world. John von Neumann, another famous mathematician, was also a great prodigy. The Teaching Company's own Art Benjamin was something of a child prodigy, as well.

o   In chess, the most famous child prodigy was Bobby Fischer, but other children have become grand masters at even younger ages than Fischer.

•   What is it that math, music, and chess have in common that seems to engender prodigies? The answer may be: patterns.

o   When you're listening to music, your mind is continuously predicting what is next, and it does that based on what you have just heard in that piece, what you have heard before in pieces of the same style, and so on.

o   Mathematical patterns are usually more explicit. Some of them we know well—1, 2, 3, 4, 5—and we know what comes next. The Fibonacci sequence was a pattern we needed in order to understand octave: 1, 1, 2, 3, 4, 5, 8, 13.... The pattern 2, 3, 5, 7, 11, 13, 17... is the primes in order, the numbers that have only 1 and themselves as divisors.

o   Sometimes, simple patterns lead to difficult mathematics. For example, Goldbach's conjecture says that every even number can be written as the sum of two primes. This statement has been checked with computers up to extremely large numbers, but we do not know that it is always true.

- The combination of musical and mathematical patterns results in something like the work of David Cope, which is at the boundary between music and artificial intelligence.
  - Cope has written computer programs that will compose melodies in the style of certain composers or predict melodies based on rules about continuing patterns. In emulating Mozart, Cope's program gets between 64 and 71 percent of the notes correct.

  - This work tells us that when we predict the end of a musical phrase, we are doing mathematical thinking. It's a mathematical-style algorithm that does this prediction of patterns.

Practice

- The need to practice is another feature that is shared by both math and music. The psychologist K. Anders Ericsson at Florida State University has noted that it takes about 10,000 hours of practice to become an expert in any endeavor.

Psychologists estimate that it takes about 10,000 hours of practice—3 hours a day for 10 years—to become an expert in any endeavor.

- One of the keys to Ericsson's theory is that it is not just practice that is required—not just mindless repetition—but deliberate practice, time spent breaking down, assessing, and refining one's craft.

- Again, it seems as if people can imagine musicians practicing much more easily than they can mathematicians. For most mathematicians, practice consists of pondering puzzles and mathematical ideas, playing games that require strategic thinking or geometrical reasoning, and asking questions of their favorite teachers. Practicing math is not so constrained as other types of practice.

- Of course, there are limits to the argument about gaining expertise through 10,000 hours of practice. Most of us couldn't get in the NBA, even with 1 million hours of basketball practice!

Creativity

- Both mathematics and music have elements of creativity, and this creativity in the two disciplines seems similar. In both cases, practitioners work within structured systems that have patterns.
  o On the musical side, the system includes scales, keys, and tempos. On the mathematical side, it includes definitions and logic.

  o Further, both mathematicians and musicians try to construct something new and original, and if they succeed, what they create is studied and emulated by others.

- One of the implications of creativity in these fields is that we will never run out of math or music. In fact, we can actually use mathematics to quantify the fact that we will never run out of music.
  o How many 10-note melodies can we create with just 12 notes and three note lengths? The answer is 36^{10} different melodies.

  o It would take 1 million songwriters writing 1,000 melodies a day for more than 10,000 years to write out all of those melodies.

- Which endeavor is more creative? Of course, we can't answer that question. But whether you are playing well with a string quartet or attacking a math problem from a new direction, the sense of creativity is exhilarating.

Abstractness

- In addition to patterns and creativity, math and music share the curious trait of abstractness. Both can be expressed intrinsically, and in both, there is no necessary reference to the natural world, although that reference may be present.

- The fact that 5 is a prime number is independent of any part of our physical reality. So is the fact that Beethoven's Fifth Symphony exists. Even if all the copies of Beethoven's Fifth were destroyed, it would still exist in our minds.

- In some sense, music is the most abstract of the arts and math is the most abstract of the sciences. The arts, with some exceptions, largely refer to the human experience. The sciences study physical objects. But both mathematics and music are built around abstract patterns.

Beauty

- Musical beauty seems fairly identifiable. When you hear a soprano soaring through an aria, it evokes a sense of beauty that somehow reaches in and touches your soul. Many people also know that there are different styles of musical beauty: Renaissance music, Baroque, classical, Romantic, and so on.

- What most people don't know is that mathematics has different styles also; it has different aesthetic sensibilities.
  o Mathematicians who study logic—sets, relations, and so on— are sort of like Baroque purists, playing period instruments and making sure that the A they use is not today's 440 A but the A of that particular period.

o   Topologists, the mathematicians who study rubber-sheet geometry, give loose, imprecise proofs, similar to the fluid rhythms of Chopin or Debussy.

o   Those who study abstract algebra—group theory—and write amazingly perfect proofs are more like Beethoven, who spun his melodies into perfect symphonies.

o   The category theorists are the most abstract of mathematicians. Their thinking about such abstract concepts as functions is akin to the work of the atonal and pantonal composers, who work in their own cerebral worlds.

- We end with the Bach Chaconne that we discussed in Lecture 1. As you listen, think about the fact that math tells us what sounds will emanate from a vibrating string. Think about the chords constructed in part because of the mathematics behind the tuning systems used in Bach's time. Think about how scales are constructed using mathematical principles and Bach's use of ideas akin to group theory to transform melodies and put them together. Listen, in other words, for how mathematics informs the musical experience.

Suggested Reading

Harkleroad, *The Math behind the Music*, chapter 9.

Lakoff and Núñez, *Where Mathematics Comes From*.

Levitin, *This Is Your Brain on Music*.

Rothstein, *Emblems of Mind*.

Sacks, *Musicophilia*.

1. In what ways are the types of thinking done in mathematics and music similar? In what ways are they different?

2. In what ways are the abstractness and beauty of mathematics and music similar? In what ways are they different?

Math, Music, and the Mind
Lecture 12—Transcript

Welcome to this, the culminating lecture on math and music. We've talked through all of the components of music. We have talked through notes, scales, chords, rhythms, transformations, and now we are ready to put them all together in a performance and so I thought I would dress up for the occasion. In the spirit of performance, let's listen to some music.

That's a delightful tune. What did you notice about it? You know before watching these math and music lectures you might have already known lots of things. You might have been able to say things about this piece. It's a beautiful little melody and most would agree that it is beautiful. It's written in the classical style. Composers like Haydn; it's after the Baroque style of Bach and Handel and before the romantics, Brahms, Rachmaninoff, Tchaikovsky. If you really knew your music well you might recognize it as the work of a child prodigy. This tune was written by 5-year-old Wolfgang Amadeus Mozart in 1761. What you might not have realized is that all three of these aspects, beauty, style, and prodigies help us to relate mathematics to music.

Today, we look at these types of relations and how they relate to human thinking. Today, we look at math, music, and the mind. Now, you might remember at the very beginning of this lecture series we were looking at the central question, how can mathematics help us understand music. Now, so far these first 11 lectures have given us a lot of evidence for connections between math and music, vibrations, scales, compositional techniques, today instead of those details we're looking at big-picture connections between these two areas of math and music.

If this were a trial then the first 11 lectures would have been like the detailed forensic evidence, the DNA, the fingerprints, the expert witnesses, the photographs of the crime scene. Strings, drumheads vibrating in particular modes and the modes of the gamelan leading to very different scales and different music. Today, we are going to give you the closing arguments, the big picture. In this final lecture, we are going to look at deep connections between mathematics and music. We're going to refer back to everything we've learned, all of those details, but all to make a larger point. The connections we make between mathematics and music, they really are here in our minds.

Before we get to our argument, let's let the other side have a little bit of time before the court. Let's talk about the limits of this connection between math and music because math and music are simply not the same thing. In what ways are math and music different? What aspects of music are completely nonmathematical? There are many. Can mathematics compose a melody, an elegant simple one like the one Mozart composed at age 5? I think that composing a melody is simply not mathematical. What if it were? What if we let mathematics compose melodies? I will play you a little piece here. This was computed, it was not composed. It was computed using mathematical algorithms and I think you will notice that there is no theme, there is no coherence. There is no musical point being made here.

That's pure mathematics. That was computed; that was not composed, by the mathematician Dr. Marcus Pendergrass. It's not what we traditionally think of as music. It's even more disjointed than that piece that I composed with the help of dice. There are a lot more dissimilarities between mathematics and music. If you remember back in lecture 2 we talked about the Fourier Transform. Now, the Fourier Transform can explain how the overtones of an oboe are different from those of a clarinet; remember the oboe has a conical bore and the clarinet's is cylindrical.

What tells a composer which instrument to give the melody to? The active orchestrating, choosing which instrument should play which part, orchestrating a melody is a very nonmathematical art. There are lots more differences. Mathematics can guide us in tuning a piano. It can help us understand the beats we get from two notes that are really close to each other, wawawawawa. It can predict the sound that will come out when we hit a key. It can tell us where we should put the hammers in order to eliminate the 7th harmonic. But, when a pianist is playing a Chopin etude math cannot tell her how hard to strike each note, or how the tempo should ebb and then flow in some places.

On the other hand, there are things that math does that music simply can't. Virtually all scientific advances rely on some form of mathematics and music cannot make that claim at all. Music can and should be seen as the pinnacle of civilization's creative works, along with other arts, but it doesn't turn out to be useful in the same way that mathematics so frequently does.

The last difference I want to talk about today is the difference of accessibility. You see everybody likes music, some form of music. I have been at plenty of parties to indicate that when I have conversations with people that is simply not true of mathematics, not everybody loves mathematics. A lot of people had some pretty bad experiences in middle school. Millions of people appreciate music without understanding it or being able to play it themselves. Math, you do not see crowds of fans lining up to buy tickets to Mathapalooza or filling up football stadiums in the summer. Only mathematicians really truly appreciate the beauty of math in that way.

There is an accomplished jazz pianist who is also a mathematician named Rob Schneiderman. What he says is math is like music that only musicians can hear. So, we have this difference between utility and accessibility. In mathematics, math is so vital to so many fields. It has a high level of utility, but yet few people understand it. It's not particularly accessible and this is sometimes a real problem for mathematicians, especially when we are trying to get funding in the National Science Foundation.

For music, it goes the other way. It's universally accessible. At least some forms of music, on some level, are loved and appreciated by many, many people, but the utility is not immediately apparent. That is a real problem for musicians when they are trying to get extra funding for the arts.

With that disclaimer about the ways in which math and music are dissimilar, let's go back to this closing argument of this trial, back to math, music, and the mind. When we use the word mind we must remember the distinction between the mind and the brain. The brain is the physical organ, the nervous tissue, all of the neurons that fire, all of the things inside of our skull. The mind is consciousness, thought, reason. Now, we're going to see similarities between math and music on both levels, the brain and the mind. The structures in our brains that are put in place somehow to understand both subjects as well as the thinking that our minds do when we experience mathematics and music.

In this final lecture, let's explore the connections among math, music, and the mind. As we'll see, we can draw connections among these three subjects in many different ways from the way our brains develop to the thinking done by the best mathematical minds and the best musical minds out there.

That, of course, was the Brahms' "Lullaby," something you might play to a baby. It is something I play to my own baby Ellie sometimes. Let's talk about babies and development of children and what that tells us about the connections between mathematics and music.

What do small children, infants know about math and music? It turns out that practically from birth, babies start thinking both mathematically and musically. Humans come hardwired for both math and music. You might wonder how we know something like this, after all infants can't talk. We infer it in part from how long infants look at something. You see, if infants see the same thing over and over again, they tend to look away quicker as they see it over and over again. That is called habituation. If they see something unexpected and something changes, they look longer and that is called fixation.

When babies are just three or four days old they can distinguish three dots from two dots. The way researchers do this is they show babies two dots repeatedly, two, two, two, and the babies get habituated and they stop looking very long at the two dots when they are shown and then all of a sudden they switch to three and the babies are fixated; they look longer when they switch to three than if they had just shown two. This is evidence of something that mathematics educators have a word for. It's called subitizing, instantly counting without counting out the individual things.

Subitizing would be looking and saying that is three apples, not counting, which would be that is one, two, three apples. Subito, subitizing comes from subito; it is Latin and it is actually a musical term that musicians know. Subito forte means to play suddenly loud. Now, adults subitize three, four, even five items. I can look out in a classroom, you can do this if you practice and count out groups of five and you can count people very quickly like that. If you try to do this with three, four, or five you have virtually no errors and incredibly fast reaction time. But, if you try to do this with more than five, most adults have a lot more errors and a much longer reaction time.

Infants are subitizing at three or four days old. They have some innate numerical ability. Okay, they can sort of count in some sense, or subitize, but can they add? Can they combine groups and count them? You would think that would be much harder, but by five months infants can tell that $1 + 1$ is 2. They can do basic addition. This comes from the work of Karen Wynn. She is a psychologist at the Infant Cognition Center at Yale. The test she does involves the violation of expectation. Again, the babies will look longer at unexpected images.

The setup looks something like this. There are dolls going behind a screen and the screen can rise and fall and you can model something like $1 + 1 = 2$ in the following way. You have one doll showing and then the screen goes up and hides that doll and then you see a second doll entering the scene and the second doll goes behind the screen and then the screen comes down and of course you would think that two dolls should now be revealed. But, what if there was only one doll there? That would be unexpected and by five months babies are looking longer at these unexpected results.

If you're skeptical you might ask, how do we know it is really about the numbers and not just some innate counting of dolls, something like that. They actually have done some really interesting tests to eliminate that possibility. They have switched objects and with five months old if you have 1 doll plus 1 doll and then drop the screen and show the baby two blocks instead of dolls, they do not look very long. There's a shorter gaze. On the other hand, if you have 1 doll plus 1 doll and then drop the screen and there is 1 block there is a longer gaze. That is unexpected to them. These young babies, they do not know the difference between a doll and a block, but they somehow know that $1 + 1$ is 2.

Older babies look longer at both. Older babies by about a year know that a doll and a block are different. And so they know that 1 doll plus 1 doll should not equal 2 blocks. This sort of addition these babies, these infants, are doing that at five months old. Addition is nearly innate.

What about music? Are there musically innate structures in the brain? We don't really have a good idea about this. I guess you could raise somebody without hearing any music and ask would they develop their own sense of music, but we do know that there are early preferences about music and babies like fast, loud, and familiar music. In order to understand this, they have developed what is called a conditioned head turning experiment. This is work in the early 2000s of Alexander Lamont in the UK.

A baby's head controls the music. Look left and the baby hears one song. Look right and the baby hears a different song. Babies about one year old quickly learn how to control the system, how turning their heads tells them what music they're going to hear. When they can control the music they prefer upbeat, loud, and familiar music. It sounds like they are sort of like teenagers. The upbeat and the loud, you can imagine babies figuring this out fairly quickly and it is interesting that babies can distinguish these very musical traits so early.

But what about familiar? That seems very different. To test for that, they had mothers play music in utero. It was maybe Mozart or maybe reggae like UB40 for the last three months of their pregnancies. Then the babies did not hear that music again for a full year. That one year they put these babies in this head turning experiment and the babies preferred the music that they had heard in the womb over similar styled and similar tempoed music, other classical music or other reggae music. Babies in utero were storing musical memories. Now, this research got taken way out of control and we heard about the Mozart effect, which was not entirely well-reported in the media. But, this research is saying that infants have musical structures in their brains that they can make use of and they can store these musical memories.

What's the big picture take home message from all of this? It points to a connection between math and music. Infant brains are structured in ways that allow them to process these early, these fundamentally important aspects of both math and music. Before language, before walking, these infant brains have abilities in both math and music. The brain somehow comes wired to process, to remember, and maybe even to understand both math and music.

How does this melody finish? If you recognize it you might know from memory exactly how it finishes. If you do not know it you can still make a pretty good guess because our brains are marvelous pattern matchers and pattern predictors. This pattern matching is the core of both mathematics and music. One place we see the importance of pattern matching is with prodigies. These are children who perform at an adult level in any particular field. Think for a second, which field has prodigies, who are the prodigies? When I have asked the most common answer I hear is Mozart, but what about others? Well, the answers that I have heard almost always come from three different fields and those are music, math, and chess.

Music, we have prodigies like Mozart, Cézanne was also a prodigy. More modern examples include the cellist Yo-Yo Ma and the violinists Hillary Hahn and Sarah Chang. In math, we have the Indian Ramanujan who grew up in very poor conditions in India and eventually moved to England to work with the most renowned mathematicians in the world. He rediscovered Euler's equation on his own. John von Neumann, a famous mathematician, was also a great prodigy. The Teaching Company's own Art Benjamin was something of a child prodigy as well.

In chess, we have the most famous child prodigy Bobby Fischer, but other children have come along to become grand masters at even younger ages than Bobby. You do not see prodigies in biochemistry, psychology, electrical engineering. What is it that math, music, and chess have in common? I think it is patterns.

What are musical patterns? When you're listening to music your mind is continuously predicting what is next and it is doing that based on what you have just heard in that piece, what you have heard before of pieces in that same style, things like that. Maybe you did not recognize the opening music to this section as Mozart's 40th Symphony. You might still be able to correctly predict how he finishes this phrase based on patterns. Here's the opening of the music, and this time I'll finish it.

Those are musical patterns. What about mathematical patterns? Mathematical patterns are usually more explicit. Some of them we know well 1, 2, 3, 4, 5, we know what comes next; 1, 2, 4, 8, 16, here we are doubling. That was the pattern we needed in order to understand octave; 1, 1, 2, 3, 4, 5, 8, 13, the Fibonacci sequence. We saw this in the lecture on rhythm, on Indian poetry. How about 2, 3, 5, 7, 11, 13, 17? These are the primes in order; the numbers which have only 1 and themselves as divisors.

Sometimes simple patterns lead to very difficult mathematics. If we take an even number that is bigger than 2, say 6, we could write that as 3 + 3, that is the sum of two primes. Ten is 7 + 3. If we take 12, that is 5 + 7, 14 is 3 + 11. Every even number we take, we can write as the sum of two primes. Can we always do that? Nobody knows. It is a famous conjecture in mathematics. That is Goldbach's conjecture and nobody has been able to prove that we can always do it. We can check with computers up to extremely large numbers, but we do not know that it will always happen.

What if we combine musical and mathematical patterns? Then we're doing something sort of like what David Cope has done. He is at the boundary between music and artificial intelligence. He has programmed many different computer programs that will predict, that will write music based on music that has already been written. He will take a composer and try to compose melodies in that style. He programmed one thing called the Melody Predictor. If you feed it a short portion of a melody, the Melody Predictor will finish it using fairly simple rules about continuing these patterns.

How well does it do in emulating Mozart? It actually gets between 64 and 71 percent of the notes correct. Let's look more closely at an example of that. Here is an example; it's from a Mozart piano sonata, but I will play it on violin and Cope fed the computer just the first five notes and then the rhythm for the entire five measures and the computer chose the pitches for all but those first five notes. I'll play the original, this is Mozart.

And this is Cope's Melody Predictor predicting what Mozart would write from just the first five notes and from the rhythm. Not far off.

What does this tell us? It tells us that when we predict the end of a musical phrase we are doing mathematical thinking. Cope's work shows that it's a mathematical style algorithm that can do this prediction of patterns. If you have ever had to sight read music very fast, you know that you become a very good pattern predictor. When you're reading a long run of notes in a Bach piece you do not see each individual note, you're already aware of which key you are in, that limits you to a particular scale. You're aware that it is a Baroque piece that gives you certain patterns. You know it is Bach and that limits you to particular patterns. You probably see what note the run starts on and what note it ends on and your brain just sort of fills in the rest. It predicts the pattern. If you try to sight read 20th-century music, or at least when I do, it is much harder for me to sight read. The patterns are, sometimes by design, very much less predictable.

Now, what's the big picture in terms of patterns? In both math and in music patterns are key. We see that infants are practically born with abilities in both mathematics and music and now we see that those with extraordinary pattern matching skills, the prodigies, they excel in a couple of different subjects, math, music, and chess, all of which patterns are key at. Patterns in mathematics and music are probably connected in here, in your brain, and how the brain processes, how the brain interprets, how it understands and predicts patterns.

I have vivid memories of learning to play this section of the Mendelssohn Violin Concerto. Slurs where you play consecutive notes when your bow is all traveling in one direction. They are normally smooth like this. But, in this section they are supposed to be separate, they are supposed to be bouncing and getting your bow to bounce while you go from one string to the next it took me months of practice. I remember doing this section again and again and again for hours at a time all so that I could do something like this.

That exhibits one of the qualities that are similar between math and music, practice. Practice is so important for musicians that it's the punch line of the most well-known musical joke out there. How do you get to Carnegie Hall? Practice. Parents spend endless hours getting their young musicians to practice. In mathematics, we do not usually call it practice. We have other names. Exercises, problems, homework, these are all forms of practice.

People have studied practice and recently the psychologist K. Anders Ericsson at Florida State, his work has become more widely known about experts in the field, in different fields, academic fields, artistic fields, sports.

There is a substantial body of academic work on the traits of experts. Ericsson has encapsulated that all in what is now an oversimplified phrase: in any endeavor it takes 10,000 hours of practice to become an expert. Now, it is just referred to as the 10,000 hours theory. If you are wondering, if you want to do the math, it is about three hours a day for 10 years before you get to 10,000 hours. You may have heard of Ericsson's work. His theories date back to his work in the 1990s, but it has more recently gained attention in Malcolm Gladwell's book *Outliers* and in Geoff Colvin's book *Talent is Overrated.*

One of the keys to Ericsson's theory is that it is not just practice, not just mindless repetition, but the concept of deliberate practice, time spent breaking down, assessing, refining, whatever one's craft is. Let's think back to math and music. When I talk with musicians and mathematicians this is one thing almost everyone has in common. They all spent extensive time, maybe 10,000 hours, maybe more, maybe less, but they all spent time practicing. I think it's much easier for most people to imagine what this looks like for musicians. You play pieces again and again, you work on particular passages at very slow tempos and then you start speeding them up. You concentrate on skill like bouncing your bow in the slurred passage of the Mendelssohn.

You know, even musical practice is more accessible than mathematical practice. What would deliberate practice in math look like? I think for most mathematicians practice isn't the exercises that you find at the back of the section in the book. For most mathematicians, practice was pondering puzzles and mathematical ideas, playing games that required strategic thinking or geometrical reasoning. Mulling over a concept around in their heads, talking with teachers about their favorite questions, that is really brilliantly described for the non-expert in Steven Strogratz's memoir *The Calculus of Friendship.* Practicing math is not so constrained as other types of practice. You know, I have actually solved a lot of mathematical problems

317

I was working on while out running with my dogs through the woods. I do not think I have made it to 10,000 hours of running practice yet.

Now there are limits to this argument. Nobody really argues that even with deliberate practice 10,000 hours will make you an expert in any field. A million hours of practice wouldn't have gotten me into the NBA. If you do not believe me do the math about a million hours. So, practice plays a key role in developing expertise and that is true in both mathematics and in music.

Don't recognize that tune? I bet you don't. I just made it up. I just created that. What is creativity? Now, there are lots of different kinds of creativity. You could have architectural creativity, diplomatic creativity. We've all heard about creative accounting, but both mathematics and music have elements of creativity. I think the creativity in math and the creativity in music are very similar. Let me explain what I mean.

Think about the ultimate in creativity moments in math and music. In music, it might be a jazz musician or maybe in Baroque times a violinist. Improvising, well other musicians around him played in the background. Think of Miles Davis the opening solo in "So What," bum, bum, badabadumbabum. That's such a great solo. On the math side of creativity, think about a mathematician sitting down and attacking an open question, something that nobody knows, nobody understands, and attacking it in some new way. That is a creative act.

In both the musical case and the mathematical case, they are working within a structured system that has patterns. On the musical side, those are things like scales, keys, tempos. On the mathematical side, those are definitions, logic. They are both trying to construct something new and original and if they succeed, if what they created is really good, others will study and emulate it. Think of how Thelonious Monk's percussive piano with all that dissonance changed jazz music and other people have worked to encapsulate that and to push that further. On the math side, think about Kurt Gödel's incompleteness theorem and how that opened up entire vistas of new mathematics, new places for mathematicians to go.

One of the implications of creativity is that we're never going to run out of math and we're never going to run out of music. We can actually use mathematics to quantify the fact that we are never going to run out of music. Suppose we have 12 notes, A, A#, all the way through G and G#, and let's just take three note lengths, eighth notes, quarter notes, half notes. Now, how many 10-note melodies are there? We can do a quick calculation. For each note there are 12 different pitches we could choose and three different note lengths. That gives us 36 choices for each note, and now there are 10 notes and so we have to multiple 36 times itself, 10 times. We get 36^{10} different melodies. If you do a quick computation it would take a million songwriters writing a thousand melodies a day over 10,000 years to write out all of those melodies. We will never run out of melodies.

Math and music, which one is more creative? Most people would say music, but an old friend of mine, my friend Jeff recently reminded me that when I chose to pursue mathematics over music back when I was about 17 years old, part of my reasoning was that math allowed for more creativity than playing classical music. No matter where you stand on this argument, when you play in a string quartet and you feel like the four of you are a single instrument and you are together interpreting the music or when you are sitting down and you attack a math problem from a new direction that you hadn't thought of before, that maybe nobody had thought of before, that sense of creativity is just exhilarating.

What did Tchaikovsky mean with this opening? This is his Violin Concerto. What is this melody referring to? I think this illustrates something shared by math and music and that is abstractness. In addition to patterns and creativity, math and music share this curious trait. Both math and music can be expressed intrinsically. There's no necessary reference to the natural world, they are both abstract. That's not always true. There is a lot of mathematics and some music that refers directly to the natural world. Think about the differential equations we looked at back in lectures 1 and 2; those models vibrating strings, those are a physical thing. Think about Vivaldi's *Four Seasons*; that was direct reference to the natural world.

But, much of both mathematics and music are abstract. They are living in some platonic plane that is separate from the one that we live in. Rob

Schneiderman, the jazz pianist and mathematician I mentioned earlier, he makes this point in a really excellent article that math and music can both be expressed intrinsically. What do we mean by abstractness? Well, in mathematics if you think about 5 being a prime number, it has just factors 1 and itself, 5 being prime is independent of any part of our physical reality. If humans were walking around with three heads and we lived underwater and we ate plankton 5 would still be prime.

On the music side, Beethoven's Fifth exists, it just does and it exists independent of any physical reality. If all copies of Beethoven's Fifth, all printed copies, all of the copies that could be played on a Victrola, all of the ones online, if it were all destroyed Beethoven's Fifth would still exist because it is in our minds. Math and music, even both show up as abstract in extraterrestrial communication and it is because of their abstractness that comes up. In Carl Sagan's *Contact* aliens communicate using a sequence of prime numbers. It's used as a universal language that exists independent of our or their contexts.

When we sent the Voyager up, the Voyager record was included. It was launched in 1977 and it prominently features music of many different traditions. One of the challenges on the Voyager record was to provide instructions on how to play the record and the instructions look surprisingly like the Victrola we have here.

Let's go back to Schneiderman's point about the intrinsic nature of math and music. Now, you might disagree, but you must admit that there is some negative truth in here; math and music are both very abstract. In some sense, music is the most abstract of the arts and math is the most abstract of the sciences. The arts, they largely refer to the human experience. Now, there are some exceptions, modern dance, maybe very abstract modern paintings. In science, the very objects that they're studying are physical. Without those, you would not have anything. Think biology, chemistry, physics.

Mathematics and music, much of both subjects, are abstract in a very similar way. There's no reference needed to the natural world. This adds to what we have seen before; both mathematics and music are built around patterns and they are built around abstract patterns.

That is Jules Massenet's "Meditation" from his opera *Thais*. I think most would describe this melody as beautiful. I have played it at many weddings. What makes it beautiful? What makes anything beautiful? What makes any piece of music beautiful? What makes a particular mathematical proof beautiful? What is beauty?

Well, let's step back from those big philosophical questions. What is beauty? That is such a large question, but what is beauty to mathematicians and to musicians? I think musical beauty is fairly well-known. When you hear a soprano soaring through some aria, think of Puccini's "O Mio Babbino Caro." It evokes a sense of beauty, somehow that beauty just reaches in and touches your soul. Many people also know that there are different styles of musical beauty, Renaissance music, Baroque, classical, romantic. These are all different aesthetic sensibilities. But, what is mathematical beauty?

What does style mean in the mathematical worlds of hard truths and cold counter-examples. This isn't particularly well-known to the general public, but mathematics has its different styles. It is different aesthetic sensibilities. Mathematicians who study logic, these are the foundations of mathematics, sets and relations and things like that, they are sort of like the Baroque purists playing with their period instruments making sure that the A they use is not today's 440 A, but the A of that particular period.

The topologists, the mathematicians who study rubber-sheet geometry where donuts are the same things as coffee mugs because they both have one hole poked through them. They give these loose, imprecise proofs, sort of like the fluid rhythms of Chopin or Debussy. Abstract algebra, the algebraists, people who do group theory, they write proofs where the precise definitions setup these surprisingly perfect proofs, sort of like the way Beethoven uses his melodies and spins them into these perfect symphonies. The category theorists, these are the most abstract of mathematicians. They deal in abstract ways to think about already abstract concepts like functions. These folks are like Webern and Schoenberg, the atonal composers, the pantonal composers, proud to be working as far removed from tradition as possible, working in their own cerebral worlds.

What is it about mathematical beauty and musical beauty? I am certainly not saying that mathematical beauty and musical beauty are the same thing, but the beauty in mathematics and music are similar. They have aesthetic sensibilities and those aesthetic sensibilities mirror each other. Way back in lecture 1, I told you a story about the Bach Chaconne and I mentioned Brahms's take on the Chaconne. Here is something else Brahms said about this masterful piece. He said, "If I imagined that I could have created, even conceived the piece, I am quite certain that the excessive excitement and earth shattering experience would have driven me out of my mind." That was Brahms talking about the Chaconne.

Remember, the Chaconne was a piece that Richard Stark asked me about in my job interview at St. Mary's College in Maryland. Can you play the Bach Chaconne? Well, now I can play the Bach Chaconne; I also have tenure, as you know; I am not sure if those are related. But I wanted to close with the last bit of the Bach Chaconne and while you listen I want you to think about how math tells us what sounds emanate from a vibrating string. I want you to think about the chords constructed in part because of mathematics behind the tuning systems that Bach was using at the time.

I want you to think about how scales are constructed using mathematical principles. How Bach used ideas akin to group theory to transform melodies and put them together. I want you to think about how violin sounds that I am making here are encoded on the DVD that you have or the download that you have using brilliant error correcting codes so that all of the errors you hear are my responsibility because we are not going to use Auto-Tune here.

The last thing I want you to listen for is I want you listen to how the mathematics informs the musical experience because my greatest hope for you is that you hear the world differently because of these 12 lectures; that you continue to listen to beautiful music and appreciated mathematics, but you now see more clearly how these two wonderful subjects are intimately connected. So, here is end of the Bach Chaconne.

I wanted to thank my family, Sarah, Cy, and Ellie who never complained when I got home late after working on these lectures again, and again, and again. I also wanted to thank my fantastic team at The Teaching Company especially Jay, Zach, Chris, and Nancy, and on behalf of them I want to thank you for joining us on this mathematical journey through the musical experience. I am honored to have been given the privilege of guiding you through this journey. Thank you.

Bibliography

Five of the books in this bibliography have been written as textbooks for Math and Music courses or "complete" views of mathematics and music and provide excellent additional resources for many of the topics covered in this course. Of these, Wright's *Mathematics and Music* and Harkleroad's *The Math behind the Music* are the most accessible, with the former reading more like a textbook (it assumes no mathematical or musical background but explains concepts quite quickly) and the latter as more of a general-interest book.

Three other volumes are significantly more technical and assume mathematical knowledge at roughly an undergraduate-degree level. Of these, Forster's *Musical Mathematics* is the least mathematically technical because the author brings the perspective of an instrument maker and focuses on the physics of instruments and the scales that can be played as a result. Unlike Forster's book, Benson's *A Mathematical Offering* does delve into mathematical compositional techniques in relatively readable manner. Loy's two-volume *Musimathics* is the most complete reference in existence for connections between mathematics and music from a mathematics or physics perspective; it includes significant material on signal processing and the electronics of digital sound production.

In terms of these five texts, here is a quick guide to how the lecture material matches up with the chapters:

Lecture No.	Wright	Harkleroad	Forster	Benson	Loy
1–2	10	2	1–2	1–3	V1: 1–2, 4–8 V2: 2–3, 6
3				4	V1: 6
4–5	4–6, 11–12	3	9–11	4–6	V1: 3
6				1	V1: 6
7	2, 8				
8		4		9	
9					
10	6	5–6			V1: 9
11				7	V2: 1
12		9			

Barbour, J. M. *Tuning and Temperament: A Historical Survey.* Mineola, NY: Dover, 2004. Originally published in 1951, this is the bible of piano tunings and temperaments, including technical analysis of subtly different "microtunings."

Benson, D. *Music: A Mathematical Offering.* Cambridge, UK: Cambridge University Press, 2006 (available for free at http://www.abdn.ac.uk/~mth192/html/maths-music.html). An excellent overview of mathematics and music, written for someone with a mathematical background equivalent to an undergraduate degree in mathematics. Includes sections on synthesized sound not covered in this course.

Deutsch, D. "Diana Deutsch's Audio Illusions." http://philomel.com/musical_illusions/. One of the world's preeminent researchers in psychoacoustics maintains a website with examples of auditory illusions.

Duffin, R. W. *How Equal Temperament Ruined Harmony (and Why You Should Care).* New York: W. W. Norton & Co., 2008. A popular treatise that argues for the less-equal temperaments popular during the pre-20th-century eras.

Dunne, E., and M. McConnell. "Pianos and Continued Fractions." *Mathematics Magazine* 72, no. 2 (1999): 104–115. A complete, mathematically rigorous account of the mathematics of equal-tempered scale systems of *n* notes and the connection with continued fractions.

Fischer, J. C. *Piano Tuning: A Simple and Accurate Method for Amateurs.* New York: Dover Publications, 1907. The classic text on piano tuning written in simple language, allowing the amateur tinkerer to adequately tune a piano.

Fletcher, N. H., and T. D. Rossing. *The Physics of Musical Instruments.* New York: Springer Verlag, 1998. A thorough look at the ways in which different musical instruments produce sound through vibrating strings, air columns, solid beams, hollow cylinders, and circular membranes. Assumes significant knowledge of physics and mathematics.

Bibliography

326

Forster, C. *Musical Mathematics: On the Art and Science of Acoustic Instruments*. San Francisco: Chronicle Books, 2010. A thorough reference written from the perspective of an instrument maker (which Forster is), including the use of English units (inches, feet, slugs, and so on). Of all these references, this is the most complete description of the vibration of wound strings (like most piano strings) and of non-Western scales.

Forte, A. *The Structure of Atonal Music*. New Haven, CT: Yale University Press, 1973. A thorough examination of the (sometimes mathematical) principles behind atonal music. Requires a significant background in music theory and some knowledge of set theory.

Harkleroad, L. *The Math behind the Music*. New York: Cambridge University Press, 2006. Like this course, a gentle introduction to the connections between the two subjects, assuming little knowledge of either subject.

Hofstadter, D. R. *Gödel, Escher, Bach: An Eternal Golden Braid*. New York: Basic Books, 1979. The groundbreaking, Pulitzer Prize–winning, fancifully constructed tour through three seemingly disconnected masters. Sections of Socratic dialogue are interspersed with more technical discussions of the types of self-reference and strange loops seen in mathematics, music, and art.

Lakoff, G., and R. E. Núñez. *Where Mathematics Comes From: How the Embodied Mind Brings Mathematics into Being*. New York: Basic Books, 2000. A linguist and a cognitive scientist combine forces in an attempt to explain how abstract mathematics arises starting with bodily experiences. Early chapters include overviews of the mathematical abilities of infants.

Levitin, D. J. *This Is Your Brain on Music: The Science of a Human Obsession*. New York: Dutton Adult, 2006. A popular book exploring what the emerging field of neuroscience says about how humans process music.

Lewin, D. *Generalized Musical Intervals and Transformations*. New York: Oxford University Press, USA, 2010. Originally published in 1987, this standard work of music theory sets out an ambitious agenda of analyzing music with mathematical tools. Assumes a significant knowledge of music theory.

Loy, G. *Musimathics: The Mathematical Foundations of Music.* Volumes 1–2. Cambridge, MA: MIT Press, 2006, 2007. The most complete and current encyclopedia of math/music connections. Assumes a significant knowledge of both mathematics and music theory. The material throughout the two-volume set is meticulously and thoroughly referenced.

Magadini, P. *Polyrhythms: The Musician's Guide.* Milwaukee, WI: Hal Leonard Corporation, 2001. A guide to playing and practicing polyrhythms, primarily for percussionists.

Nagel, E., J. R. Newman, and D. R. Hofstadter. *Gödel's Proof.* New York: University Press New York, 1958. A popular and accessible overview of Gödel's groundbreaking work on the incompleteness of axiomatic systems of mathematics. Coauthored by a leading philosopher and the future author of *Gödel, Escher, Bach.*

Perle, G. *Serial Composition and Atonality: An Introduction to the Music of Schoenberg, Berg, and Webern.* Berkeley: University of California Press, 1991. A detailed look at the theories behind atonal music. Not for the musical novice or the mathematically faint of heart.

Pohlmann, K. C. *Principles of Digital Audio.* 6th ed. New York: McGraw-Hill/TAB Electronics, 2010. A thorough, mathematically dense tour through all aspects of digital audio, including CD encoding and various types of compression.

Rothstein, E. *Emblems of Mind: The Inner Life of Music and Mathematics.* New York: Times Books, 1995. A philosophical look at the connections between the subjects, focusing on the similarities for the participant. Both the musical analysis and mathematical arguments are written for the non-expert but remain complicated and impenetrable to the novice.

Sacks, O. *Musicophilia: Tales of Music and the Brain.* New York: Alfred A. Knopf, 2007. The bestselling physician, author, and neurologist takes us on a tour of unusual neurological conditions and how they affect people's ability to process music.

University of New South Wales, http://www.phys.unsw.edu.au/music/. The best online resource for the latest research in the physics of sound. Includes detailed explanations of technical acoustical phenomena.

Wright, D. *Mathematics and Music*. Volume 28. Providence, RI: American Mathematical Society, 2009. This textbook is appropriate for an undergraduate course in mathematics and music, covering a handful of important topics without assuming much knowledge of either subject.

Notes